STUDY AND REVISION GUIDE

Working for over
25 YEARS
WITH
Cambridge Assessment International Education

Cambridge
IGCSE™ and O Level

History

Option B:
The 20th Century

Benjamin Harrison

HODDER
EDUCATION
AN HACHETTE UK COMPANY

The Publishers would like to thank the following for permission to reproduce copyright material.

Photo credits

p.2 Image courtesy of Kent Cartoon Library © Solo Syndication; **p.21** © Topham Picturepoint / TopFoto; **p.31** © Solo Syndication / Associated Newspapers Ltd; **p.64** Cartoon by Nicholas Garland, Independent, 10th August 1990 / British Cartoon Archive, University of Kent.

Although every effort has been made to ensure that website addresses are correct at time of going to press, Hodder Education cannot be held responsible for the content of any website mentioned in this book. It is sometimes possible to find a relocated web page by typing in the address of the home page for a website in the URL window of your browser.

Hachette UK's policy is to use papers that are natural, renewable and recyclable products and made from wood grown in well-managed forests and other controlled sources. The logging and manufacturing processes are expected to conform to the environmental regulations of the country of origin.

Orders: please contact Bookpoint Ltd, 130 Park Drive, Milton Park, Abingdon, Oxon OX14 4SE. Telephone: +44 (0)1235 827827. Fax: +44 (0)1235 400401. Email education@bookpoint.co.uk Lines are open from 9 a.m. to 5 p.m., Monday to Saturday, with a 24-hour message answering service. You can also order through our website: www.hoddereducation.com

ISBN: 978 1 5104 2119 6

© Benjamin Harrison 2019

First published in 2019 by
Hodder Education,
An Hachette UK Company
Carmelite House
50 Victoria Embankment
London EC4Y 0DZ

Impression number   10 9 8 7 6 5 4 3 2 1

Year   2023 2022 2021 2020 2019

Cover photo © toa555 – Fotolia

Illustrations by Aptara Inc.

Typeset in OffcianaSans-book 11/13 pts by Aptara Inc.

Printed in Spain.

A catalogue record for this title is available from the British Library.

Contents

© Benjamin Harrison/Hodder & Stoughton

Introduction

Welcome to the *Cambridge IGCSE™ and O Level Study and Revision Guide* for History: Option B. This book has been written to help you revise everything you need to know for your History examinations. Following the History syllabus, it covers all the key content as well as offering sample questions and answers and exam-style practice questions to help you learn how to answer questions and to check your understanding.

How to use this book

Key point

A summary of the main information.

Tips

Advice to help you give the perfect answer.

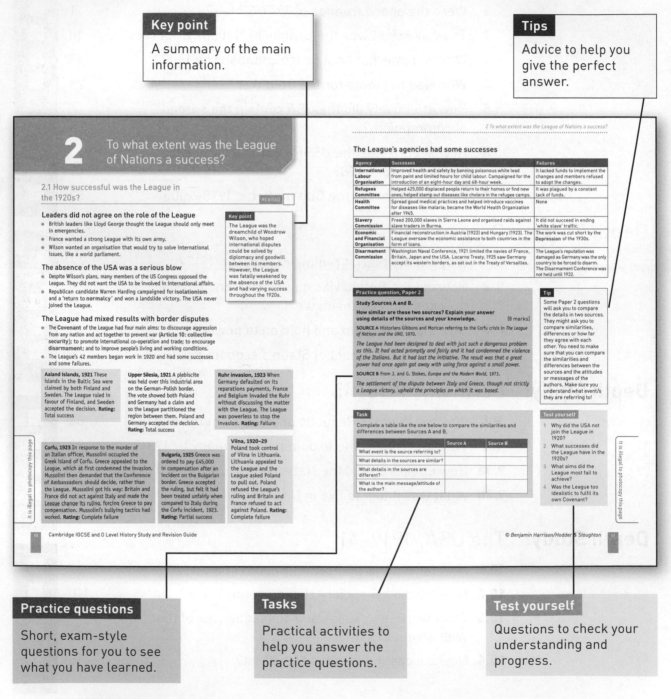

Practice questions

Short, exam-style questions for you to see what you have learned.

Tasks

Practical activities to help you answer the practice questions.

Test yourself

Questions to check your understanding and progress.

Answers

Sample answers to the practice questions are given on pages 124–155.

1 Were the peace treaties of 1919–23 fair?

1.1 What were the motives and aims of the Big Three at Versailles?

At the end of the First World War the Paris Peace Conference was held

- An armistice was signed on 11 November 1918 between the Allies (principally Britain, France and the USA) and the Central Powers of Germany, Austria–Hungary, Turkey and Bulgaria.
- There was great optimism for a lasting peace, especially from US President Woodrow Wilson who outlined his **Fourteen Points** in a speech in 1918.
- Thirty-two nations representing over two-thirds of the world's population met at the Paris Peace Conference in January 1919 to prepare five peace treaties collectively known as the Versailles settlement. The most important of these was the **Treaty of Versailles** which dealt with Germany.

The Big Three had different aims and motives for the Treaty terms

- The **Big Three** of David Lloyd George (British prime minister), Georges Clemenceau (French prime minister) and Woodrow Wilson (US president) were the main peacemakers.
- The Big Three had different aims and motives and clashed on many of the terms of the peace treaties, especially the Treaty of Versailles.

> **Key point**
>
> The peacemakers at the **Paris Peace Conference** had different aims and motives. Wilson was an **idealist** who wanted future peace in Europe; Clemenceau wanted revenge for the huge war damage inflicted on France; Lloyd George was a **realist** who wanted to punish Germany, but not too harshly, to prevent a future conflict. These leaders would have to find common ground if the peace treaties were to be agreed on.

Big Three	Aims	Motives
Britain – Lloyd George ('the realist')	To punish Germany but not too harshly; wanted Britain and Germany to be trading partners; Germany to lose its naval power and colonies	Didn't want Germany to seek revenge or have a communist revolution as in Russia if the Treaty was too harsh BUT wanted to appease anti-German feelings at home; wanted jobs for people in Britain; wanted to protect the British Empire
Clemenceau ('the uncompromising')	To cripple Germany economically and territorially; ensure France's borders were secure against future attack; demand Germany takes blame for starting the war and pays **reparations**	For Germany not to be able to build up its armed forces again and threaten France, which had been invaded twice (in 1870 and 1914); French people had suffered huge casualties (1.4 million killed) and had lost farmland and industry in north-east France
Wilson ('the idealist')	To create a 'far and lasting peace' in Europe by implementing his Fourteen Points, which included **disarmament** for all European nations, no **secret treaties** and a **League of Nations**	To remove the causes of conflict in Europe to prevent future wars; increase trade between Europe and the USA to prevent the spread of communism; strengthen **democracy** and **self-determination** to break up empires

The result was a compromise

Terms of the Treaty of Versailles

Military: The German army was reduced to 100,000 soldiers; no conscription; no tanks; no air force; only six battleships; the Rhineland was to be demilitarised and the west bank of the Rhine occupied by an Allied army for 15 years.

Financial: Reparations for war damage to be paid to the Allies, agreed in 1921 at £6.6 billion; the coal in the Saar region went to France for 15 years.

League of Nations: The League was set up in 1920 to enforce the Treaty and keep international peace. Germany was not allowed to join until 1926.

Territory: All of Germany's colonies were taken away and controlled by the League of Nations (run by Britain and France); Alsace-Lorraine returned to France; Poland to be given access to the sea by the creation of a Polish Corridor; land given to Denmark, Belgium, Lithuania and Czechoslovakia; Danzig to become a free city; union between Germany and Austria forbidden (*Anschluss*).

War guilt: Article 231 said Germany had to take full responsibility for starting the war.

Practice question, Paper 2

Study Source A.

What is the message of the cartoonist? Explain your answer using source details and your own knowledge. [8 marks]

Task

Study Source A.

Draw a line from the annotation next to the cartoon to the relevant detail in the image then add some more notes.

SOURCE A A cartoon published in 1919 in an Australian newspaper.

The title 'Melting Pot' and the label 'Peace Soup' suggest that the Treaty was …

The figures on the right and the left represent …

THE MELTING POT.

Italy, France and Britain have pots labelled 'National Sentiment' which represent …

The figure on the 'Peace Soup' bowl is Wilson; his bottle of 'Sweet Oil of Brotherhood' suggests …

Tip

For interpretation questions that ask you to work out the cartoonist's message, make sure that you think about whether it is supporting, criticising or commenting on a particular event at a particular time. Use the provenance, the source details and your own knowledge to explain the message.

Test yourself

1 Which countries had peace treaties imposed on them by the Allies at the Paris Peace Conference?

2 Who were the Big Three and what problems did they face at the Conference?

3 List two aims and motives of the Big Three.

4 List what you think were the three harshest terms of the Treaty of Versailles.

1.2 Why did the victors not get everything they wanted?

The British and French leaders were influenced by public opinion in their home countries

- Britain had suffered hugely in the First World War. Lloyd George had won the 1918 general election by promising to 'make Germany pay'.
- The French public wanted a treaty that would severely punish Germany. Over two-thirds of the men who had served in the French army had been killed or wounded.
- America had not suffered as much as Britain or France in the war and Wilson had a more generous attitude towards Germany.

> **Key point**
>
> The Big Three were forced to compromise over the terms of the Treaty. Each achieved some of their aims but were forced to make concessions in order to get everyone to sign.

The Big Three's aims for the Treaty terms were too different to be reconciled

- Clemenceau and Wilson clashed over what to do about the **Rhineland** and Germany's coalfields in the **Saar**. Wilson gave in, and in return Clemenceau and Lloyd George conceded over eastern European self-determination.
- Clemenceau and Lloyd George also disagreed. Clemenceau argued that Britain was happy to treat Germany fairly in Europe, against France's interests, but stricter when it came to Germany's navy and colonies, which threatened British power.
- Wilson's views on self-determination threatened the British Empire, which ruled millions of people across the world.

As a result, each leader had to compromise

Clemenceau

- Clemenceau was content with the return of Alsace-Lorraine, which helped secure France's border with Germany.
- He also received two of Germany's overseas colonies (Togoland and the Cameroons), which expanded the French Empire.
- The reparations helped pay for the war damage France suffered and the military terms helped reduce the threat of a future invasion.
- *But* Clemenceau wanted the reparations to be higher and was concerned that Germany would recover its economic and military strength, especially as the Rhineland was only **demilitarised** and not given to France.
- He was also concerned that the French people would not think the Treaty was harsh enough – this led to his defeat in the French presidential elections in 1920 and his resignation soon afterwards.

Lloyd George

- British imperial interests were helped as a result of the Treaty – its empire in Africa gained an additional 13 million new subjects. The reduction of the German navy also secured Britain's rule of the seas.

- The German economy had not been totally destroyed by the Treaty, which allowed Britain and Germany to trade again. This would help stop the spread of communism and promote British businesses.

- *But* Lloyd George did not like the fact that German-speaking people were now under the control of countries such as Poland and France – he thought this would lead to resentment and future conflict.

- He was also under public pressure to punish Germany after Britain had suffered over 1 million casualties in the First World War, meaning he would have to balance his desire for a fair treaty with demands at home for harsher terms.

Wilson

- Wilson had managed to get some of his Fourteen Points into the different peace treaties, such as the requirement to disarm and the setting up of a League of Nations.

- He also managed to get concessions from France such as lowering the reparations figure and only demilitarising the Rhineland.

- Wilson achieved self-determination for countries in eastern Europe such as Estonia, Lithuania and Latvia.

- *But* France and Britain had increased the size of their overseas empires at the expense of Germany.

- Britain had also increased its control of the seas by reducing Germany's navy, which went against Wilson's principle of free navigation of the seas.

Test yourself

1 How did France benefit from the terms of the Treaty of Versailles?
2 Why might the French people not have been satisfied with the Treaty?
3 How did Lloyd George manage to increase British international power?
4 What were Wilson's most significant achievements in the terms of the Treaty of Versailles?

Practice question, Paper 1

What aims did Clemenceau achieve in the Treaty of Versailles?

[4 marks]

Task

Write the names of the Big Three at the top of three separate cards. On one side of each card draw a + sign and on the other a – sign. On each card, make a list of the terms with which each of the Big Three would have been satisfied (+) and unsatisfied (–).

Tip

Four-mark questions don't require you to explain, but to demonstrate your knowledge. Make sure you give sufficient factual details but keep your answer relatively short.

1.3 What was the impact of the peace treaty on Germany up to 1923?

The German people resented the terms of the Treaty of Versailles

- Many Germans hated the **war guilt** clause and believed other countries were as much to blame as them for starting the war.
- Germans felt the disarmament terms were too harsh. The army had been a source of German pride and none of the Allies were forced to disarm. Germany was now left defenceless and surrounded by countries with far superior armies to its own.
- Germans were bitter at the reparations and territorial losses: 10 per cent of its land in Europe; all overseas colonies; 12.5 per cent of its population; 16 per cent of its coalfields. This was a major blow to the German economy.
- Many Germans, including politicians and soldiers, saw the Treaty as a dictated peace or '**diktat**'. Germany was not allowed to attend the peace conference and was forced to accept the terms of the Treaty or face occupation.

> **Key point**
>
> The Treaty was deeply unpopular with most Germans and led to resentment and hatred towards the new Weimar Government. This caused instability, political extremism, violence and huge economic problems.

Political opposition threatened to destabilise the Weimar Government

- **Right-wing** nationalists opposed the Treaty and the new Weimar Government by attempting several coups.
- The anti-communist *Freikorps*, made up of ex-soldiers, under the command of Wolfgang Kapp, launched the **Kapp Putsch** in 1920 and managed to seize Berlin. The army refused to fire on them, and it was only defeated when the workers called a **general strike**.
- In 1922, the foreign minister Walter Rathenau was murdered by right-wing extremists.
- In November 1923, Hitler's Nazi Party attempted to seize control during the Munich Putsch.
- Left-wing extremists (communists), inspired by the Spartacists' failed uprising in January 1919 and taking advantage of anti-Weimar feeling, attempted a rebellion in the **Ruhr** in 1920.

The Treaty led to economic instability in Germany

- Many Germans claimed that the reparations bill of £6.6 billion would be impossible to pay and together with the other harsh economic terms would lead to instability.
- Germany paid its first instalment of the reparations bill in 1921 but claimed it could not make the 1922 payment.
- France and Belgium decided to occupy the Ruhr region in January 1923 to take its raw materials and goods as payment. This occupation was legal under the terms of the Treaty of Versailles, so the League of Nations did nothing to stop the French and Belgian forces. The occupation of the Ruhr was a disaster for Germany.
- Ebert ordered German workers to use passive resistance so the French could take nothing. France reacted by killing over 100 workers and expelling over 100,000 strikers.

- The Weimar Government printed money to pay the striking workers, which contributed to a period of **hyperinflation** in Germany.
- The prices of goods rocketed, making the currency worthless – one US dollar was worth over 4 trillion marks by November 1923. Many Germans used worthless banknotes as wallpaper or burnt them as fuel. Those with debts and mortgages were able to pay off their debts easily, but trade was made impossible, people had to be paid daily, and the middle classes and pensioners lost their savings.
- The Ruhr occupation and the period of hyperinflation allowed political extremists to point the finger of blame towards the Weimar politicians and the Treaty of Versailles.

Task

Complete a table like the one below to summarise and explain the impact of the Treaty on Germany up to 1923.

Impact	Details	Effect on Germany by 1923
Social		
Political		
Economic		

Practice question, Paper 1

Why did the Treaty of Versailles make Weimar Germany unstable up to 1923? [6 marks]

Test yourself

1 What terms of the Treaty caused the most resentment in Germany?
2 Give one example of a right-wing and one of a left-wing uprising up to 1923.
3 How did the occupation of the Ruhr help lead to hyperinflation?
4 Who lost out and who benefited from German hyperinflation in 1923?

Tip

Six-mark questions require you to explain your reasons using your own knowledge to support your answer. Make sure you use full paragraphs and explain more than one reason in your answer.

1.4 Could the treaties be justified at the time?

> **Key point**
>
> The other treaties imposed similar terms on the other defeated Central Powers as Versailles had done on Germany. Many, especially the defeated powers, saw the treaties as overly harsh, but others saw their terms as fair or even not harsh enough after the devastation of the First World War.

Germany's allies in the First World War also had harsh treaties imposed on them

- The peace treaties forced Germany's allies to accept some responsibility for the war. Austria was made to sign Article 177 and accept war guilt along with Hungary and the other Central Powers.

Treaty/Country	Financial terms	Military terms	Territorial terms	War guilt
Treaty of Saint Germain, 1919 (Austria)	Reparations to be paid to the Allies	**Conscription** abolished; limit of 30,000 soldiers	Austria–Hungary separated; union with Germany forbidden; **territory** given to Czechoslovakia, Poland, Yugoslavia, Italy and Romania	Article 177 forced Austria and the Central Powers to accept blame for the war
Treaty of Neuilly, 1919 (Bulgaria)	£100 million to be paid to the Allies	Army reduced to 20,000 soldiers	Land lost to Yugoslavia, Romania and Greece	Bulgaria was forced to accept responsibility with other Central Powers
Treaty of Trianon, 1920 (Hungary)	Ordered to pay reparations but it was too weak to do so; loss of raw materials	Limited to 35,000 soldiers and no navy	Hungary forced to accept separation from Austria; loss of land to Romania, Slovenia, Croatia and Czechoslovakia; over 3 million Hungarians displaced	Like Austria, Hungary was forced to accept joint responsibility for the war
Treaty of Sèvres, 1920 (Turkey)	Financial system to be controlled by the Allies; property owned by Central Powers was turned over to the Reparations Commission	Army reduced to 50,000 soldiers; no air force and a limited navy	Turkey's empire was broken up and lost to its neighbours; much of it controlled by Britain, France and Italy in separate zones	Forced to accept blame for the war
Treaty of Lausanne, 1923 (Turkey)	No war reparations; minor debts to be paid off and some tariff restrictions	Restrictions from Treaty of Sèvres were removed by Treaty of Lausanne	Treaty of Lausanne returned some of its European land to Turkey in 1923, but land in the Middle East was lost	

Many at the time saw the treaties as unfair and too harsh

- Germany, Austria, Hungary and Turkey resented the reparation payments and the severe restrictions on their military and territory. The treaties left many nationals outside of their borders and led to economic problems and political instability.
- In Germany and Turkey, the treaties led to nationalist uprisings and political violence.
- The defeated nations hated the war guilt clause as they believed other countries were to blame for starting the war as well.
- In Britain, some politicians and journalists criticised the harshness of the Treaty of Versailles and claimed it would lead to a future war with Germany.

However, some onlookers thought the treaties let the defeated nations off too easily

- Many in France took this view and claimed that when Germany imposed the **Treaty of Brest-Litovsk** on Russia in 1918, its terms were far harsher than those in the Versailles settlement.
- Marshal Foch of the French army claimed Versailles was merely a 20-year ceasefire and did not protect France sufficiently from future invasion.

Some believed that the peace treaties were fair and the best that could have been achieved

- Some journalists in Britain commented that Germany and its allies got off relatively lightly and would be able to afford the economic and territorial costs of the treaties.
- Some in the USA saw the treaties as the only possible compromise that could be made between the Allies after the war.

Test yourself

1 What similarities were there between the Treaty of Versailles and the other peace treaties?
2 Were all the peace treaties equally harsh?
3 Why might many Germans see the Treaty of Versailles as unfair?
4 Why might France view the treaties as not harsh enough?

Practice question, Paper 1

'Germany suffered the most in the peace settlements after the war.'

How far do you agree with this statement? Explain your answer.

[10 marks]

Task

Write a list of the treaties from the table on page 7. For each treaty write an answer to the question: 'Was this treaty fairer than the terms of the Treaty of Versailles?'

Add an explanation using evidence from the previous pages to support your judgement. Then write a conclusion to reach an overall judgement about which peace treaty was the fairest/harshest.

Tip

Ten-mark questions require a balanced and structured response supported by your own knowledge. Try to think of a counter-argument to the one in the question.

8 Cambridge IGCSE and O Level History Study and Revision Guide

Key terms

Make sure you know these terms, people or events and can use them or describe them confidently.

Anschluss Joining of Austria and Germany as one state – forbidden by the Treaty of Versailles 1919 but carried out by Hitler in 1938.

Big Three Three main leaders at the Paris Peace Conference 1919 – Lloyd George (Britain), Wilson (USA), Clemenceau (France).

Conscription Compulsory service in the armed forces.

Demilitarised zone Area of land where troops cannot be stationed, e.g. Rhineland area of Germany after the First World War.

Democracy Political system in which the population votes for its government in elections held on a regular basis.

Diktat Term used in Germany to describe the Treaty of Versailles because Germany had no say in the terms of the Treaty.

Disarmament Process of scrapping land, sea or air weapons.

Fourteen Points The statement of principles for the peace negotiations after the First World War, made by Woodrow Wilson.

General strike Large-scale co-ordinated strike by workers designed to stop essential services like power, transport, etc.

Hyperinflation Process of money becoming worthless; most notable instance was in Germany in 1923.

Idealist/realist An idealist is motivated by particular beliefs, e.g. commitment to right of peoples to rule themselves. A realist is a politician who accepts a particular course of action even though it is not what they would prefer to do.

Kapp Putsch Attempt to overthrow democratically elected government in Germany in 1920.

League of Nations Organisation set up to manage international disputes and prevent wars after the First World War. Brainchild of US President Woodrow Wilson

Paris Peace Conference Conference which ran 1919–23 to decide how to officially end the First World War. Resulted in Treaty of Versailles with Germany and three other treaties.

Public opinion View of majority or large section of population on an issue, most important in democracies where politicians often must win over public opinion.

Reparations Compensation to be paid by Germany to France, Belgium, Britain and other states as a result of the First World War.

Rhineland Area of Germany that bordered France. Under Treaty of Versailles it was demilitarised – no German forces were allowed there.

Right-wing Political groups or individuals with beliefs in national pride, authoritarian government and opposed to communism.

Ruhr Main industrial area of Germany.

Saar Region on the border between France and Germany. Run by League of Nations from 1920 to 1935 when its people voted to become part of Germany.

Secret treaties International agreements between countries that are not made public to other nations.

Self-determination The right for people to choose which nation they belong to, often by vote.

Territory An area of land or country controlled by another nation.

Treaty of Brest-Litovsk Treaty between Germany and Russia in 1918 which ended war between the two. Germany took massive amounts of land and reparations.

Treaty of Versailles Treaty that officially ended war between Allies and Germany in 1919. Controversial because of the terms, which Germany claimed were excessively harsh.

War guilt Clause in Treaty of Versailles which forced Germany to accept blame for the First World War.

To what extent was the League of Nations a success?

2.1 How successful was the League in the 1920s?

Leaders did not agree on the role of the League

- British leaders like Lloyd George thought the League should only meet in emergencies.
- France wanted a strong League with its own army.
- Wilson wanted an organisation that would try to solve international issues, like a world parliament.

The absence of the USA was a serious blow

- Despite Wilson's plans, many members of the US Congress opposed the League. They did not want the USA to be involved in international affairs.
- Republican candidate Warren Harding campaigned for **isolationism** and a 'return to **normalcy**' and won a landslide victory. The USA never joined the League.

The League had mixed results with border disputes

- The **Covenant** of the League had four main aims: to discourage aggression from any nation and act together to prevent war (**Article 10: collective security**); to promote international co-operation and trade; to encourage **disarmament**; and to improve people's living and working conditions.
- The League's 42 members began work in 1920 and had some successes and some failures.

> **Key point**
>
> The League was the dreamchild of Woodrow Wilson, who hoped international disputes could be solved by diplomacy and goodwill between its members. However, the League was fatally weakened by the absence of the USA and had varying success throughout the 1920s.

Aaland Islands, 1921 These islands in the Baltic Sea were claimed by both Finland and Sweden. The League ruled in favour of Finland, and Sweden accepted the decision. **Rating:** Total success

Upper Silesia, 1921 A plebiscite was held over this industrial area on the German–Polish border. The vote showed both Poland and Germany had a claim and so the League partitioned the region between them. Poland and Germany accepted the decision. **Rating:** Total success

Ruhr invasion, 1923 When Germany defaulted on its reparations payments, France and Belgium invaded the Ruhr without discussing the matter with the League. The League was powerless to stop the invasion. **Rating:** Failure

Corfu, 1923 In response to the murder of an Italian officer, Mussolini occupied the Greek island of Corfu. Greece appealed to the League, which at first condemned the invasion. Mussolini then demanded that the **Conference of Ambassadors** should decide, rather than the League. Mussolini got his way: Britain and France did not act against Italy and made the League change its ruling, forcing Greece to pay compensation. Mussolini's bullying tactics had worked. **Rating:** Complete failure

Bulgaria, 1925 Greece was ordered to pay £45,000 in compensation after an incident on the Bulgarian border. Greece accepted the ruling, but felt it had been treated unfairly when compared to Italy during the Corfu incident, 1923. **Rating:** Partial success

Vilna, 1920–29 Poland took control of Vilna in Lithuania. Lithuania appealed to the League and the League asked Poland to pull out. Poland refused the League's ruling and Britain and France refused to act against Poland. **Rating:** Complete failure

The League's agencies had some successes

Agency	Successes	Failures
International Labour Organisation	Improved health and safety by banning poisonous white lead from paint and limited hours for child labour. Campaigned for the introduction of an eight-hour day and 48-hour week.	It lacked funds to implement the changes and members refused to adopt the changes.
Refugees Committee	Helped 425,000 displaced people return to their homes or find new ones; helped stamp out diseases like cholera in the refugee camps.	It was plagued by a constant lack of funds.
Health Committee	Spread good medical practices and helped introduce vaccines for diseases like malaria; became the World Health Organization after 1945.	None
Slavery Commission	Freed 200,000 slaves in Sierra Leone and organised raids against slave traders in Burma.	It did not succeed in ending 'white slave' traffic.
Economic and Financial Organisation	Financial reconstruction in Austria (1922) and Hungary (1923). The League oversaw the economic assistance to both countries in the form of loans.	The work was cut short by the **Depression** of the 1930s.
Disarmament Commission	Washington Naval Conference, 1921 limited the navies of France, Britain, Japan and the USA. Locarno Treaty, 1925 saw Germany accept its western borders, as set out in the Treaty of Versailles.	The League's reputation was damaged as Germany was the only country to be forced to disarm. The Disarmament Conference was not held until 1932.

Practice question, Paper 2

Study Sources A and B.

How similar are these two sources? Explain your answer using details of the sources and your knowledge. [8 marks]

SOURCE A Historians Gibbons and Morican referring to the Corfu crisis in *The League of Nations and the UNO,* 1970.

The League had been designed to deal with just such a dangerous problem as this. It had acted promptly and fairly and it had condemned the violence of the Italians. But it had lost the initiative. The result was that a great power had once again got away with using force against a small power.

SOURCE B From J. and G. Stokes, *Europe and the Modern World,* 1973.

The settlement of the dispute between Italy and Greece, though not strictly a League victory, upheld the principles on which it was based.

Tip

Some Paper 2 questions will ask you to compare the details in two sources. They might ask you to compare similarities, differences or how far they agree with each other. You need to make sure that you can compare the similarities and differences between the sources and the attitudes or messages of the authors. Make sure you understand what event/s they are referring to!

Task

Complete a table like the one below to compare the similarities and differences between Sources A and B.

	Source A	Source B
What event is the source referring to?		
What details in the sources are similar?		
What details in the sources are different?		
What is the main message/attitude of the author?		

Test yourself

1 Why did the USA not join the League in 1920?

2 What successes did the League have in the 1920s?

3 What aims did the League most fail to achieve?

4 Was the League too idealistic to fulfil its own Covenant?

2.2 How far did weaknesses in the League's organisation make failure inevitable?

The League was limited by its membership

- The USA, the most powerful and wealthy country in the world, never joined, which severely reduced the League's ability to deal with aggressive nations (see Factfile on page 13).
- The Treaty of Versailles forbade Germany to join (until 1926).
- The communist Soviet Union was refused membership, for ideological reasons, until 1934.
- Britain and France were the most powerful countries in the League. Both were severely weakened by the First World War and both had other priorities: for Britain, its empire; for France, the threat of Germany.
- Both Britain and France felt only the USA had enough influence and resources to head up the League. This would lead both countries to bypass the League when it suited them.

> **Key point**
>
> Wilson had envisaged the League to be a world parliament that could stop conflict before it started, but without the USA it was dominated by Britain and France. The League's organisation and structure also meant it was often slow to act on international disputes.

The League's structure was democratic, but it had weaknesses

- The League's Covenant set up three main bodies: the **Assembly**, the **Council** and the **Secretariat**. A Permanent Court of Justice and International Labour Organisation (ILO) were also attached to the League along with various agencies, committees and **commissions** (see table below).
- The League was funded by member states and budgets set by the Assembly.

Key body	Roles and functions	Strengths	Weaknesses
Assembly	The League's 'parliament'; each country had one representative in the assembly (there were 42 founding members); could admit new members; discussed and decided general policies	Very democratic – each member had one vote so no one country could dominate decisions	Only met once per year and decisions had to be **unanimous**, meaning it was slow to act
Council	Smaller 'executive' (government) body that met more often and in emergencies to resolve disputes. Had a variety of powers to stop aggressive nations (see Factfile on page 13)	Met up to five times per year and could react more quickly than the Assembly	Permanent members (Britain, France, Italy and Japan) could dominate the Council's decisions; each member had a veto so one member could stop a decisive action
Secretariat	Civil service of the League – kept records and administered all the different bodies	Lots of experts brought together	Expensive to run and grew larger as the League's roles expanded over time
Permanent Court of International Justice	Based in The Hague in the Netherlands. Judges settled disputes and provided legal advice to the Council	Made up of legal experts from member states; held in high regard by many	Lacked the power to follow up its rulings
International Labour Organisation	Brought together employers, employees and governments to improve working conditions	See focus point 2.1 (pages 10–11)	See focus point 2.1 (pages 10–11)
Agencies	Commissions and committees set up to deal with social and economic issues caused by the First World War and peace settlements	See focus point 2.1 (pages 10–11)	See focus point 2.1 (pages 10–11)

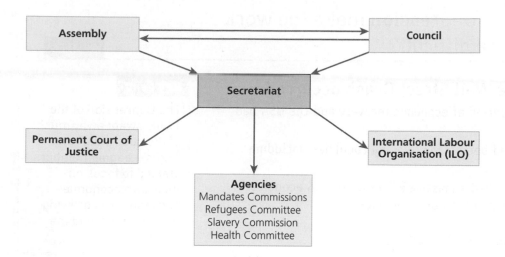

Task

Use each letter of the word LEAGUE below to write a sentence about the League's organisation and membership. Try to write three strengths and three weaknesses. The first has been done for you.

League of Nations' members each had a vote in the Assembly meaning it was very representative.

E _____

A _____

G _____

U _____

E _____

Practice question, Paper 1

Describe the main features of the organisation and structure of the League of Nations. [4 marks]

Tip

Four-mark questions require you to give accurate and relevant detail. You do not need to write long answers or explanations. Save more of your time for the questions that carry higher marks.

Test yourself

1 Which were the most important bodies in the League's organisation?

2 In what ways was the League a representative organisation?

Factfile

League of Nations' sanctions

Moral condemnation: The Council could use the might of world opinion to condemn aggressive actions.

Trade sanctions: The Council could impose trade boycotts on the aggressor (but the USA could continue to trade with them).

Military force: Member countries could raise a force against the aggressor (difficult without the USA's military might).

2.3 How far did the Depression make the work of the League more difficult?

In October 1929, the Wall Street Crash occurred

- The 1920s had been a period of economic recovery and the USA had grown wealthy.
- As a result, US loans had been made to many countries, including Germany.
- The **Wall Street Crash** had a massive effect on the US economy, leading to bankruptcies and high unemployment.

A worldwide depression followed

- The USA saw unemployment rise by over 600 per cent between 1929 and 1932, meaning 30 per cent of the working population were without jobs and US loans were called back as banks collapsed.
- In Germany, unemployment reached nearly 6 million in 1932, which led to chaos on the streets and a surge in support for extremist parties like the Nazis and Communists.
- In Japan, the Depression led to a drop in its main export, silk. Japan was unable to buy important raw materials and food to survive.
- Britain and France, the League's two leading powers, were unwilling to help sort out international disputes while their economies were suffering.
- Many countries cut expenditure as worldwide trade dropped over 50 per cent between the world's major powers. Some countries put up **tariffs** on imports and this made things worse.
- The spirit of international co-operation was lost.

Some countries turned to extremism and militarism

- Britain, Germany, Japan and Italy all started to rearm to help solve their unemployment problems.
- In Japan, the military wanted to expand Japan's overseas empire to access the raw materials and food it needed.
- In Italy, the fascist government under Mussolini believed that an empire in the Mediterranean and Africa would help solve economic problems.
- In Germany, the Nazis came to power under Hitler in 1933. He promised to solve Germany's economic problems by rearming and winning back territory lost in the Treaty of Versailles.

Many nations were now weak and aggressive

- The League had failed in the 1920s when more aggressive nations had used force – now leading members like Japan, Italy and Germany were threatening military expansion.
- Britain and France had been weakened by the Depression and were not willing to spend money or send forces to stop international aggression.
- Nationalism was on the rise in many countries leading to **dictatorships** that were preparing their countries for war – the League lacked an army or the might of the USA to stop them.

Key point

The Depression of the 1930s swept away much of the goodwill of the 1920s. League members started to focus on their own economies and ignore the growing militarism around the world.

Task

Draw a spider diagram with 'How the Depression impacted the League' in the centre and 'Unemployment', 'Extremism' and 'Militarism' as branches. Add some facts.

Test yourself

1 How did the Wall Street Crash lead to worldwide depression?

2 Why did Germany, Italy and Japan believe military expansion would solve their problems?

3 Why would the League's ability to solve international disputes be made more difficult?

Practice question, Paper 1

Explain why the Depression led to problems for the League of Nations. [6 marks]

2.4 How successful was the League in the 1930s?

The League, weakened by the Depression, faced its first crisis when Japan invaded Manchuria

Why Manchuria?

1 **Economic:** Japan lacked food and raw materials and the Depression had ruined its silk trade with the USA. Manchuria had rich natural resources and links to Asian markets.

2 **Military:** China's military was inferior to Japan's modern armed forces.

3 **Geographical:** Japan had controlled Korea, which was on the border of Manchuria, since 1905, and had access to the South Manchurian Railway which carried food and fuel to Japan.

> **Key point**
>
> The League would face its biggest challenges in the 1930s as the Depression led to powerful nations turning to rearmament and imperialism to solve their economic problems. The League, without an army or the USA, was left to rely on Britain and France to try to stop Japan and Italy.

What happened?

| **September 1931:** Mukden incident – Japan blamed China for a staged attack on the South Manchurian Railway. | **January–March 1932:** Japan occupied all of Manchuria and renamed it Manchukuo. | **March 1932:** China appealed to the League for help. | **April 1932:** Lord Lytton sent by League to investigate. | **September 1932:** Lytton Report condemned invasion and asked Japan to withdraw. | **February 1933:** Japan ignored the report and invaded more of China. | **March 1933:** Japan vetoed the actions of the League and resigned its membership. |

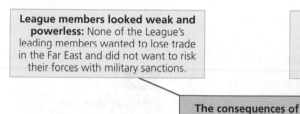

League members looked weak and powerless: None of the League's leading members wanted to lose trade in the Far East and did not want to risk their forces with military sanctions.

Britain and France looked self-interested: Both countries had colonies in the Far East and did not want to be drawn into a war with Japan.

The consequences of the Manchurian crisis for the League

No USA or USSR: Both countries had the resources to remove Japan, but neither were members of the League.

Future aggression: Italy and Germany both saw the League's members were not willing to stop powerful nations when they acted aggressively.

The League also failed in its aim to disarm countries

- The League's Covenant was committed to disarmament, but only Germany was forced to disarm.
- In 1932, the Disarmament Conference was convened in Geneva.
- Germany proposed that all nations disarm to its level. The Conference failed to agree.
- In 1993, Hitler started to rearm Germany in secret. He left the Conference and the League.
- France was concerned over its security with Germany and refused to disarm. Poland and Czechoslovakia were also concerned as they bordered Germany.
- By 1934, the major countries had failed to reach any agreement and many countries began to rearm.

Italy's invasion of Abyssinia was the final blow to the League's reputation

Why Abyssinia?

1 **Historical:** In 1896, the Italian army had been defeated by a poorly equipped Abyssinian army. Mussolini wanted revenge and a military victory to boost his prestige at home.

2 **Economic:** Abyssinia had rich mineral deposits and fertile land that could be added to Italy's empire.

3 **Geographical:** Abyssinia was bordered by two other Italian colonies – Eritrea and Italian Somaliland. This would give Mussolini a stronger foothold in East Africa, which was dominated by British colonies.

What happened?

| **December 1934:** Mussolini claimed Abyssinia after a border dispute at the Wal-Wal oasis. | → | **January–October 1935:** Italy prepared for invasion while negotiating with the League to settle the dispute; Mussolini rejected the League's judgements. | → | **October 1935:** Italy invaded Abyssinia in a ruthless attack that included the use of chemical weapons. | → | **November–December 1935:** The League condemned the invasion and imposed economic sanctions. | → | **December 1935:** Hoare–Laval Pact signed but it was leaked to the French press and Britain and France were blamed. | → | **May 1936:** Abyssinian capital, Addis Ababa, captured. |

Britain and France: The Hoare–Laval Pact was a secret deal to give Mussolini two-thirds of Abyssinia in return for ending the war. When it was leaked it looked like the League's leading members were following their own interests rather than the League's.

Stresa Pact, 1935: Britain and France wanted Italy as an ally against Hitler and did not take the situation seriously enough. They didn't even close the Suez Canal, so Italy was able to continue to supply its troops. They were prepared to ignore the League, which weakened its authority.

The consequences of the Abyssinian crisis for the League

No USA: The League had banned arms sales and loans to Italy but not oil over fear the USA would not support the sanctions. The delays in a decision were fatal for Abyssinia. The League's sanctions were ineffective without the membership of the USA.

Hitler's actions: Hitler saw the League was preoccupied and launched an invasion of the Rhineland in 1936, which broke the terms of the Treaty of Versailles. In November, angered by Britain and France, Mussolini allied himself with Hitler to form the Rome–Berlin Axis and Italy left the League in 1937.

Practice question, Paper 1

'The weak leadership of France and Britain was the main reason the League failed in Manchuria and Abyssinia.'

How far do you agree with this statement? Explain your answer.

[10 marks]

Test yourself

1 How similar were the causes of the Manchurian and Abyssinian invasions?

2 Why did Britain and France fail to act against Japan?

3 What were the main reasons for the failure of the Disarmament Conference?

4 Were Britain and France the main reason why the League failed over the Abyssinian crisis?

Tip

Remember, ten-mark questions require you to write a balanced, essay-style response. It is worth spending a few minutes planning your answer. To plan for this question you could draw up a table with evidence and explanations for three factors: 'The weak leadership of France and Britain'; 'No USA in the League'; 'The League's weak structure and organisation'. Make sure you use relevant examples in your paragraphs to explain the different factors and write a conclusion to make an overall judgement.

Key terms

Make sure you know these terms, people or events and can use them or describe them confidently.

Abyssinian crisis International tensions resulting from invasion of Abyssinia (present-day Ethiopia) by Italy in 1935.

Article 10 Article of League of Nations Covenant which promised security to League members from attack by other states.

Assembly Main forum of the League of Nations for discussing important issues.

Collective security Key principle of the League of Nations that all members could expect to be secure because the other members of the League would defend them from attack.

Commissions Organisations set up by the League of Nations to tackle economic, social and health problems.

Conference of Ambassadors Organisation involving Britain, France, Italy and Japan which met to sort out international disputes. Worked alongside League of Nations.

Council Influential body within the League of Nations which contained the most powerful members of the League.

Covenant Agreement or set of rules.

Depression Period of economic downturn where trade between countries and inside countries declines, often leading to unemployment.

Dictatorship System in which one person runs a country.

Disarmament Process of scrapping land, sea or air weapons.

Isolationism Policy in the USA in the 1920s which argued that the USA should not get involved in international disputes.

Manchurian crisis International crisis sparked off when Japan invaded the Chinese province of Manchuria in 1931. Despite investigating, the League of Nations failed to stop Japanese aggression.

Military force Use of armed force (e.g. troops, bombing by aircraft) as opposed to political or economic methods.

Moral condemnation Criticism of a state for actions against another state – prelude to stronger action such as economic sanctions or military force.

Normalcy Term used by US President Warren Harding in the 1920s to describe the return to normal life after the First World War.

Secretariat The section of the League of Nations which carried out administrative tasks and also the agencies of the League.

Tariffs Taxes on imported goods which made them more expensive – often designed to protect makers of home-produced goods

Trade sanctions Restricting sale of goods to a nation or sales from a nation.

Unanimous Agreed by all.

Wall Street Crash Collapse in value of US companies in October 1929, which led to widespread economic distress.

3 Why had international peace collapsed by 1939?

3.1 What were the long-term consequences of the peace treaties of 1919–23?

The Versailles settlement left many major powers dissatisfied

- Italy had hoped to gain more out of the peace settlement, especially more colonies from Germany and Turkey.
- Japan had its racial equality clause rejected at the Paris Peace Conference.
- Germany resented the Treaty of Versailles. It opposed the harsh territorial, military and financial terms. Since the end of the First World War, Weimar politicians had been accused of stabbing Germany in the back for signing the armistice and the Treaty and were referred to as the '**November Criminals**' by right-wing nationalists like Hitler.
- Germans had been split apart by the Treaty which led to nationalism: East Prussia had been separated by the **Polish Corridor** and nearly 4 million Germans lived in the **Sudetenland** in Czechoslovakia.
- Many in Britain began to feel that the Treaty was too harsh on Germany. They wanted to see Germany return as a power to defend against the threat of the Soviet Union.
- In France, the public felt the Treaty was not harsh enough and wanted reassurances, especially from Britain, that their borders would remain secure.

Hitler became the German Chancellor in 1933 and promised to destroy the terms of the Treaty

- Hitler laid out his plans to overturn the terms of the Treaty in *Mein Kampf* (1925).
- Some terms of the Treaty were already being ignored, for example reparation payments had already ceased.
- Hitler wanted to rearm and felt it was unfair that Germany was surrounded by countries with more powerful armies, while Germany was defenceless with only 100,000 soldiers and no air force.
- Hitler's desire to reunite all German-speaking people, create living space in the East (*Lebensraum*) and destroy **communism** would mean the terms of the Treaty would be violated.

Hitler destroys the Treaty of Versailles

| **1933:** Germany leaves the League of Nations and begins to secretly rearm. | **1934:** Hitler tries to annex Austria but is stopped by Mussolini. | **1936:** Hitler reintroduces conscription and occupies the Rhineland. | **1937:** Hitler tests new air force in Spanish Civil War. | **1938:** Hitler annexes Austria (*Anschluss*) and takes over the Sudetenland. | **1939:** Hitler takes over all of Czechoslovakia and invades Poland – war begins! |

> **Key point**
>
> The peace settlement had been a compromise and left many parties dissatisfied. In Germany, in particular, the Treaty of Versailles had bred resentment and Hitler promised to overturn its terms and make Germany a world power again.

> **Task**
>
> Create a spider diagram with 'Hitler destroys the Treaty of Versailles' in the centre and the branches labelled: Rearmament, League of Nations, **Anschluss**, German territory. Add dates and examples.

> **Practice question, Paper 1**
>
> **Describe how Hitler destroyed the terms of the Treaty of Versailles.**
> [4 marks]

> **Tip**
>
> Four-mark questions should have short answers. Only spend a few minutes answering them and do not waste time writing lots of background information.

18 Cambridge IGCSE and O Level History Study and Revision Guide

3.2 What were the consequences of the failures of the League in the 1930s?

The League was supposed to uphold collective security and stop aggressive nations, but ...

- The League had been seriously weakened by the effects of the worldwide depression. Member states, including Britain and France, concentrated on solving their own economic problems rather than concerning themselves with collective security.
- Britain increasingly viewed the Treaty as unfair and too harsh. The League was supposed to enforce the Treaty of Versailles but failed to stop Germany when it reoccupied the Rhineland in 1936.
- The League failed to stop Hitler rearming. Britain, France and Italy had formed the Stresa Pact in 1935 to try to condemn Hitler, but they were not prepared to go to war. Britain, France and Italy all began to rearm.
- The crises in Manchuria and Abyssinia had shown the world the League was powerless to stop aggressive nations and that Britain and France were not prepared to use military force. This encouraged Japan, Italy and Germany to take further actions.

The Saar region of Germany had been run by the League since 1919, but ...

- In 1935, the League held a plebiscite for people in the Saar region to vote on whether they wanted to be run by Germany again. Many opponents of Hitler were living in the Saar region and he was fearful of a negative result.
- Hitler allowed the plebiscite to take place and over 90 per cent of the population voted to return to German rule. This was a great propaganda success for Hitler and another blow to the League.
- Hitler promised to make no further claims to French territory, but it encouraged him to take further gambles in the future – the Rhineland would be next in 1936.

Task

The factors in the first column of the table are reasons why the League failed. Use the second column to explain the impact this would have on Hitler's foreign policy. Remember to add examples. The first one has been done for you.

Factor	Explanation
Depression	*The Depression caused high unemployment in many countries, especially Germany where it reached nearly 6 million in 1932. This led to Hitler promising to rearm Germany and expand its borders to help solve the unemployment problem. The League members were too focused on problems in their own countries to effectively oppose Hitler.*
Treaty of Versailles	
Disarmament	
Manchuria and Abyssinia	
Saar	

Key point

The League of Nations was supposed to maintain world peace through its system of collective security, but the Depression made its work almost impossible as leading members looked inwards to solve their countries' problems. This gave Hitler the opportunity to begin his aggressive foreign policy unopposed.

Practice question, Paper 1

Explain why the League of Nations' failures encouraged Hitler's aggressive foreign policy. [6 marks]

Tip

Remember that for six-mark questions you need to explain the reasons you give. Use full paragraphs and provide relevant knowledge to support your explanations.

Test yourself

1 How far was the Depression the cause of all the League's problems in the 1930s?

2 Do you think the Manchurian and Abyssinian crises would have encouraged Hitler?

3 How was the Saar plebiscite a body blow for the League?

3.3 How far was Hitler's foreign policy to blame for the outbreak of war in 1939?

As Chancellor, Hitler wanted to make Germany a great power again

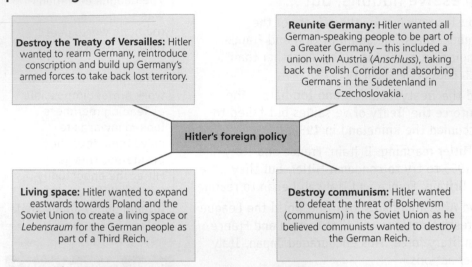

Destroy the Treaty of Versailles: Hitler wanted to rearm Germany, reintroduce conscription and build up Germany's armed forces to take back lost territory.

Reunite Germany: Hitler wanted all German-speaking people to be part of a Greater Germany – this included a union with Austria (*Anschluss*), taking back the Polish Corridor and absorbing Germans in the Sudetenland in Czechoslovakia.

Hitler's foreign policy

Living space: Hitler wanted to expand eastwards towards Poland and the Soviet Union to create a living space or *Lebensraum* for the German people as part of a Third Reich.

Destroy communism: Hitler wanted to defeat the threat of Bolshevism (communism) in the Soviet Union as he believed communists wanted to destroy the German Reich.

> **Key point**
>
> Hitler's foreign policy was simple – take back what Germany lost in the peace treaty and expand the German Reich, especially in the East. Hitler was prepared to gamble that Britain, France and the League would do little to stop him and waited for international crises to distract the major powers from Germany's expansion.

Hitler's initial foreign policy moves were seen as reasonable

- Hitler began rearming Germany in secret. After withdrawing Germany from the League of Nations, he staged a military rally in 1935 and reintroduced **conscription** in 1936.
- Nothing was done in response as other countries were rearming and Britain believed the Treaty had punished Germany too severely.
- Hitler didn't achieve everything he wanted. In 1934, Mussolini moved Italian troops to the Austrian border, which forced Hitler to back down in his attempt to annex Austria.

Hitler's first foreign policy gamble was the Rhineland

- The Rhineland had been demilitarised as part of the terms of the Treaty of Versailles and accepted by Germany as part of the 1925 Locarno Treaties. It was designed to protect France from German invasions.
- Hitler used the alliance between France and Russia in 1935 as an excuse to invade. He said Germany was surrounded by hostile forces.
- Germany's invasion went unimpeded – the League of Nations was busy with the Abyssinian crisis, Britain believed Germany had a right to the Rhineland and France was about to hold an election so politicians did not want to start a conflict with Germany.

In 1936, Germany tried out its weapons in the Spanish Civil War

- The **Spanish Civil War** was fought between the left-wing Republican Government and the right-wing nationalist rebels led by General Franco.
- The Soviet leader, Stalin, sent weapons and aircraft to support the Republicans and Mussolini and Hitler declared their support for Franco.
- Britain and France refused to get directly involved.

> **Test yourself**
>
> 1 Did Hitler's foreign policy aims suggest war was inevitable?
>
> 2 Why do you think Hitler's early foreign policy was not as aggressive as later on?
>
> 3 How did the success of the Rhineland invasion encourage Hitler to become more aggressive in his foreign policy?
>
> 4 How did Hitler manipulate events in Austria to his advantage in 1938?

- Germany sent pilots and aircraft from the new *Luftwaffe* (air force) to take part in bombing raids on civilian populations.
- The bonds between Mussolini and Hitler strengthened and Britain and France increased the scale and speed of their **rearmament**.
- At the same time, in 1936, Germany allied itself with Japan to form the anti-communist **Anti-Comintern Pact** and then made an alliance with Italy in 1937 called the Axis alliance.

Hitler, spurred on by his success and good luck, turned his attention to Austria again in 1938

- Many in Austria supported the idea of a union with Germany and there was already a strong Nazi Party there. Hitler told the Nazis to stir up trouble in Austria and demand the union.
- The Austrian Chancellor, Schuschnigg, appealed to Britain and France for help. No help was offered, and Schuschnigg held a plebiscite. Hitler feared losing the vote so demanded Schuschnigg's resignation. He was replaced by the Nazi leader Seyss-Inquart who requested help from Germany to restore order. Hitler's troops marched into Austria unopposed in March 1938.
- The plebiscite was held and over 99 per cent voted in favour of a union.
- The British prime minister, Neville Chamberlain, said it had been wrong to not allow a union in the Treaty of Versailles in the first place. Hitler's gamble had paid off again.

Practice question, Paper 2

Why was this photo published in 1937? Explain your answer using details of the source and your knowledge. [7 marks]

SOURCE A A postcard published in France to mark the bombing of Guernica in 1937. The text reads 'The Basque people murdered by German planes. Guernica martyred 26 April 1937'.

What year was the photograph published? What event is it referring to?

What message is the photograph giving the audience? How is it achieving this?

How does the photographer want the audience to react? What does the photographer want to persuade or convince the audience to do or to think?

Is the photo supportive or critical of the event? What details suggest this?

It is illegal to photocopy this page

Britain and France were not prepared to defend the Treaty of Versailles or the League

- The **remilitarisation** of the Rhineland and the union with Austria showed Hitler that Britain and France were prepared to appease his demands. This policy of Appeasement was particularly associated with British prime minister Neville Chamberlain (see Profile).

> **Profile**
>
> **Neville Chamberlain**
>
> - Chamberlain was an able government minister but was not good at listening to others.
> - He served in the governments of the 1920s and 1930s; he was the main supporter of the policy of Appeasement in the 1930s.
> - In 1937, he became prime minister. He believed Germany had been treated harshly by the peace treaty.
> - He is most famous for declaring 'peace for our time' after the Munich Conference in 1938, which has caused controversy among historians.
> - In 1940, he resigned and was replaced as prime minster by Winston Churchill.
> - Many politicians and the British public were in favour of the policy of Appeasement, but some critics, such as Winston Churchill, were strongly opposed.

> **Key point**
>
> Britain and France followed a policy of **Appeasement** towards Hitler – they gave into his demands to avoid a war. Some historians think this was because Britain and France needed time to rearm and that war was inevitable. Other historians think that Britain and France were prepared to do anything to avoid war, even allowing Hitler a free hand in Europe.

Chamberlain (arguments for Appeasement)

Threat of communism: Hitler is our best defence against the spread of communism into Europe from Stalin and the USSR.

British arms: We need time to rearm. Germany has been building up its army and air force since 1933. We are not ready for a war with Germany.

Fear of another World War: The people have suffered enough after the Great War of 1914–18. War must be avoided at any cost.

Treaty of Versailles: This Treaty was unfair on Germany and its terms too harsh. Hitler is just taking back what is Germany's so it can defend itself.

Cost of war: Britain and France are struggling economically due to the Depression and cannot afford another conflict.

Trust in Hitler: We believe Hitler will stop his demands and not risk war.

Churchill (arguments against Appeasement)

Hitler cannot be trusted: Hitler has broken his promises and asks for more and more. He aims to conquer the East and the rest of Europe and we must stand up to him.

German rearmament: Hitler is building up his armed forces quickly. We should stop him now before it is too late.

We look weak: If we do not stand up to Hitler the rest of the world will think we are cowards who are not confronting a tyrant.

Hitler's next aim was the Sudetenland

- Geographically, Czechoslovakia's borders pushed into the side of Germany. Hitler wanted to protect Germany from the threat of invasion.
- Economically, the Sudetenland had rich mineral deposits and fertile land, which would benefit Germany.
- Militarily, the Sudetenland contained much of Czechoslovakia's defences and fortifications. The Czech army was modern and well equipped and taking the Sudetenland would weaken it.
- Socially, over 3.5 million Sudeten Germans lived in the Sudetenland. Hitler wanted them to be absorbed into the German Reich.

Hitler finally took control of the Sudetenland as a result of the Munich Agreement

- Britain, France and the USSR had all promised to defend Czechoslovakia against a German invasion and the Czechs were also ready to fight. Crisis talks began to try to avoid war in Europe.

15 September 1938: Chamberlain met Hitler in Bavaria, Germany and agreed that parts of the Sudetenland would be given to Germany if the British, French and Czech governments agreed.	**September 1938:** Hitler demanded all of the Sudetenland immediately and claimed the Czechs were mistreating German citizens. Chamberlain ordered the British Government to prepare for war.	**29 September 1938:** The Munich Conference was held with the help of Mussolini. Britain, France, Italy and Germany were present, but Czechoslovakia and the USSR were not invited.

- At the Munich Conference, the four countries decided on terms that would prevent war, known as the **Munich Agreement**.
- Germany would receive the Sudetenland and the borders of the rest of Czechoslovakia would be guaranteed. The Agreement was presented to the Czech Government – it had no choice but to agree.
- Hitler marched his troops into the Sudetenland on 1 October 1938. Poland and Hungary helped themselves to Czech territory where they claimed their citizens were living.

The Munich Agreement avoided war, but not for long

- On his return to London, Chamberlain declared that the Munich Agreement had guaranteed 'peace for our time', much to the delight of many in Britain. War had been temporarily averted.
- The Czech Government fell into chaos over the Agreement and its leader Beneš resigned.
- Britain and France continued to rearm – clearly they believed that the Agreement only delayed war, rather than prevented it. Trust in Hitler and his promises had been discarded.

Practice question, Paper 1

'Appeasement was a necessary policy that could be justified at the time.'

How far do you agree with this statement? Explain your answer.

[10 marks]

Test yourself

1 What do you think was the main reason Hitler demanded the Sudetenland?

2 How might the public have reacted to the Munich Agreement in a) Germany; b) Britain; c) Czechoslovakia?

Task

Use the arguments from the speech bubbles on page 22 to create a table to plan for the practice question. Remember that you will need to reach a conclusion about how far you agree with the statement in the question.

Tip

For ten-mark questions on Paper 1 make sure that you explain why you agree or disagree with the statement in the question and explain other factors as a counter-argument. This will give your answer balance and depth. Use your own knowledge to give examples that support both sides of the argument.

Hitler took over the rest of Czechoslovakia in March 1939

- The policy of Appeasement ended when Hitler marched troops into the rest of Czechoslovakia.
- Britain and France realised that Hitler's next ambition would be to take over Poland. They told him they would go to war if that happened.

Hitler's next foreign policy aim was the Polish Corridor

- The Polish Corridor was German land that had been given to Poland in the Treaty of Versailles.
- Despite their threats, Hitler was convinced that Britain and France would not go to war over Poland after the Munich Agreement, but did fear war with the USSR if he invaded.

In August 1939, Hitler and Stalin signed the Nazi–Soviet Pact

- This Pact was a non-aggression pact. Germany and the Soviet Union agreed not to attack each other and secretly divided up Poland between them. Stalin was also allowed the Baltic states.
- Hitler had ensured that he would not face a war on two fronts if he invaded Poland. He could invade Poland and then concentrate on invading the West.

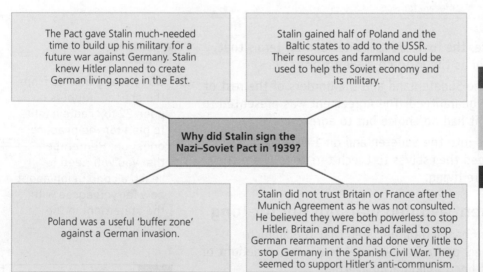

The Pact gave Stalin much-needed time to build up his military for a future war against Germany. Stalin knew Hitler planned to create German living space in the East.

Stalin gained half of Poland and the Baltic states to add to the USSR. Their resources and farmland could be used to help the Soviet economy and its military.

Why did Stalin sign the Nazi–Soviet Pact in 1939?

Poland was a useful 'buffer zone' against a German invasion.

Stalin did not trust Britain or France after the Munich Agreement as he was not consulted. He believed they were both powerless to stop Hitler. Britain and France had failed to stop German rearmament and had done very little to stop Germany in the Spanish Civil War. They seemed to support Hitler's anti-communism.

> **Key point**
>
> The **Nazi–Soviet Pact** is seen by some historians as a catalyst for the outbreak of war in 1939. Two ideological enemies made a temporary alliance, which gave Hitler the excuse he needed to invade Poland.

> **Practice question, Paper 1**
>
> **Explain why Stalin signed the Nazi–Soviet Pact in 1939.** [6 marks]

> **Tip**
>
> Six-mark questions require structured responses. Make sure you explain more than one reason and use your own knowledge to support your explanations.

Task

The factors in the first column of the table are reasons why Stalin signed the Pact. Use the second column to explain the impact this had on Hitler's foreign policy. Remember to add examples. The first one has been done for you.

Factor	Explanation
Time	The Pact gave Stalin the time he needed to build up his armed forces against a future German invasion.
Territory	
Trust	

> **Test yourself**
>
> 1 Why did Hitler want to invade the Polish Corridor?
> 2 Give reasons why Hitler was prepared to sign a non-aggression pact with the USSR.

It is illegal to photocopy this page

3.6 Why did Britain and France declare war on Germany in September 1939?

REVISED

Hitler ignored Britain and France's ultimatum

- On 1 September 1939, Hitler invaded Poland. Britain and France gave Hitler an ultimatum: withdraw immediately or we will declare war.
- After three years of Appeasement, Hitler still did not believe them. It took him by surprise when on 3 September 1939, Britain and France declared war on Germany and the Second World War began.

There were both long-term and short-term causes of the outbreak of war in 1939

> **Key point**
>
> Hitler invaded Poland in 1939 and Britain and France declared war. There were many long-term and short-term causes for the outbreak of the Second World War. The question many onlookers had been asking was not 'if' there would be a war in Europe but 'when'.

The Treaty of Versailles
The harsh terms of the Treaty had led to economic and political problems in Germany as well as great resentment. Some British leaders such as Lloyd George had warned this could lead to future conflict.

The failure of the League of Nations
The League's failures in the 1930s in Manchuria, Abyssinia, the Rhineland and the Spanish Civil War demonstrated to Hitler that it was powerless to stop strong nations with a powerful military, especially without the membership of the USA. This encouraged Hitler to make demands on Britain and France, who seemed to ignore the League for their own interests.

Causes of the Second World War

Nazi–Soviet Pact
The Nazi–Soviet Pact gave Hitler the opportunity he needed to invade Poland in September 1939. Hitler signed the non-aggression pact to avoid facing a war on two fronts (against the Soviet Union, and against Britain and France) at the same time.

The policy of Appeasement
Britain and France's policy of Appeasement 1936–39 gave Hitler the Rhineland, Austria and the Sudetenland without a shot being fired or a German life lost. Hitler believed Britain and France to be weak and so was encouraged to make greater demands. It also gave time for all sides to rearm.

Hitler's foreign policy
Hitler was clearly focused on retaking lost German territory and expanding eastwards towards Poland and the Soviet Union to create *Lebensraum* and destroy communism. Hitler's creation of a new German air force, the *Luftwaffe*, the reintroduction of conscription and the huge expenditure on armaments meant war in Europe was always on the cards.

> **Tip**
>
> Ten-mark questions will require you to examine several different factors, not just the one in the statement. The question asks, 'How far …?', so be prepared to compare the different factors to reach a judgement. A plan is a great idea for these essay questions.

> **Practice question, Paper 1**
>
> 'Long-term factors were the main cause of the outbreak of war in 1939.'
>
> How far do you agree with this statement? Explain your answer.
>
> [10 marks]

1   Make your own copy of the spider diagram on page 25. Colour code or label each branch as either a short-term factor or a long-term factor.
2   Add details and examples next to each by adding more branches and then a separate branch to explain how each factor helped cause the outbreak of war in 1939. You could write this in a different colour.
3   Draw lines to show any links between the factors. Explain how the factors link by writing on the line.
4   Then, using your diagram, answer the practice question. Use the table below to help you structure your answer.

'Long-term factors were the main cause of the outbreak of war in 1939.' How far do you agree with this statement? Explain your answer.

Plan	Details to include
Introduction	*Examine the different factors that helped cause the outbreak of war in 1939. Make sure you have long-term and short-term causes to show balance.*
Paragraph 1	*Examine one long-term cause such as the Treaty of Versailles, Hitler's foreign policy or the failure of the League.*
Paragraph 2	*Examine a different long-term cause.*
Paragraph 3	*Now balance your argument by examining a short-term cause, such as the policy of Appeasement or the Nazi–Soviet Pact.*
Paragraph 4	*Examine a different short-term cause.*
Conclusion	*Decide here if any of the reasons link together. Make a judgement about which factor(s) is/are the most important cause for the outbreak of war in 1939 and justify your choice.*

1   Why did Hitler believe Britain and France would do nothing if he invaded Poland?
2   Make a list of the long-term and short-term causes for the outbreak of war in 1939.
3   Do you think that war with Germany could have been avoided? Explain your answer.

Key terms

Make sure you know these terms, people or events and are able to use them or describe them confidently.

Anschluss Joining of Austria and Germany as one state – forbidden by the Treaty of Versailles 1919 but carried out by Hitler in 1938.

Anti-Comintern Pact Alliance between Germany, Italy and Japan in 1936 to combat the spread of communism.

Appeasement Policy of Britain and France in the 1930s allowing Hitler to break the terms of the Treaty of Versailles.

Communism/communist Political, economic and social system involving state control of the economy and less emphasis on individual rights than capitalism.

Conscription Compulsory service in the armed forces.

Lebensraum Living space – became part of Hitler's plans to conquer an empire for Germany in the 1930s.

Mein Kampf '*My Struggle*': the autobiography of Adolf Hitler in which he set out his theories about power and racial superiority.

Munich Agreement Agreement in October 1938 in which Britain and France agreed to Hitler's demands to control the Sudetenland area of Czechoslovakia. This is generally seen as the final stage of the policy of Appeasement.

Nazi–Soviet Pact Agreement in 1939 between Hitler and Stalin to not attack each other and to divide Poland between them.

November Criminals The German politicians who signed the Treaty of Versailles. This was a term of abuse exploited by extreme parties in Germany, especially the Nazis, to undermine democracy.

Polish Corridor Strip of land which, under the Treaty of Versailles 1919, gave Poland access to the sea but separated East Prussia from the rest of Germany.

Rearmament Building up arms and armed forces, used as a means to fight unemployment by many states in the 1930s, including Nazi Germany and Britain.

Remilitarisation Reintroduction of armed forces into the Rhineland area of Germany in 1936, even though this was banned by the Treaty of Versailles.

Spanish Civil War Conflict in Spain which was seen as a rehearsal for the Second World War when German and Italian forces intervened to support General Franco.

Sudetenland Area of Czechoslovakia which bordered Germany and contained many German speakers. Taken over by Hitler in 1938 as part of the Munich Agreement.

Who was to blame for the Cold War?

4.1 Why did the USA–USSR alliance begin to break down in 1945?

REVISED

The USA and USSR had united to defeat Nazi Germany, despite their ideological differences

- For most of the war the Grand Alliance consisted of British Prime Minister Winston Churchill, US President F.D. Roosevelt and Soviet leader Joseph Stalin.
- Britain and the USA were capitalist countries with democratic governments and were ideologically opposed to Stalin's one-party-state communist system.

> **Key point**
>
> The Grand Alliance was fragile. Defeating Hitler kept it united, but once Germany was defeated, ideological differences and the strong personalities of Truman and Stalin led to a breakdown in trust and co-operation.

	The USA and Britain	The USSR
Government and elections	Government elected by the people from a choice of many political parties (**democracy**).	One-party state with no free elections, just the Communist Party.
Economy	Capitalist system where property and industry were privately owned. There were rich and poor.	Communist system where the state owned and ran industry for the good of everyone (equality).
The people	Citizens had individual rights and freedoms guaranteed by law.	The state controlled every aspect of life with no individual rights or freedoms.
Ideology	Wanted other nations to adopt democratic governments, **capitalism** and stop the spread of **communism**.	Wanted other nations to adopt Soviet-style communism and stop the spread of capitalism.

- However, they were all prepared to work together in a strategic **alliance** to defeat Hitler, which they had done by May 1945.

Cracks in the wartime alliance were beginning to show even before the end of the Second World War

- Many in Britain and the USA did not trust Stalin and feared the spread of communism across Europe after the war.
- Stalin did not trust Roosevelt or Churchill. They had been openly hostile to communism and before the Second World War Britain had appeased Nazi Germany and ignored the USSR, for example, the Soviet Union was not invited to the Munich Conference, 1938.
- Stalin refused to share his wartime strategies with Britain and the USA during the war and Churchill did not share his knowledge of German troop movements with Stalin.
- However, to the public, the wartime alliance seemed to be positive and united.

> **Test yourself**
>
> 1 What factor kept the alliance united during the Second World War?
>
> 2 What differences in ideology between the USA and the USSR might have led to increased tension?
>
> 3 Do you think that the Yalta Conference was a success? Which leader was the most successful in achieving their aims?
>
> 4 Was it Truman or Stalin that was most to blame for the disagreements at Potsdam? Explain your choice.

At the Yalta Conference the Big Three were able to negotiate and agreements were made

Germany: The **Big Three** agreed to divide Germany and Berlin into four occupation zones run by Britain, France, the USA and the USSR. Germany would also be de-Nazified and war criminals would be brought to trial.

Japan: Stalin agreed to join the war against Japan after Germany's defeat.

Polish territory: Stalin wanted to absorb east Poland into the USSR.

Agreements at Yalta

Disgreements at Yalta

United Nations: They agreed to all join the new United Nations Organisation (UNO) to try to keep world peace after the war.

Eastern Europe: They agreed there would be free elections in occupied countries after the war. It was also agreed that eastern Europe would be part of the USSR's 'sphere of influence'.

Polish elections: Roosevelt and Churchill did not want Poland under Soviet control and wanted free elections.

- Poland was the main point of disagreement. A compromise was reached, however, and Churchill persuaded Roosevelt to accept some of Stalin's demands in return for promises that Stalin would not help the communists in Greece.

The Potsdam Conference in July 1945 was dominated by rivalry between Stalin and Truman

- The Soviet 'Red Army' had occupied most of eastern Europe as it advanced towards Germany. Stalin began setting up pro-Soviet communist governments, including in Poland.
- Roosevelt died and was replaced by Harry Truman. He was more openly anti-communist and was prepared to stand up to Stalin's aggressive expansion into eastern Europe.
- The USA had successfully tested the first **atomic bomb** as part of the Manhattan Project. Truman told Stalin about America's new weapon, although Stalin had already been told by his spies.
- Halfway through the Conference, Churchill was replaced in Britain with the Labour leader Clement Atlee.
- In Churchill's absence, the Conference was dominated by the rivalry between Truman and Stalin.
  - **Germany:** Stalin demanded crippling reparations and access to the Ruhr, but Truman did not want to repeat the mistakes of the Treaty of Versailles.
  - **Reparations:** Stalin wanted compensation from Germany for the devastation it had caused to the USSR. Truman again was reluctant to impose harsh reparation terms.
  - **Eastern Europe:** Stalin had won agreement at Yalta that he could set up pro-Soviet governments in eastern Europe. Truman, however, was very opposed to this.
- However, there were some agreements made. All three leaders agreed that the plans made at Yalta to de-Nazify Germany and bring war criminals to trial should go ahead. They also agreed that Germany would be governed by an Allied Control Council in Berlin with equal representation.

Practice question, Paper 1

Why did the alliance between the Big Three begin to break down at the Potsdam Conference in July 1945? [6 marks]

Task

To help you plan for the practice question, create a table with two columns. In the first column, write the reasons why the alliance between the Big Three began to break down at Potsdam: Red Army in eastern Europe; Truman; Atlee; The atomic bomb. In the second column write an explanation of each factor.

Tip

Remember that six-mark questions require explanation, rather than just a list of reasons or a description of what happened. Use full paragraphs to properly develop your answer and use examples.

Stalin increased his hold over eastern Europe after the Potsdam Conference

- In October 1947, Stalin set up **Cominform** (Communist Information Bureau) to co-ordinate the communist parties in eastern Europe to ensure they followed orders from Moscow. Only Yugoslavia, under Marshal Tito, resisted this and he was expelled from Cominform in 1948. Yugoslavia remained a communist state outside of the Soviet bloc.

> **Key point**
>
> Stalin used various methods to establish pro-Soviet regimes in eastern Europe after the Second World War. Britain and the USA saw this as evidence that communism needed to be contained, whereas Stalin proclaimed that eastern Europe was in the **Soviet 'sphere of influence'** and was necessary for defence against future invasions from the West.

Country	Date Soviet control established	Methods used
East Germany	1945	The Red Army remained after liberation and the Allies gave the eastern sector of Germany to the USSR to control. Red Army control was handed over to the Socialist Unity Party (SED), which was dominated by the communists in 1948 and the German Democratic Republic (GDR) was formed in 1949.
Poland	1947	The Red Army remained after liberation and the communists joined a coalition government. Opposition leaders were later murdered, and rigged elections gave the communists control.
Romania	1947	The Red Army remained after liberation. A communist was made prime minister in a left-wing coalition. Elections were rigged, putting communists in control. Communists took over control of the police and security forces. The monarchy was abolished.
Bulgaria	1947	The Red Army remained after liberation. A left-wing coalition won the elections. The communists executed leaders of other parties and destroyed the democratic system.
Hungary	1948	The Red Army remained after liberation. Communists won 17 per cent of the vote in 1945 and used the Ministry of the Interior to remove rival politicians. In 1948, they were the largest single party after merging with the Social Democrats.
Czechoslovakia	1948	The Red Army left after the war. A left-wing coalition won the elections in 1945 and by 1946 the communists were the single largest party. In 1948, non-communist members of the Government were removed or resigned, and Czechoslovakia became a one-party communist state.
Albania	1948	Communists gained power in Albania after the war with the backing of Yugoslavia and the USSR. Albania broke relations with Yugoslavia when it left Cominform in 1948 and became dependent on Soviet aid. It adopted a Stalinist-style government.

Churchill saw Soviet expansion as a threat to the West

- The **Western powers** were alarmed by Stalin's actions. After the war they had agreed that eastern Europe would be a Soviet 'sphere of influence' but they had not expected complete Soviet domination.

- In March 1946, while touring the USA, Churchill gave his famous '**iron curtain**' speech with President Truman in the audience.

- Churchill proclaimed that 'From Stettin on the Baltic to Trieste on the Adriatic, an iron curtain has descended.' Churchill suggested that the USSR had established communist governments behind this 'iron curtain' that threatened the liberated states in western Europe, and this would lead to conflict. President Truman agreed.

- Stalin thought differently. He viewed the **Soviet Union**'s control over eastern Europe as necessary for defence against future invasion from the West.

SOURCE A A British cartoon commenting on Churchill's 'iron curtain' speech, in the *Daily Mail*, 6 March 1946.

SOURCE B A Soviet cartoon. Churchill is shown with two flags, the first threatening an 'iron curtain' and the second proclaiming that 'Anglo Saxons must rule the world'. Notice who is formed by his shadow!

Task

Use a copy of the table below to help you compare the differences between Sources A and B.

	Source A	Source B
How is Churchill portrayed in the sources?		
What is the main message/attitude of the author?		
What is the provenance of the source?		
What is the author's purpose?		

Test yourself

1 What was the role of Cominform?
2 How did Stalin's view of Soviet control in eastern Europe differ from Churchill's and Truman's?
3 Study Sources A and B. What different messages do these two cartoons suggest?

Practice question, Paper 2

Study Sources A and B.

How far do these two sources agree? Explain your answer using details of the sources.
[7 marks]

Tip

Paper 2 questions that ask you to compare the similarities or differences between sources want you to go beyond just comparing the details. You need to try to compare the different message and purpose of each source for a stronger response.

The West was horrified at the complete communist domination of eastern Europe

- Britain and the USA were prepared to accept that eastern Europe was part of the Soviet 'sphere of influence'. This had been agreed at Yalta and Potsdam. However, it seemed like Stalin was attempting a complete communist take-over, rather than the establishment of Soviet-friendly democratic regimes.
- Greece would be a turning point for US foreign policy. Since 1946, Greece had been fighting a civil war between communists, who wanted Greece to be a Soviet republic, and monarchists, who wanted the return of the King of Greece.
- Britain had been supporting the monarchists and Stalin had protested to the UN over British intervention. The UN took no action.

Truman introduced a policy of containment

- Britain announced it was withdrawing its troops from Greece. This would have given Greece to the communists. Truman took action to stop the spread of communism and paid for the British troops to remain and prop up the monarchist government.
- This new policy of containment was known as the '**Truman Doctrine**'.
- The USA committed itself to help any country threatened by communist take-over by sending money, supplies, weapons and advice.

Containment would be the cornerstone of US foreign policy during the Cold War

- Truman believed that if the economies of Europe could be stabilised, then communism would not threaten European democracies.
- Secretary of State, George Marshall, was sent to Europe to assess its financial situation and found that its economy was in ruins.
- Truman asked Congress for $17 billion in aid to rebuild European prosperity. Congress refused at first as many Americans did not want to get involved in European affairs after the Second World War.
- The turning point came in 1948 when the communists seized control from the coalition government in Czechoslovakia and purged the government of all anti-Soviet leaders.
- Congress reacted and approved the **Marshall Plan**, making $17 billion available in Marshall Aid. For four years, the USA would provide loans to European countries. In return, these countries would create a strong market for US goods.
- Stalin refused to allow Soviet bloc countries to receive Marshall Aid as he feared that it would lead to closer ties with the Western powers.

> **Key point**
>
> The US policy of containment began in 1947 and was put into action in 1948 in the form of **Marshall Aid**. The USA hoped that this would help stop Stalin spreading communism further into eastern Europe.

Containment can be viewed from two perspectives

Stalin's Soviet view of Marshall Aid

I will not allow countries in eastern Europe to receive Marshall Aid. It will weaken my grip over their governments.

It is an attempt by the USA to spread capitalist ideas in Europe.

The USA will dominate Europe by making it dependent on the US dollar.

Truman's US view of Marshall Aid

This will halt the spread of communism in poorer countries by making them prosperous.

We will have new European markets to sell US goods to and prevent another depression like in the 1930s.

Europe will embrace democracy and free-market capitalism like the USA.

Task

The factors in the first column are reasons why the USA introduced Marshall Aid. Use the second column to explain the reasons. Remember to add examples. The first one has been done for you.

Factor	Explanation
Soviet expansion	Stalin had seized control of most of eastern Europe by the end of 1947 and established pro-Soviet communist governments. In his 'iron curtain' speech Churchill saw this as an attempt to dominate Europe and Truman believed that communism had to be contained.
Greece, 1946–47	
Post-war Europe	
Truman Doctrine	
Communist take-over of Czechoslovakia, 1948	

Practice question, Paper 1

Why did the USA introduce Marshall Aid in 1948? [6 marks]

Tip

Six-mark questions will ask you to explain reasons why or how something happened. Make sure you can give multiple reasons in your answer.

Test yourself

1 What events led to the formation of the Truman Doctrine?
2 What problems in post-war Europe might lead to a communist take-over?
3 How did the views of the USA and the Soviet Union differ towards Marshall Aid?

4.4 What were the consequences of the Berlin Blockade?

The Western powers united the Western zones of Germany

- It had been agreed at Yalta and Potsdam that Germany would be divided into four zones. Berlin, which was deep inside the Soviet zone, was also divided into four zones. An Allied Control Council which represented Britain, France, the USA and the USSR would decide matters.
- By 1947, with the USSR dominating most of eastern Europe, Truman had decided that a strong Germany would be a useful ally.
- In January 1947, Britain and the USA joined their zones together. This was called Bizonia. France joined a year later. Stalin's suspicions of the Western powers grew when Marshall Aid was made available to the Western zones.
- By June 1948, the Western zones had introduced their own currency. Stalin refused to accept this.

> **Key point**
>
> The division of Germany and Berlin was to become the focal point of the Cold War in Europe. The **Berlin Blockade** and the **Berlin airlift** demonstrated that neither side was willing to lose their grip over Germany.

In response, Stalin blockaded Berlin

- Stalin created his own currency in his zone and blockaded West Berlin. This cut off supplies by road, rail and canal from the Western zones. If the USA tried to destroy the blockade it would be an act of war.
- It was an aggressive move, but Stalin expected Truman to announce a withdrawal from Berlin. This would be a great propaganda win for the USSR.

But Truman was prepared to test his policy of containment

- Truman believed that if the West allowed Stalin Berlin, then West Germany might be next.
- Britain, France and the USA quickly decided not to back down over West Berlin and began a huge operation to bring supplies to West Berliners by air, known as the Berlin airlift.
- For 11 months, nearly 300,000 flights took place from West Germany and dropped over 2 million tons of fuel, food and other supplies to the 2 million West Berliners.
- Stalin, realising he had failed in his goal, lifted the blockade in May 1949.
- Stalin created the Council for Mutual Economic Assistance (Comecon) in 1949 for eastern European communist states. This tied all of the economies to Moscow in response to a strengthened West Germany and the availability of Marshall Aid.

North Atlantic Treaty Organisation: In 1949, 12 nations joined a military alliance that promised to defend each other against attack. Stalin did not react, but a Soviet defensive alliance – the Warsaw Pact – was formed in 1955 when West Germany joined NATO.

Federal Republic of Germany: In May 1949, the Western zones merged to form a single political union (West Germany) which was pro-American and democratic.

Consequences of the Berlin Blockade

German Democratic Republic: Stalin responded to the creation of West Germany by creating East Germany out of the Soviet zone. Germany, and especially Berlin, were now the flashpoints for the Cold War in Europe.

Proxy war: The crisis in Berlin had shown that the two superpowers would not start a direct war against each other. Both sides would instead support any state or group around the world opposed to the other side.

Test yourself

1 What evidence is there to suggest that the USA was more to blame for the crisis in Berlin?

2 What evidence is there to suggest that the USSR was more to blame for the crisis in Berlin?

Practice question, Paper 1

'The Cold War began with the crisis in Berlin in 1948.'

How far do you agree with this statement? Explain your answer.

[10 marks]

Task

Use your own copy of the following table to plan and then write your answer to the practice question.

'The Cold War began with the crisis in Berlin in 1948.' How far do you agree with this statement? Explain your answer.	
Plan	**Details to include**
Introduction	*Use this space to examine the different reasons for the beginning of the Cold War. You can use all of the information from Chapter 4.*
Paragraph 1	*Examine how far the crisis in Berlin in 1948 was responsible for beginning the Cold War.*
Paragraph 2	*Now balance your argument by examining a different reason, such as the breakdown of the Grand Alliance at Yalta and Potsdam.*
Paragraph 3	*Examine another reason, such as the conflict in ideology between the USA and the USSR (capitalism and communism).*
Paragraph 4	*Examine a final reason, such as Soviet expansion into eastern Europe or the US policy of containment (Truman Doctrine and Marshall Plan).*
Conclusion	*Decide here which reason was the most significant or important in beginning the Cold War. When did it actually begin? Was it always inevitable? Are all of the reasons equally significant or important?*

Tip

Ensure that you give plenty of time in the exam to answer ten-mark questions. You will need to plan and write a balanced essay-style answer using relevant and detailed evidence to support your arguments.

4.5 Who was the more to blame for starting the Cold War: the United States or the USSR?

The argument over who was to blame has divided historians

- The US view was that Stalin was to blame. The Soviet Union aggressively tried to extend its control over eastern Europe after the Second World War to try to make communism the dominant ideology. Many in the West during the Cold War adhered to this view.

- The Soviet view was that US imperialism was to blame. The USSR was merely defending itself against aggression from the West. The Truman Doctrine and the Marshall Plan were US attempts to spread capitalist ideas in Europe and destabilise the USSR.

There is evidence for and against each interpretation

US view – USSR to blame	Soviet view – USA to blame
The USSR broke the Yalta agreements over Poland and set up a Soviet government there.	Truman was much more anti-communist than Roosevelt.
After the Second World War the Red Army remained in eastern Europe and, with the use of terror, pro-Soviet regimes were set up.	Effect of announcement of atomic bomb by Truman at Potsdam.
	Doctrine of containment viewed as attempt to isolate USSR in Europe.
Cominform created, 1947. Eastern European communist countries took their orders from Moscow.	US supported anti-communist forces in 1947 Greek Civil War.
Stalin tried to absorb West Berlin into the Soviet zone with the 1948 blockade.	Marshall Aid was an attempt to extend US control over European markets and spread capitalist ideology.
Ideologically, Stalin was a dictator, fixated on spreading Soviet-style communism.	Creation of Bizonia in 1947.
	Creation of new currency in Bizonia in 1948.
BUT	**BUT**
USSR had suffered hugely in Second World War. Stalin was trying to defend communism.	Truman only developed his policy of containment and the Marshall Plan after aggressive Soviet expansion, fear of Soviet intervention in the Greek Civil War in 1947 and the communist take-over of Czechoslovakia in 1948.
Eastern Europe was part of the agreed upon Soviet 'sphere of influence'.	
After Truman's atomic bomb announcement and Churchill's iron curtain speech, Stalin couldn't trust Western leaders.	The Truman Doctrine was also a policy to help the war-torn countries of Europe.
Truman was openly hostile to communism.	Stalin had broken agreements at Yalta and Potsdam by preventing free elections in eastern Europe and setting up a pro-Soviet regime in Poland after the defeat of Germany.

Tip

Question 6 of Paper 2 will ask you to study all of the sources A–G. Make sure you refer to each source directly and use details from the sources to explain whether each supports the view in the statement or not. The best answers also evaluate the reliability or purpose of some of the sources by examining the provenances to question the content.

Key point

A key area for debate for historians studying the Cold War has been who was to blame for starting it. The USA and its allies have always pointed the finger at Stalin and his aggressive expansion, whereas the Soviets have pointed the blame at US foreign policy. Recent historians have revised earlier interpretations and seen that both sides share the blame. Some also suggest that ideological differences after the Second World War made conflict inevitable.

Practice question, Paper 2

Study all the sources on page 37.

How far do these sources provide convincing evidence that the Soviet Union was to blame for the start of the Cold War? Use the sources to explain your answer.

[12 marks]

Task

Study all of the sources carefully before tackling the Paper 2 question on page 36. Draw your own table using the following column headings:

- Source
- Inference: what/who does the source suggest is to blame for the start of the Cold War?
- Evidence (source details or quotes)
- Evaluation: does the provenance make you question the source's reliability?

SOURCE A Historian Eleanor Hore of the University of Essex, UK.

For Americans, private property was sacred and formed the basis for the rule of law, while for the Soviets private property was the source of all evil and inequality, preventing the development of all humanity to a bright and fair future. While in the West people were taught that if you work harder you better yourself, in the East people were taught that if they work harder, society gets richer and they would share in that. Both systems advocated freedom and democracy, but their understanding of these terms was totally different. Both sides believed that government should be for the benefit of the majority of the population. For the USA, this was ensured by free choice through the ballot box. For Communists, there was no need for free choice because the Communist party understood the hopes and needs of the people even better than the people themselves.

SOURCE B Stalin speaking soon after the end of the Second World War about the take-over of eastern Europe.

This war is not as in the past; whoever occupies a territory also imposes on it his own social system. Everyone imposes his own system as far as his army has power to do so. It cannot be otherwise.

SOURCE C A Soviet cartoon from 1947. It shows (from left to right) the USA, Britain and France. The three sticks tied together are labelled 'American zone', 'British zone' and 'French zone'. The building is labelled 'Yalta and Potsdam Agreements'.

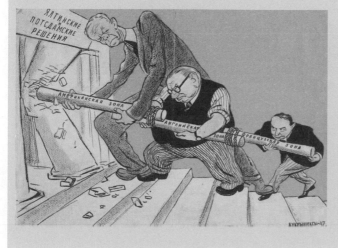

SOURCE D A British cartoon commenting on Churchill's 'iron curtain' speech, in the *Daily Mail*, 6 March 1946.

SOURCE E An American cartoon commenting on Stalin's take-over of eastern Europe. The bear represents the USSR.

SOURCE F President Truman speaking on 12 March 1947, explaining his decision to help Greece.

I believe that it must be the policy of the United States to support free peoples who are resisting attempted subjugation by armed minorities or by outside pressures … The free peoples of the world look to us for support in maintaining those freedoms. If we falter in our leadership, we may endanger the peace of the world.

SOURCE G Churchill writing to Roosevelt shortly after the **Yalta Conference**. Churchill ordered his army leader Montgomery to keep German arms intact in case they had to be used against the Russians.

The Soviet Union has become a danger to the free world. A new front must be created against her onward sweep. This front should be as far east as possible. A settlement must be reached on all major issues between West and East in Europe before the armies of democracy melt.

Key terms

Make sure you know these terms, people or events and are able to use them or describe them confidently.

Alliance Arrangement between two countries to help or defend each other, usually in trade or war.

Atomic bomb/hydrogen bomb Nuclear weapons; the atomic bomb was only used in the Second World War by the USA against Japan but was a constant threat in the Cold War.

Berlin airlift Operation in 1948–49 using aircraft to transport supplies to West Berlin, which had been cut off by USSR.

Berlin Blockade Action by USSR to cut road, rail and canal links between West Berlin and the rest of Germany. The aim was to force the USA and its allies to withdraw from West Berlin.

Big Three Leaders at Yalta and Potsdam Conferences 1945 – Roosevelt/Truman (USA), Churchill/Atlee (Britain), Stalin (USSR).

Capitalism/capitalist Political, social and economic system centred on democracy and individual freedoms such as free speech, political beliefs and freedom to do business.

Cominform Organisation to spread communist ideas and also make sure communist states followed the ideas of communism practised in the USSR.

Communism/communist Political, economic and social system involving state control of the economy and less emphasis on individual rights than capitalism.

Democracy Political system in which the population votes for its government in elections held on a regular basis.

Iron curtain Term used by Churchill in 1946 to describe separation of eastern and western Europe into communist and non-communist blocs.

Marshall Aid Programme of US economic aid to western Europe 1947–51. Aim was to aid economic recovery, but also to prevent more states becoming communist.

Marshall Plan The plan behind Marshall Aid. Although it was an economic programme it was also political. Some commentators argued it was an economic form of imperialism designed to allow the USA to dominate western Europe.

North Atlantic Treaty Organisation (NATO) An alliance formed by USA and other Western states which promised to defend members against any attack, particularly from the USSR.

Potsdam Conference Conference held in August 1945 between President Truman (USA), Stalin (USSR) and Churchill, then Atlee (Britain). Discussed major issues including the atomic bomb and Soviet take-over of eastern Europe.

Soviet 'sphere of influence' Terms agreed at Yalta Conference in 1945 – Western powers agreed that Poland and other parts of eastern Europe would be under Soviet influence.

Soviet Union The former Russian Empire after it became a communist state in the 1920s.

Truman Doctrine Policy of US President Truman from 1947 to promise help to any state threatened by communism.

West/Western powers Term generally used to refer to USA and its allies in the Cold War.

Yalta Conference Conference between USA, USSR and Britain in 1945 to decide the shape of the world after the Second World War ended.

5.1 America and events in Korea, 1950–53

At the end of the Second World War, Korea became a hotspot for the emerging Cold War

- By 1948, the north of Korea had been occupied by the Soviet Union and was controlled by the communists under Kim Il Sung. The south was supported by the USA because it was led by the anti-communist leader, President Syngman Rhee. Both sides claimed to be the legitimate government of all Korea.
- The dividing line between North and South was called the 38th Parallel.
- In 1950, North Korea invaded South Korea. The North had the support of the Soviet Union under Stalin and China under Mao. They sent military and financial aid to North Korea, whose armies were much stronger than those of South Korea.
- Kim Il Sung was convinced that as the Soviets had had the **atomic bomb** since 1949, the USA would not involve itself over Korea.

The USA responded and pressured the United Nations to act

- The policy of containment was put to the test. Truman first sent advisers, supplies and warships to South Korea, but he needed international support if there was going to be a war.
- As the USA contributed more to the **United Nations** (UN) budget than any other country, Truman used this to pressure the UN Security Council to act against the aggression of North Korea.
- As the USSR was boycotting the UN, it could not use a veto against any action. Resolution 84 was therefore passed, and the UN used armed force to stop the invasion. Eighteen member states provided troops or military support including Britain, France, Australia and South Africa.
- The USA, under General MacArthur (see Profile on page 40) made up the largest part of the UN force.

The war saw both sides on the offensive and defensive

> **Key point**
>
> The Korean War saw the **Cold War** spread beyond the confines of Europe. The USA was prepared to commit itself to a policy of **containment** and use force to try to stop the spread of **communism**. This would be the first of many 'proxy wars' in which the USA and communist countries were prepared to involve themselves.

1. North Korean success	2. UN counter-attack	3. Attack from China	4. UN counter-attack	5. Stalemate and armistice
(June–September 1950) Most of South Korea was overrun by the communists except a small area around Pusan in the south-east.	(September–October 1950) MacArthur launched an attack from behind enemy lines with UN forces heading northwards from Pusan. The capital Seoul was captured, and the communists were pushed back across the 38th Parallel.	(November, 1950–January 1951) Mao launched a counter-attack as he feared an invasion. Seoul was recaptured by the communists and the UN forces were forced to retreat back across the 38th Parallel.	(January–July 1951) The UN forces re-took Seoul. MacArthur argued for the use of a nuclear attack against China. He was relieved of his command by Truman, who feared Soviet involvement.	(July 1951–July 1953) There was little tactical advantage gained by either side. Peace talks began. Stalin's death in 1953 helped push North Korea to sign an armistice.

The Korean War ended a stalemate but had consequences for the continuing Cold War

- The USA showed it was willing to use force to oppose the communists and South Korea was protected – a success for containment.
- The UN had shown that it was more successful than the League of Nations had ever been when faced with an aggressive nation.

BUT ...

- North Korea remained under communist control with Chinese support. The USA strengthened its alliance with Japan and the Cold War was now in South-east Asia as well as Europe.
- Nearly 4 million casualties and massive damage to infrastructure demonstrated to the USA that it would be harder than it thought to fight off the threat of communism.
- The USA furthered its anti-communist alliances by setting up **SEATO** in South-east Asia and **CENTO** in Central Asia and the Middle East. The new Soviet leader, Khrushchev, believed the USA was surrounding the Soviet Union with anti-communist enemies and created the **Warsaw Pact** in 1955.
- Both the USA and the USSR began a nuclear **arms race**, developing more powerful weapons such as **hydrogen bombs** and Inter Continental Ballistic Missiles (**ICBM**s) that threatened world peace.
- The war showed Americans that containment had its limits and was not able to completely push back communist expansion by force.

Practice question, Paper 1

Describe the consequences of the Korean War. [4 marks]

Task

Complete a diagram like the one below to summarise the impact the Korean War had on the course of the Cold War.

> The USA showed it was serious with its policy of containment. It was willing to use force and the UN to stop the spread of communism in Asia.

Consequences of the Korean War

5.2 America and events in Cuba, 1959–62

Cuba became a communist nation

- Cuba had long been an American ally. There was a US naval base on the island and many American-owned businesses.
- The USA supported the **dictator**, Batista, as he was anti-communist. In 1959, communist Fidel Castro overthrew Batista.
- As a result, thousands of anti-communist Cubans fled into the USA and formed powerful pressure groups, demanding American action against Castro.
- Castro nationalised many American businesses and distributed US land to Cuban **peasants**.

President Eisenhower tried to destabilise Castro's regime

- Eisenhower used the Central Intelligence Agency (**CIA**) to find ways of overthrowing Castro. He started by imposing economic sanctions on Cuba and trade between the USA and Cuba stopped.
- The US media also criticised Castro and his regime.
- Eisenhower drew up plans with his National Security Council to remove Castro. The CIA began by training Cuban exiles for an invasion.
- Castro responded by allying himself with the Soviet Union in 1960 and Khrushchev, the Soviet leader, signed a trade agreement with Cuba worth $100 million in economic aid.
- Khrushchev also sent arms to help Cuba defend itself in the hope it would become a Soviet ally on the doorstep of the USA.

President Kennedy decided to act on Eisenhower's plans

- In January 1961, the new president, J.F. Kennedy, broke off all **diplomatic relations** with Cuba. He had approved Eisenhower's plan for 1400 US troops, including Cuban exiles, to land on a beach called the **Bay of Pigs**. They would march on Havana with the support of the air force and paratroopers.
- Kennedy hoped the plan would take Castro by surprise and in the confusion the Cuban people would join the US invasion force and overthrow Castro's regime.
- The plan failed miserably. Twenty thousand Cuban troops with tanks and an air force easily stopped the invasion force. Khrushchev watched the events closely.
- The failure of the Bay of Pigs invasion helped convince Khrushchev that Kennedy was young and naive. He also believed that the USA was not prepared to risk its own troops in Cuba.

> **Key point**
>
> The Cuban Missile Crisis was considered by many onlookers as the tensest period of the entire Cold War. The leaders of the USA and the USSR were locked in a stand-off over Soviet missiles placed in Cuba, which brought the superpowers to the brink of nuclear war.

Khrushchev decided to arm Cuba

To defend Cuba: Castro had allied Cuba with the communist USSR. Khrushchev wanted to ensure Cuba could defend itself against a US invasion after the Bay of Pigs.

To close the missile gap: Cuba was in 'Uncle Sam's backyard'. If Khrushchev put nuclear missiles in Cuba, they would be in range for a 'first strike' against the USA. This would close the missile gap as the USA had nuclear missiles in Turkey on the Soviet border.

Why did Khrushchev put nuclear missiles in Cuba?

To strengthen his position: Some in the Soviet Communist Party felt Khrushchev was not aggressive enough towards the USA. Placing missiles in Cuba as a deterrent would be a show of strength by the Soviet leader.

To bargain: Khrushchev thought that Kennedy was weak after his failed Bay of Pigs invasion. He wanted to take advantage of this and force the USA to make concessions.

Test yourself

1 Why was the Batista regime so unpopular with many Cubans?
2 Why did the USA try to destabilise Castro's regime?
3 What were the tensest moments of the 13-day crisis? Explain your answer.
4 Describe a positive and a negative outcome for Kennedy, Khrushchev and Castro after the crisis was over.

The USA discovered the missile sites and '13 days' of crisis followed

16 October: Kennedy was informed of the missiles and Ex Comm formed.

20–22 October: Kennedy decided on the use of a **blockade** and demanded the USSR withdraw its missiles.

23 October: Khrushchev replied saying the blockade would be ignored.

24 October: 20 Soviet ships approached but then received orders to turn around.

26 October: Khrushchev sent a first letter to Kennedy asking him to promise not to invade Cuba. In return, the missiles would be removed.

27 October: Khrushchev sent a second letter demanding that US missiles needed to be removed from Turkey as well. A U2 spy plane was shot down over Cuba.

27–28 October: Kennedy accepted the terms of the first letter and Khrushchev agreed to dismantle the missiles.

This was the last direct confrontation between the superpowers in the Cold War

● Khrushchev had been forced to back down, which upset many in the Communist Party and the Soviet military who thought he looked weak against the USA. The **missile gap** had not been closed. He was removed from power in 1964.

● The USSR succeeded in removing US missiles from Turkey, but it was forced to keep this a secret.

● Kennedy had successfully avoided a nuclear war and kept world peace as well as standing up to the USSR. Some hardliners in the Government thought he had been humiliated by giving concessions to the USSR.

● Castro's Cuba remained a Soviet ally and Kennedy promised not to invade. Cuba remained a communist state.

Tip

Make sure your answer is a balanced one when tackling ten-mark questions. These should be short essay-style responses using full paragraphs. You need to reach a judgement in your conclusion.

Practice question, Paper 1

'The Cuban Missile Crisis was a success for the US policy of containment.'

How far do you agree with this statement? Explain your answer.

[10 marks]

5.3 American involvement in Vietnam

Vietnam had a long history of fighting outside forces

- Before the Second World War, Vietnam was ruled by the French and known as **Indochina**.
- During the war the Japanese occupied Vietnam.
- In 1941, a communist, anti-Japanese resistance army, the Viet Minh, was set up and led by Ho Chi Minh. In 1945, after the defeat of Japan, they declared independence for Vietnam.
- France wanted its colony back when the Japanese left and between 1945 and 1954 a war was fought between the Viet-Minh-controlled north and the French-controlled south (Indochina War). The USA supported the French financially, as part of its policy of containment.
- In 1954, the French pulled out of Vietnam and the Geneva Peace Accord was signed. This temporarily partitioned the country into north and south in preparation for free elections.

The USA believed in the domino theory

- President Eisenhower and his Secretary of State John Dulles feared the communists would win in the elections. They believed in the **domino theory** – if one country fell to communism, other neighbouring countries were more likely to do the same.
- In 1955, the USA backed the anti-communist and Catholic Government in the South. They helped set up the Republic of South Vietnam under Ngo Dinh Diem.
- Diem was very unpopular with Vietnamese peasants who were Buddhist. His regime was very corrupt.

The Viet Cong was formed to oppose the South Vietnamese Government

- The **Viet Cong** was created in 1960 comprising peasants in the South as well as communists in North Vietnam who took their orders from Ho Chi Minh.
- The new US president, J.F. Kennedy, responded in 1961 by sending more money to help the South. They increased the size of their army and more advisers were sent to train the soldiers.
- The Viet Cong launched a **guerrilla warfare** campaign against South Vietnamese troops, officials and government buildings and attacked US supplies. In 1962, Kennedy sent 12,000 more military advisers to the South and equipped them with US helicopters.
- The Viet Cong were sent supplies from the North via the **Ho Chi Minh Trail**.
- In 1963, Diem's government was overthrown by a military coup and Diem was murdered.

President Johnson escalated US involvement in Vietnam

- President Johnson was more prepared to commit the USA to a military conflict. In 1964, communist patrol boats opened fire on US ships in the Gulf of Tonkin. The US Congress passed the Gulf of Tonkin Resolution, which allowed Johnson to launch a full-scale war against North Vietnam.

> **Key point**
>
> The war in Vietnam was a humiliation for the USA and the policy of containment. The superior technology and wealth of the USA was expected to successfully stop the communist take-over of Vietnam, but the tactics of the Vietnamese communists and negative world opinion towards US involvement turned the US public against the war.

It is illegal to photocopy this page

- In 1965, **Operation Rolling Thunder** saw the US air force bomb the cities and factories of North Vietnam. By 1968, there were over half a million US troops in Vietnam.

The Americans found it difficult to overcome the Viet Cong

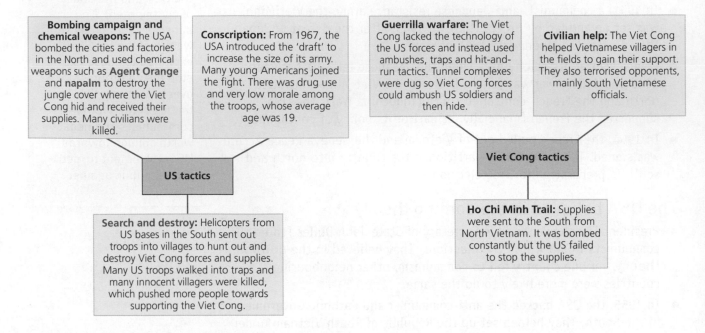

Bombing campaign and chemical weapons: The USA bombed the cities and factories in the North and used chemical weapons such as **Agent Orange** and **napalm** to destroy the jungle cover where the Viet Cong hid and received their supplies. Many civilians were killed.

Conscription: From 1967, the USA introduced the 'draft' to increase the size of its army. Many young Americans joined the fight. There was drug use and very low morale among the troops, whose average age was 19.

Guerrilla warfare: The Viet Cong lacked the technology of the US forces and instead used ambushes, traps and hit-and-run tactics. Tunnel complexes were dug so Viet Cong forces could ambush US soldiers and then hide.

Civilian help: The Viet Cong helped Vietnamese villagers in the fields to gain their support. They also terrorised opponents, mainly South Vietnamese officials.

US tactics

Viet Cong tactics

Search and destroy: Helicopters from US bases in the South sent out troops into villages to hunt out and destroy Viet Cong forces and supplies. Many US troops walked into traps and many innocent villagers were killed, which pushed more people towards supporting the Viet Cong.

Ho Chi Minh Trail: Supplies were sent to the South from North Vietnam. It was bombed constantly but the US failed to stop the supplies.

The American public turned against the conflict in 1968–70

- In early 1968 the Viet Cong launched the **Tet Offensive** – attacking over 100 cities and military targets.
- The Viet Cong was weakened by the attack, but it proved a turning point in the USA as the media began to question whether the sacrifice, expense and purpose of the war was worth it.
- US anti-war feeling and anti-war protests peaked during 1968–70 and were particularly fuelled by the events of the My Lai massacre in 1968.

A peace agreement was signed in January 1973

- In 1968, the new president, Nixon, and his National Security Adviser, Kissinger, wanted to pull US troops out of Vietnam but not make it look like they had failed in the policy of containment.
- By 1973, the number of US troops in Vietnam had been reduced to under 30,000. Nixon signed a peace treaty with North Vietnam in Paris and described the withdrawal as 'peace with honour'.
- By 1975, the whole of Vietnam had fallen to the communists. Vietnam's neighbours, Cambodia and Laos, became communist states the same year.
- US military and economic strength had failed to contain the spread of communism. It was a propaganda disaster for US foreign policy and the atrocities of the war had been exposed.

Practice question, Paper 2

Study Source A.

Are you surprised by this source? Explain your answer using details of the source and your knowledge.   [7 marks]

SOURCE A Reaction to the agreement of January 1973 in the influential American news magazine *Newsweek*, 5 February 1973.

FOR WHOM THE BELL TOLLS ... the nation began at last to extricate itself from a quicksandy war that had plagued four Presidents and driven one from office, that had sundered the country more deeply than any event since the Civil War, that in the end came to be seen by a great majority of Americans as having been a tragic mistake.

... but its more grievous toll was paid at home – a wound to the spirit so sore that news of peace stirred only the relief that comes with an end to pain. A war that produced no famous victories, no national heroes and no strong patriotic songs, produced no memorable armistice day celebrations either. America was too exhausted by the war and too chary of peace to celebrate.

Task

Use a copy of this table to help you analyse Source A.

Questions to ask	Answers
When was the source made and who made it? What event happened on this date?	
What is the overall message or opinion being presented in the source?	
What information in this source is surprising? Explain why, based on who made the source.	
What information in this source is not surprising? Explain why, based on who made the source and when it was made.	

Tip

This type of question wants you to decide if you are surprised or not at the attitudes or opinions being expressed in the source details. You need to use your knowledge and understanding of the historical context to help you explain. Make sure you carefully read the provenance. Look at the date to help you link the source to a specific event – is the source surprising or not now? Consider the author – is what they are suggesting surprising or not?

Test yourself

1 Briefly describe the domino theory.
2 Why was the Viet Cong created in 1960?
3 Create a brief timeline of US involvement in Vietnam from 1945 to 1965.
4 What were the turning points in the war?
5 Describe the differences between US and Viet Cong tactics.
6 Make a list of the reasons for US failure in the Vietnam conflict.

Key terms

Make sure you know these terms, people or events and can use them or describe them confidently.

Agent Orange Poisonous chemical used by US forces in Vietnam to defoliate (remove leaves) from forest areas to deprive enemy of cover.

Armistice End to fighting.

Arms race Competition to build stockpiles of weapons.

Atomic bomb/hydrogen bomb Nuclear weapons; the atomic bomb was only used in the Second World War by the USA against Japan, but was a constant threat in the Cold War.

Bay of Pigs Bay in Cuba, scene of a disastrous attempt by Cuban exiles to overthrow Fidel Castro. Caused humiliation for USA, which backed the attack.

Blockade Tactic involving cutting off supplies to a city or country, usually by sea but can also be a land or air blockade.

CENTO Central Treaty Organisation – alliance of countries including Britain, Turkey and Pakistan designed to resist the spread of communism.

CIA The Central Intelligence Agency is a US government department, formed in 1947, which gathers information (intelligence) about threats to the USA, but which also funds direct action (such as the Bay of Pigs invasion) to support US foreign policy.

Cold War Conflict that ran from c.1946 to 1989 between the USA and the USSR and their various allies. They never fought each other but used propaganda, spying and similar methods against each other. Also sponsored other countries in regional wars.

Communism/communist Political, economic and social system involving state control of economy and less emphasis on individual rights than capitalism.

Containment US policy in the Cold War to stop the spread of communism.

Dictator Leader of a state who has total control and does not have to listen to opponents or face elections.

Diplomatic relations How countries discuss issues with each other. Breaking off diplomatic relations can sometimes be a first step towards war.

Domino theory Policy in which the USA believed it had to stop countries becoming communist otherwise other nearby countries would fall to communism like dominoes.

Guerrilla warfare Type of warfare which avoids large-scale battles and relies on hit-and-run raids.

Ho Chi Minh Trail Route in Cambodia used by North Vietnamese and Viet Cong forces to supply forces fighting South Vietnamese and US forces.

ICBM Inter Continental Ballistic Missile – nuclear missiles capable of travelling through space and almost impossible to stop.

Indochina Former name for Vietnam.

Missile gap Term to describe the alleged advantage of the USSR over the USA in nuclear missiles. Historians doubt whether the missile gap was as real as was claimed.

Napalm Highly explosive chemical weapon which spread a fireball over a large area. Used extensively in the Vietnam War.

Operation Rolling Thunder Huge-scale bombing campaign by USA against North Vietnam during the Vietnam War.

Peasants Poor farmers who worked their own small plots of land and usually had to work the lands of landlords as well.

Search and destroy Type of tactic used by US military in Vietnam to locate Viet Cong fighters and kill them.

SEATO South East Asia Treaty Organisation – alliance formed in 1954 designed mainly to block the spread of communism.

Tet Offensive Attack launched by Viet Cong and North Vietnamese forces in 1968. Seen by many as the turning point in the Vietnam War as the US public turned against the war.

United Nations (UN) Organisation that succeeded the League of Nations in 1945 and whose aim was to solve international disputes and promote humanitarian causes.

Viet Cong/Viet Minh Underground army fighting against French rule in the 1950s and then government of South Vietnam and its US allies in Vietnam War.

Warsaw Pact Alliance of USSR and eastern European states to defend against attack and preserve communist control in eastern Europe.

6.1 Why was there opposition to Soviet control in Hungary in 1956 and Czechoslovakia in 1968, and how did the USSR react to this opposition?

In 1956, events in Hungary tested Khrushchev's new approach to the Soviet rule of eastern Europe

- Hungary was a member of the Warsaw Pact, set up in 1955. This was a defensive alliance between communist countries in the **Soviet bloc**.

- Many in Hungary resented Soviet interference and the communist policies of the hard-line leader Rákosi. They lost their **freedom of speech**, had Soviet troops permanently stationed in their country and lived in fear of the **secret police**. An estimated 2000 people had been executed and over 100,000 were in prison.

- The Catholic Church had been banned and priests imprisoned. Standards of living were poor, and the Russian language and culture were being imposed on the Hungarian population.

- Some reformers and opponents were encouraged by Khrushchev's new approach and the fact that he had allowed Gomulka, a reformer, to be appointed leader in Poland.

The outcome ...

- Estimates suggest that nearly 3000 Hungarians and 1000 Soviet soldiers were killed in the fighting; 200,000 Hungarians fled the country to Austria.

- The West did not send help as it was preoccupied with the Suez Crisis in the Middle East.

- The protest was successfully stopped, and a pro-Soviet regime installed. Nagy was executed and replaced by another hard-liner, János Kádár. He introduced some reforms but arrested anti-communist opponents. Over 300 were executed. Hungary remained in the Warsaw Pact.

> **Key point**
>
> **Communist** rule in eastern Europe was one of repression and poor living standards for many. After Stalin's death, fresh calls for reform emerged in some eastern European countries, including Poland and Hungary in 1956 and Czechoslovakia in 1968. Both Khrushchev and later Brezhnev had to ensure that the **Warsaw Pact** remained intact and were prepared to use force to keep Soviet control alive.

Timeline of the Hungarian uprising

June, 1956:	**23 October 1956:**	**24 October 1956:**	**25 October 1956:**	**29 October 1956:**	**4 November 1956:**
Moscow forced Rákosi to 'retire' after reformers appealed to Khrushchev.	Students in the capital, Budapest, demanded an end to Soviet occupation and the implementation of 'true socialism'. The police made arrests and opened fire on the protesters.	Soviet troops in Hungary were used to protect key buildings and roads. Hungarian soldiers and workers joined the protesters. The USSR allowed the appointment of a new leader, the well-respected Imre Nagy.	Nagy promised reforms to the communist system such as free elections and the withdrawal of Soviet troops.	Nagy's government began to introduce reforms. Some political prisoners were released and Nagy announced Hungary's intention to leave the Warsaw Pact.	Khrushchev refused to allow Hungary to leave the Warsaw Pact. He sent in over 1000 tanks and more troops. Fierce fighting took place between Soviet forces and the protesters.

In 1968, the new Soviet leader, Leonid Brezhnev, faced an uprising in Czechoslovakia

- The hard-line Czech leader was replaced with a reformer, Alexander Dubček after student protests. He promised changes to the communist system such as the removal of **censorship**, freedom of speech, rights for **trade unions** and freedom of movement known as **'socialism** with a human face'.

- Dubček was a committed communist and did not want Czechoslovakia to leave the Warsaw Pact. He had seen that years of harsh Soviet-style communist rule, a poor economy and low wages had resulted in very low standards of living for many citizens.

- The relaxation of censorship resulted in open criticism of communist rule and the spread of new and radical ideas – the **Prague Spring**. The USSR became very suspicious of Dubček's intentions.

Under pressure from East German and Polish leaders, Brezhnev responds ...

- On 20 August 1968, Brezhnev ordered Warsaw Pact troops and tanks to move into Czechoslovakia. There was very little violent resistance and the West did not interfere, seeing events as part of the Soviet 'sphere of influence'.

- Brezhnev and other Warsaw Pact leaders were worried that the ideas and reforms from the Prague Spring would spread into other Soviet bloc countries. This might weaken the Warsaw Pact and Soviet control of eastern Europe.

- Dubček was removed from power and expelled from the party. The USSR sent security forces over to monitor the Czech Government and ensure loyalty to Moscow.

- The **Brezhnev Doctrine** was announced in eastern Europe as new Soviet foreign policy:

  - Communist countries should have a **one-party system** (no democracy).

  - All countries were to remain members of the Warsaw Pact.

  If any Soviet bloc country threatened to break these conditions, other Warsaw Pact countries could use force to re-establish control.

Practice question, Paper 2

Study Sources A and B.

How far does Source A prove Source B is wrong? Explain your answer using details of the sources and your knowledge. [8 marks]

SOURCE A A Prague radio report, 21 August 1968.

Yesterday troops from the Soviet Union, Poland, East Germany, Hungary and Bulgaria crossed the frontier of Czechoslovakia ... The Czechoslovak Communist Party Central Committee regard this act as contrary to the basic principles of good relations between socialist states.

SOURCE B A Soviet news agency report, 21 August 1968.

The party and government leaders of the Czechoslovak Socialist Republic have asked the Soviet Union and other allies to give the Czechoslovak people urgent assistance, including assistance with armed forces. This request was brought about ... by the threat from counter revolutionary forces ... working with foreign forces hostile to socialism.

Test yourself

1 Create a spider diagram with three branches to list the social, economic and political causes for the uprisings in 1956 and 1968.

2 Compare and contrast the reforms announced by Nagy and Dubček.

Tip

Many Paper 2 questions require you to compare two different sources. Make sure you can compare the details in the sources, the provenances and the motives of the different authors to help you write a good answer. In this question, you will need to use your knowledge of the event to explain whether you think one source proves the other is incorrect. Is it lying or twisting the truth? Why is it saying something different?

6.2 How similar were events in Hungary in 1956 and in Czechoslovakia in 1968?

Key point

The uprisings in Hungary and Czechoslovakia have many similarities. Both countries attempted to reform the Soviet-style regime in different ways, but both were seen in the same way by the USSR and some Warsaw Pact leaders – as a direct threat to communist rule.

Events in Hungary and Czechoslovakia have been compared by modern historians

	Hungary, 1956	Czechoslovakia, 1968
Causes	Rebels were inspired by the reforms in Poland and hoped Khrushchev would allow changes. Many Hungarians hated restrictions on freedom and the secret police. The people resented the presence of Soviet troops and Soviet culture. Poor living standards.	Failure of communists to improve living standards and basic welfare. Economic depression. Desire for political reform to make communism less restrictive.
Aims of the rebels	Nagy wanted to have free elections and create impartial courts. His government wanted the removal of Soviet troops and withdrawal from the Warsaw Pact. Nagy also hoped the West would support the cause.	Dubček wanted 'socialism with a human face' – a less authoritarian form of communism with more rights for the people. To ease censorship and encourage new ideas – the Prague Spring. To possibly set up a rival Social Democratic Party. Czechoslovakia to remain a loyal member of the Warsaw Pact.
Events and actions by the rebels	Students and reformers in the Communist Party began the protests. Thousands of Hungarian soldiers joined the rebels. They forced the USSR to remove Rákosi and replace him with Nagy. The rebels were ready to fight the Soviet troops.	Communist Party under Dubček led the reforms. Prague Spring led to new ideas and criticism of the communist regime and corruption.
How the USSR and authorities responded	Khrushchev allowed Nagy to form a government and agreed to some reforms at first but refused to allow Hungary to leave the Warsaw Pact as it might destabilise the Soviet bloc. Soviet troops and tanks were sent in to fight the rebels. Nagy was removed from power and executed and replaced with pro-Soviet leader János Kádár.	Brezhnev and other Warsaw Pact leaders were concerned that the Prague Spring reforms might spread to other eastern European countries. Brezhnev tried to impose economic sanctions and moved troops to the border of Czechoslovakia. Under pressure from East German and Polish communist leaders, the USSR sent troops and tanks into Czechoslovakia. There was little resistance. Dubček was removed. Brezhnev announced the Brezhnev Doctrine.
Consequences of the uprisings	Two weeks of fighting with 3000 Hungarians killed and 200,000 fleeing the country. The USSR implemented some reforms. The West protested at Soviet intervention but took no action. Hungary remained a member of the Warsaw Pact.	No resistance or significant fighting. The West denounced the invasion but accepted Czechoslovakia as part of the Soviet 'sphere of influence'. Romania also protested at the Soviet invasion. Czechoslovakia remained a member of the Warsaw Pact.

Task

Use this activity to help you with the practice question. You will need to be able to write a balanced answer that examines the differences and the similarities between the different causes and consequences of the uprisings in 1956 and 1968. Use the bubble diagram below to help you plan your answer.

At the bottom of the diagram, there are some statements to get you started.

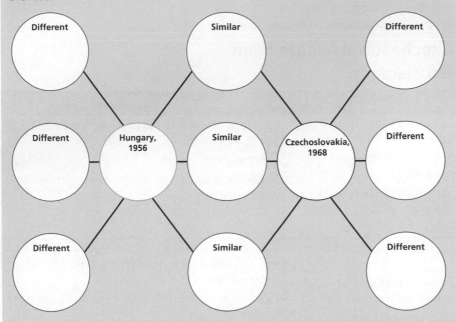

Both Nagy and Dubček were removed from their offices in the Communist Party.

The West protested against the invasions by Soviet troops and tanks.

Dubček was a committed communist and did not want to leave the Warsaw Pact.

Low standards of living for the population.

Practice question, Paper 1

'The Hungarian and Czechoslovakian uprisings had very different causes and consequences.'

How far do you agree with this statement? Explain your answer.

[10 marks]

Tip

Remember that you need to give an extended answer for ten-mark questions. Make sure you balance your response by agreeing with the statement and then disagreeing, before reaching a judgement.

Test yourself

1 Was the uprising in Hungary or Czechoslovakia more successful? Explain your answer.

2 Which uprising do you think the USSR viewed as more of a threat to the Warsaw Pact? Give reasons for your answer.

6.3 Why was the Berlin Wall built in 1961?

The differences in the standard of living between East and West Berlin caused large-scale emigration

- Many people in East Berlin suffered lower standards of living than those in the West.
- West Berlin was used by the USA as a showpiece for capitalism. Shops were filled with a variety of consumer and luxury goods.
- East Berliners also experienced the freedom and democracy present in West Berlin.
- As East Berliners could travel to West Berlin, they were very aware of the differences in the standard of living between the capitalist and communist areas.
- Many people moved from East Berlin to West Berlin and did not return. Many were well-educated young professionals and skilled workers tempted by the increased freedoms and stronger economy of the West.
- This was negative propaganda for East Germany and communist rule.

The Berlin Wall was built in response to this mass emigration from the East to the West

- Khrushchev issued President Kennedy with an ultimatum in 1961 demanding the removal of US troops from Berlin so it could become a free city. Kennedy refused.
- On Sunday 13 October 1961, East German soldiers began erecting a barbed-wire fence to prevent the free movement of people from East Berlin to the West. Soon this became a concrete wall.
- There was only one crossing point built in, known as **Checkpoint Charlie**. Border guards kept a constant lookout for people trying to cross the wall and many were killed over the next three decades.
- 27 October – both sides moved troops and tanks to Checkpoint Charlie and there was a brief stand-off as the world looked on. One by one they withdrew.
- Kennedy was prepared to accept the existence of a wall and the fact that East Berlin was permanently in the Soviet 'sphere of influence'.
- The Berlin Wall became a symbol of East–West tension. The West called the wall a prison for millions of freedom-loving East Germans. The communists saw it as a defensive barrier against capitalism.

Key point

Berlin had remained an area of division after the Second World War. The USSR wanted Berlin, which was in the Soviet zone, to become part of East Germany, but the West wanted West Berlin to remain part of West Germany, which had joined **NATO**. The 1950s saw many East Germans defect to West Germany through the frontier in Berlin and the **Berlin Wall** was built to stop this.

Practice question, Paper 1

Why did East Germany build the Berlin Wall in 1961? [6 marks]

Tip

Make sure you can provide multiple reasons 'why' when answering six-mark questions. This will make for a much stronger response. Good evidence is vital to develop your explanations.

Test yourself

1 What was the main cause of the Berlin Wall's creation in 1961?
2 Can the USA be blamed at all for the building of the Berlin Wall?
3 Do you think the Berlin Wall was inevitable? Explain your reasons.

Task

Make your own copy of the spider diagram below to gather evidence to explain why the communists built the Berlin Wall.

Political reasons

Why was the Berlin Wall built in 1961?

Economic reasons   **Social reasons**

6.4 What was the significance of Solidarity in Poland for the decline of Soviet influence in eastern Europe?

REVISED

By 1979, the economy in Poland was facing crisis and poverty was widespread

- Poland's economy had been performing well for the first half of the 1970s. But this changed in the late 1970s, leading to an economic downturn.
- The Government raised the prices of many different goods, including meat, in 1980. At the same time there was a limit on wage rises. This led to increased protests and strikes by Polish workers.

Workers at the Lenin Gdansk shipyard went on strike on 14 August 1980

- The striking workers were led by Lech Walesa. He put forward 21 demands to the communist government.
- Walesa also set up a nationwide trade union called Solidarity.
- 30 August 1980 – after negotiations, the communist government agreed to all the demands under pressure from public support for the strikers across the whole of Poland (see Factfile).
- Solidarity grew quickly and by September 1980 it had 3.5 million members. By January 1981, over a third of the workforce were members – 9.4 million workers.

Solidarity had many strengths

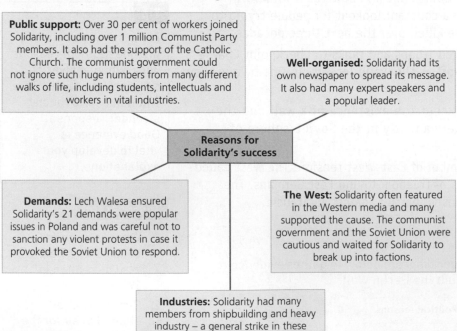

Public support: Over 30 per cent of workers joined Solidarity, including over 1 million Communist Party members. It also had the support of the Catholic Church. The communist government could not ignore such huge numbers from many different walks of life, including students, intellectuals and workers in vital industries.

Well-organised: Solidarity had its own newspaper to spread its message. It also had many expert speakers and a popular leader.

Reasons for Solidarity's success

Demands: Lech Walesa ensured Solidarity's 21 demands were popular issues in Poland and was careful not to sanction any violent protests in case it provoked the Soviet Union to respond.

The West: Solidarity often featured in the Western media and many supported the cause. The communist government and the Soviet Union were cautious and waited for Solidarity to break up into factions.

Industries: Solidarity had many members from shipbuilding and heavy industry – a general strike in these industries would have been a disaster.

Key point

Solidarity was a trade union that became a mass protest against the poor economic conditions and repression in Poland under the communists. It succeeded in gaining worldwide attention for the cause, which threatened the stability of the Soviet bloc. Once again, force was used to restore communist control.

Factfile

Main demands of the strikers

- Allow free trade unions to form independent of the Communist Party
- The right to strike
- Increased pay to compensate for price rises
- End government censorship and allow the Catholic Church to broadcast its services
- Free elections of factory managers with no Communist Party interference

The communist government crushed Solidarity

- In February 1981, the leader of the army, Jaruzelski, became prime minister. He met with Walesa and invited him to form a government of national understanding.
- In reality, Jaruzelski and the Soviet leader, Brezhnev, were growing suspicious of Solidarity and wanted it crushed.
- On 13 December 1981, the communist government introduced **martial law** and arrested nearly 10,000 Solidarity leaders including Walesa. Jaruzelski claimed he had uncovered plans for a coup. Brezhnev ordered the Soviet army to carry out training manoeuvres on the Polish border.
- The communists were not prepared to allow Solidarity any political power that might threaten the stability of Poland and the Warsaw Pact as a whole.
- Crushing Solidarity was made easier for the communists by the fact that the trade union was splitting into factions that disagreed with each other.

Solidarity was a significant event in the decline of Soviet influence

- Its popularity showed that communism was not providing a good standard of living for its population.
- It demonstrated the inefficiency and corruption of communist leaders.
- It showed that it was possible to take a stand against communism and that people would support this stand.

Task

The factors in the first column are reasons why martial law was introduced in 1981. Use the second column to add an explanation and supporting detail. One has been completed for you.

Factor	Explanation
Economic crisis	Poland was facing a severe economic downturn in the late 1970s and by 1980 the prices of goods were rising rapidly and wages were being limited. This led to widespread strikes and calls for reform which threatened communist rule in Poland.
Popularity	
Support from the West	
Factions	

Test yourself

1 Give an example of one economic and one political demand made by Walesa.
2 Create a brief timeline of events in Poland from 1979 to 1981.
3 Why did the Soviet Union get involved in crushing Solidarity? Explain your answer.

Practice question, Paper 1

Why was martial law introduced in Poland in 1981? [6 marks]

Tip

Six-mark questions require structured responses. Make sure you explain more than one reason and use your own knowledge to support your explanation.

6.5 How far was Gorbachev personally responsible for the collapse of Soviet control over eastern Europe?

In 1985, Gorbachev became leader and wanted to reform the communist system in eastern Europe

- Gorbachev saw that communism had failed to improve the lives of ordinary people. He wanted to reform the system so that it would.
- He was a committed communist who wanted to reform communism before it failed.

Gorbachev met with Warsaw Pact leaders in 1985 to announce his reforms

- Gorbachev told the leaders that they had to reform, like the Soviet Union, to improve living standards.
- He made it clear that the Soviet Union would no longer intervene to prop up communist regimes in eastern Europe.
- Many Warsaw Pact leaders did not believe Gorbachev. They thought his ideas were insane.
- Gorbachev went ahead and announced the following reforms:
  - *Glasnost* (openness): Social and political reforms. Open debate on problems with government policy.
  - *Perestroika* (restructuring): Political and economic reforms. Allowed market forces into the Soviet economy.
  - Reducing defence spending: This spending had been draining the Soviet economy. The **Red Army** was to be smaller and spending on nuclear weapons was to decrease.
  - Improving relations with the West: Gorbachev believed the Cold War could be ended if the East and West engaged in diplomatic talks and co-operation, rather than confrontation. Gorbachev and President Reagan met many times and relations between the two **superpowers** improved.

Between 1989 and 1990 people removed communist governments throughout eastern Europe

- Gorbachev intended that all Warsaw Pact countries would implement his reforms. He believed that these communist countries should be able to choose their own paths to socialism. He made it clear that the Soviet Union would not stand in their way at attempts at democracy.
- In July 1988, Gorbachev announced that Soviet troops would be withdrawn from eastern European countries. People in many countries began to call for independence in 1989.
  - **Hungary** – barbed-wire fence between Hungary and Austria dismantled. Free elections declared.
  - **Poland** – Solidarity won first free elections.
  - **Germany** – following huge demonstrations in Germany in October, the Berlin Wall was dismantled.
  - **Czechoslovakia** – government opened borders to the West and allowed formation of other political parties, following huge demonstrations.

> **Key point**
>
> By the end of 1991, Soviet control in eastern Europe had collapsed. The last decade of Soviet rule in eastern Europe had seen growing calls for independence, having been spurred on by worsening economic conditions and the political and economic reforms initiated by Gorbachev in his attempts to preserve the communist system.

- **Romania** – a bloody revolution ended with the execution of the communist dictator.
- **Bulgaria** – huge demonstrations against communism.
- **Latvia** – declared independence from the USSR.

The USA also played a part in the collapse of communism in eastern Europe

- Ronald Reagan, president from 1981 to 1988, took a tough stance against the Soviet Union and planned to end the Cold War by forcing the Soviet Union to overspend on defence.
- Reagan initiated a Second Cold War in response to the Soviet invasion of Afghanistan in 1979. He increased US defence spending by a third and called the Soviet Union an 'evil empire'. This forced the Soviet Union into an arms race. It had to spend more on defence while its economy was already overstretched.
- By the late 1980s, Gorbachev and Reagan were meeting regularly as Gorbachev realised that the economy was near collapse. Superpower relations improved and treaties were signed that reduced spending on nuclear weapons and encouraged democracy in eastern Europe.

Events in the Soviet Union itself also aided the collapse of communist control in eastern Europe

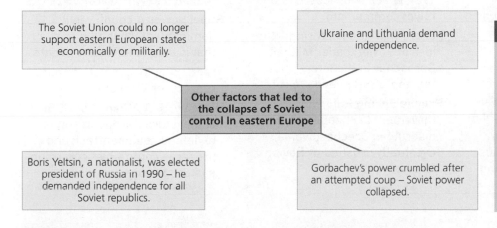

The Soviet Union could no longer support eastern European states economically or militarily.

Ukraine and Lithuania demand independence.

Other factors that led to the collapse of Soviet control in eastern Europe

Boris Yeltsin, a nationalist, was elected president of Russia in 1990 – he demanded independence for all Soviet republics.

Gorbachev's power crumbled after an attempted coup – Soviet power collapsed.

Task

Use your own copy of the following table to plan and then write your answer to the practice question.

'Gorbachev's reforms were the main cause of the collapse of communism in eastern Europe.' How far do you agree with this statement? Explain your answer.	
Plan	**Details to include**
Introduction	*Use this space to examine the different reasons for the collapse of communism.*
Paragraph 1	*Examine how far Gorbachev's social, political and economic reforms led to the collapse of communism in eastern Europe (glasnost/perestroika for example).*
Paragraph 2	*Examine some of Gorbachev's other reforms such as removing Soviet troops from eastern Europe or the ending of the Brezhnev Doctrine.*
Paragraph 3	*Give balance to your answer by examining other factors that led to the collapse of communism in eastern Europe, such as the treaties between Reagan and Gorbachev.*
Paragraph 4	*Examine a final alternative factor such as the economic pressures of the Soviet–Afghan War.*
Conclusion	*Decide here which reason was the most significant or important in the collapse of communism in eastern Europe. Was it Gorbachev's reforms or specifically one of the reforms such as glasnost? Were external factors or economic pressures more important? Do they all connect and have equal importance?*

Key terms

Make sure you know these terms, people or events and are able to use them or describe them confidently.

Berlin Wall Barrier constructed by communist East German Government to block movement between East and West Berlin. As well as a wall there were fences, dogs and armed guards.

Brezhnev Doctrine Policy of USSR from 1968 which effectively meant no eastern European states would be allowed to have a non-communist government.

Censorship System of controlling information to the public, usually employed by governments. Can refer to paper, radio, TV or online information.

Checkpoint Charlie Most famous point where travel between communist East Berlin and US-controlled West Berlin was possible.

Communism/communist Political, economic and social system involving state control of economy and less emphasis on individual rights than capitalism.

Freedom of speech Ability to publish or speak any religious or political view without being arrested.

Glasnost Openness and transparency – policy of Soviet leader Mikhail Gorbachev in the 1980s designed to allow people to have their views heard and criticise the government.

Martial law Rule by the military rather than a civil police force.

NATO North Atlantic Treaty Organisation: Alliance formed by USA and other Western states which promised to defend members against any attack, particularly from the USSR.

One-party system A system where only one political party is permitted by law such as Nazi Germany or the USSR under communism.

People power Term to describe the rise of popular action against communist regimes in 1989, which contributed to the fall of communism.

Perestroika Restructuring – the idea of Soviet leader Mikhail Gorbachev in the later 1980s that the USSR needed to reform.

Prague Spring Reform movement to change communist rule in Czechoslovakia, eventually crushed by Soviet forces.

Red Army Armed forces of the communists in the Russian Civil War 1918–21 and then the official forces of the Soviet Union.

Secret police A police force specialising in dealing with threats to the state, e.g. political opponents rather than normal crimes.

Socialism Political system in which government takes strong control of economic and social life. In theory socialist societies would eventually become communist societies.

Solidarity Polish trade union which emerged in the 1980s and opposed the communist government there.

Soviet bloc Eastern European states controlled by communist governments from the end of the Second World War to 1989.

Superpower A country in a dominant international position that is able to influence events.

Trade union Organisation that represents workers.

Warsaw Pact Alliance of USSR and eastern European states to defend against attack and preserve communist control in eastern Europe.

7.1 Why was Saddam Hussein able to come to power in Iraq?

Britain ran Iraq after the end of the First World War

- Under the terms of the Treaty of Sèvres, 1920, what we now think of as Iraq was run by the British as a League of Nations mandate. The British wanted to control the rich oil reserves in Iraq.

- The British Government invited Faisal, a member of a leading Iraqi family, to become king and head of the new government in 1921. The British hoped to use King Faisal as a collaborator so they could control foreign policy and the oil – this angered Iraqi nationalists who wanted independence.

- Under King Faisal, Iraq prospered. Education and the economy improved *but* there was a lot of inequality as the country was dominated by a small number of large landowners while most of the population remained very poor.

- Inequality and the fact that Britain supported the new Jewish state of Israel in 1948, led to a growth in **Arab nationalism** which opposed Western interference in Iraqi affairs.

> **Key point**
>
> Saddam Hussein used a variety of methods to try to establish himself as the ruler of Iraq. It took him 11 years to establish himself as president after the 1968 July Revolution. He was prepared to bide his time and manoeuvre himself into a strong position by appointing friends and family to high positions.

The growth in Arab nationalism led to the development of the Baath Party

- The **Baath Party** called for unity among Arabs in the Middle East and wanted to resist British rule. A young Saddam Hussein joined the Baathists in 1957.

- In 1958, King Faisal and his family were executed after a **coup** by leading members of the military led by General Abdul Karim Qasim. A republic was declared as part of the 14 July Revolution.

- Saddam Hussein was chosen by the Baath Party to assassinate General Abdul Karim Qasim in 1959. He failed and went into exile, but he had now emerged as a leading member of the Baath Party.

- The Baath Party was dominated by **Sunni** Muslims even though a majority of Iraq's population was **Shiite** Muslim. At first, both groups were in the Government to show unity.

Saddam built up a power base in the Baath Party and the army

- In 1963, following the death of Qasim, Saddam returned from exile and was given a minor position in the Government, now ruled by the Baath Party. He was also made head of the Iraqi Intelligence Services. Saddam now began building up alliances and friendships and by 1964 was a member of the Regional Command – the main decision-making body in the Baath Party.

- Saddam ensured that friends and family were placed in positions of power in the Baath Party and the armed forces.
- He planned to overthrow the current president of Iraq – Abdul Salam Arif – but the conspiracy was uncovered, and he was imprisoned for two years before escaping in July 1966.
- In 1968, together with army officers who were sympathetic to the Baathist cause, Arif was overthrown in a bloodless revolution called the July Revolution. The new President Bakr rewarded Saddam with the vice-presidency and vice-chairmanship of the new Revolutionary Command Council. Saddam was now the second most powerful person in Iraq after Bakr.
- By 1972, Saddam was probably the most influential man in the Iraqi Government. He used a variety of methods over the next few years to manoeuvre himself into a position to be declared president in 1979.

Saddam used popularity, control and repression to come to power

Increased his popularity: In 1972, the Government nationalised the Iraqi oil industry and used the wealth to improve healthcare, education and welfare services for the Iraqi people. Iraq's income rose from $575 million in 1972 to $26,500 million in 1980.

Increased control: The Baath Party increased its influence over the army, security forces and society. Trade unions, sports clubs and schools came under state control and promoted Arab nationalism.

What methods did Saddam Hussein use to become president in 1979?

Increased repression: Saddam was made a general in the army in 1976. He increased his control over the armed forces and the secret police to remove opposition and those suspected of disloyalty. Many were imprisoned or executed. Saddam filled the army with Sunni Muslims, including family and friends.

Task

Create a timeline from 1920 to 1979. Choose and highlight three events that you think were turning points that allowed Saddam Hussein to come to power in 1979. Then write three paragraphs explaining your choices.

Test yourself

1 What methods did the British use to control Iraq after 1920?
2 What factors led to the growth in Arab nationalism in Iraq?
3 Which group in Iraq dominated the Baath Party?
4 How did Saddam Hussein build up support in the Iraqi Government?

Practice question, Paper 1

Explain why Saddam Hussein was able to rise to power by 1979.
[6 marks]

Tip

You will need to write paragraph answers for six-mark and ten-mark questions. Make sure you can use relevant examples in your paragraphs to help explain your reasons.

7.2 What was the nature of Saddam Hussein's rule in Iraq?

Saddam used a carrot-and-stick approach to hold on to power for another 25 years

Carrot	Stick
Improving the economy Saddam used the massive $26 billion revenue from the oil industry (1980) to fund wage rises and tax cuts for many Iraqis, especially Sunni Muslims.	**Purges and show trials** Saddam used his many positions in the Government to purge the Baath Party and the army of opponents using televised show trials which resulted in imprisonment or execution – over 500 of his own party were executed!
Modernising healthcare and education The Government funded a massive building programme for schools and hospitals and increased university places.	**Personality cult** Like Stalin in Soviet Russia, Saddam used the media to portray himself as a god-like leader and defender of the Arab world. Statues, portraits, radio and TV all glorified Saddam's achievements.
Modernising the infrastructure Electrification was extended across the whole country, including rural areas, and a rail network was constructed.	**Repression** Saddam wanted complete control of the different peoples in Iraq. Over 180,000 Kurds were killed using mass executions and **chemical weapons** to stop Kurdish demands for a separate homeland. Many of the majority Shiite Iraqis, who were distrusted by Saddam after the Iranian Revolution, were deported or had their property confiscated.

Saddam wanted to convert Iraq into a major military power in the region

- Saddam was concerned over the threat posed by Iran after the Islamic Revolution in 1979 and wanted to make Iraq the greatest military power in the Gulf region.
- Saddam used oil revenues to buy weapons from the Soviet Union and major European powers such as France, to modernise his army with helicopters, artillery and tanks. The army was over 200,000 strong by 1981.
- Saddam also spent huge sums of money on building up chemical and biological weapons including mustard gas and anthrax. He also wanted to start a nuclear weapons programme, but it was destroyed by Israeli bombers in 1981.

Saddam intended to create a totalitarian regime in Iraq

- The Baath Party controlled nearly every aspect of daily life in Iraq and was dominated by Saddam Hussein and his trusted associates and family relatives.
- Children were indoctrinated in schools and in Baath Party youth organisations and censorship of the press ensured that criticism of the Government was nearly impossible.
- 'Show' elections and referendums were rigged to give Saddam 99.9 per cent approval ratings.

Key point

Saddam wanted to create a totalitarian state in Iraq like Stalin had done in Soviet Russia. He used many of the same methods to achieve this, including a system of terror and a cult of personality.

Task

Write the word 'SADDAM' vertically in your exercise book. Use each letter to start a sentence which describes a different method used by Saddam to control the Iraqi people.

Practice question, Paper 1

Describe the methods used by Saddam Hussein to control the Iraqi people. [4 marks]

Tip

For four-mark questions you will need to write a short response that focuses on factual detail. Don't spend too long on these questions.

Test yourself

1. How did the Iraqi people benefit from Saddam's rule?
2. What methods did Saddam Hussein use to control the Iraqi people?
3. Which groups in Iraq suffered under Saddam Hussein's rule?
4. How did Saddam Hussein increase Iraq's military strength?

REVISED

Iranians wanted independence from British influence

- Iran's oil fields were controlled by the British-owned Anglo-Iranian Oil Company. In 1951, the popular prime minister Mohammed Mossadeq demanded that the Shah (Iran's ruler) nationalise Iran's oil industry.
- Mossadeq became a hero to millions both in and outside of Iran, but Britain withdrew its workforce and blockaded Iran's ports.

The Shah allied himself with Western powers

- The Shah, with the help of the CIA and MI6, overthrew Mossadeq in a military coup in August 1953.
- The coup was not popular with most Iranians who now associated the Shah's regime with British and American interference.
- Iran joined an anti-Soviet alliance with Britain as part of the Cold War.
- The Shah made some land reforms and gave women the vote, but there was still a big gap between rich and poor.

The mullahs became the Shah's opposition

- By the late 1970s the contrast between rich and poor was stark, especially in the capital Tehran where the poor lived in shanty towns.
- The mullahs – Muslim religious leaders – criticised the Shah and his supporters for their wealth and corruption and their close relationship with the non-Muslim West.
- The main leader of the opposition, **Ayatollah** Khomeini, protested against the exploitation of the Iranian people by the Shah and his American allies. He encouraged street demonstrations which targeted banks, cinemas and other areas of foreign influence which was thought to be unIslamic.

Iran became an Islamic republic

- In January 1979, the Shah left the country due to ill health and Khomeini returned from exile. A referendum was held with the support of the army which abolished the monarchy and established an Islamic republic.
- Khomeini's supporters dominated Parliament and he was proclaimed the 'supreme leader' of Shiite Iran. Khomeini was keen to remove Western influences, pass new laws based on the Koran and spread the revolution to other unIslamic regimes, including Iraq.

Key point

Britain and the USA wanted to control Iran's oil fields and have the Shah as an ally against the Soviet Union during the Cold War. This led to a corrupt regime. Khomeini and the **mullahs** used opposition to it to gain support for an Islamic republic.

Test yourself

1 What problems were caused in Iran due to its oil fields?

2 What made Mossadeq so popular with the Iranian people?

3 What mistakes were made by the Shah and his Government?

4 What methods did Khomeini and the mullahs use to increase their popularity in Iran?

Practice question, Paper 1

'British influence in Iran was the main reason for the revolution in 1979.'

How far do you agree with this statement?

[10 marks]

Tip

Ten-mark questions require a balanced, essay-style response. You should devote the most time to these questions and write in full paragraphs.

Task

Complete a table like the one below to compare the different factors that led to the ending of the Shah's regime in 1979.

Factor	Detail	Explanation
Mossadeq		
Britain and the USA		
The mullahs		
Khomeini		

7.4 What were the causes and consequences of the Iran–Iraq War, 1980–88?

Saddam saw an opportunity to exploit Iran's weak position

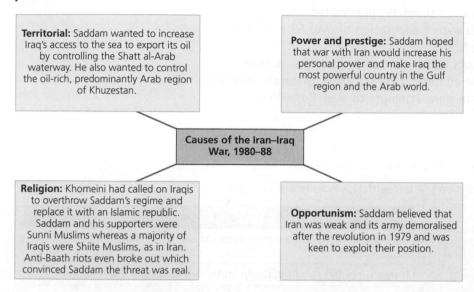

Territorial: Saddam wanted to increase Iraq's access to the sea to export its oil by controlling the Shatt al-Arab waterway. He also wanted to control the oil-rich, predominantly Arab region of Khuzestan.

Power and prestige: Saddam hoped that war with Iran would increase his personal power and make Iraq the most powerful country in the Gulf region and the Arab world.

Causes of the Iran–Iraq War, 1980–88

Religion: Khomeini had called on Iraqis to overthrow Saddam's regime and replace it with an Islamic republic. Saddam and his supporters were Sunni Muslims whereas a majority of Iraqis were Shiite Muslims, as in Iran. Anti-Baath riots even broke out which convinced Saddam the threat was real.

Opportunism: Saddam believed that Iran was weak and its army demoralised after the revolution in 1979 and was keen to exploit their position.

> **Key point**
>
> Saddam hoped for a 'whirlwind war' against Iran that would both secure his position against the threat of an Islamic revolution and make Iraq the most powerful Arab state in the Gulf region. What happened instead was a long, drawn-out war with no clear winner. There were devastating consequences for both Iran and Iraq and Saddam was left in a more vulnerable position than before.

The war lasted eight years and was bogged down in trench warfare

- The war started well for Saddam and he was confident of winning, but the huge Iranian population meant there were plenty of volunteers willing to become **martyrs** for the revolution. This was made worse by the fact that Saddam started firing missiles at Iranian cities.

- Within two years, Iran had recaptured all its lost territory and by 1984 both sides had entrenched their positions and the war reached a stalemate. Iran refused a ceasefire and wanted to overthrow Saddam's regime at any cost.

Many different foreign states became involved in the war for different reasons

- Most of the Arab states such as Saudi Arabia, Jordan and Egypt were Sunni Muslim and did not want Khomeini's Shiite version of Islam threatening them.

- The West and the Soviet Union all feared Islamic Iran controlling the oil in the Gulf region. France supplied Iraq with weapons and the USA provided satellite intelligence of Iranian movements.

- Syria supported Iran due to its rivalry with Iraq and shut down Iraqi pipelines in Syrian territory.

- By the end of the war, as a result of Western assistance, Iraq had air superiority and the most tanks and artillery. This helped force Khomeini into a ceasefire in 1988.

Both Iran and Iraq faced dire consequences after the ceasefire

- Neither side had achieved its aims – both Saddam and Khomeini remained in power. The Iran–Iraq borders remained unchanged.
- Iranian and Iraqi casualties were around 2 per cent of their total populations. Iran's economy was in ruins and Iraq was nearly $80 billion in debt. Living standards in both countries plummeted.
- Iran remained a major power with a population of over 55 million and the Islamic republic survived.
- Saddam faced strikes and riots, often co-ordinated in the mosques. Some army officers also blamed him for Iraq's failure to defeat Iran and between 1988 and 1990 there were attempts to overthrow him.

Task

Use this task to help you prepare for the practice question below.

1 Draw lines to link the factors on the left with the details on the right.

Factors	Details
Iraq	Saddam used his superior firepower to launch missiles at Iranian cities.
Iran	Iranian volunteers called Basiji mobilised to defend the revolution.
Foreign states	Most Arab states supplied money and arms to Iraq.
	Western powers also sent weapons, equipment and supplies to Iraq.

2 For each factor, write a paragraph explaining why the Iran–Iraq War became a stalemate.

Test yourself

1 Why did Saddam think that 1980 was the ideal time to invade Iran?
2 How did Saddam think a war with Iran could improve Iraq's economy?
3 What were the main reasons for foreign involvement in the Iran–Iraq War?
4 What social and economic problems did Iran and Iraq face after the ceasefire?

Practice question, Paper 1

Why was Saddam Hussein unable to achieve a quick victory in the Iran–Iraq War?　　　　　　　　　　　　　　　　　[6 marks]

Tip

Make sure your six-mark answers are written in full paragraphs that use your contextual knowledge to explain your reasons.

7.5 Why did the First Gulf War take place?

Saddam had many different motives for invading Kuwait in 1990

- Kuwait's boundaries with Iraq were established by the British. Iraq was left virtually landlocked, leading many to demand Kuwait's incorporation into Iraq.

- If Kuwait was part of Iraq, Saddam would gain more coastlines, be able to export oil more easily and be in a good position to dominate Saudi Arabia.

- Saddam was in a weaker domestic position after the Iran–Iraq War and he realised that propaganda and terror would only work for so long. He needed to secure his rule and divert people's attention.

- Iraq still had the most powerful armed forces in the Gulf region with the most advanced weapons. Saddam could use these to become the most powerful Arab leader in the Middle East.

- Saddam had over $80 billion of debt to pay off – Kuwait's rich oil fields would help reduce this and give Saddam greater control over oil prices.

> **Key point**
>
> Saddam thought that control of the Kuwaiti oil fields would solve the problem of Iraq's huge debt from the Iran–Iraq War. When he invaded Kuwait in 1990, the world reacted. The United Nations put **sanctions** on Iraq and a coalition force led by the USA quickly forced Saddam to withdraw and imposed harsh peace terms. However, Saddam was able to remain in power.

Saddam invaded Kuwait in August 1990 and the international community responded

- Saddam's 300,000-strong army overran Kuwait in three days. The United Nations Security Council condemned the invasion immediately and imposed a complete trade ban on Iraq.

- Saddam's soldiers committed atrocities against Kuwaiti citizens which caused international outcry. The Americans also feared Saddam might try to seize the Saudi oil fields.

- Operation Desert Storm launched an air and ground war against Iraq with over 700,000 troops mainly from the USA but also Britain, France and some Arab states. Iraqi civilians suffered over 100,000 fatalities.

- Saddam launched Scud missiles at Israel to try to provoke an attack so Arab states would turn their attention elsewhere, but he was unsuccessful. He then set fire to the oil fields in Kuwait but was forced to withdraw.

- President Bush encouraged the Kurds and the Shiites in Iraq to try to overthrow Saddam, leading to reprisals and 50,000 deaths.

- The coalition forces stopped short of Baghdad as many Arab allies did not want US occupation of Iraq – on 28 February 1991, President Bush called a ceasefire.

The United Nations imposed harsh peace terms on Iraq, but Saddam survived

- Iraq had to pay reparations to Kuwait and recognise its sovereignty.

- 'No-fly zones' were established to stop Saddam from committing more atrocities against the Kurds in the north and south of Iraq. The USA was trying to contain his excesses rather than topple Saddam.

- The United Nations Special Committee imposed weapons inspections on Iraq to search and destroy **weapons of mass destruction (WMD)**. Sanctions would remain in place until all WMD were destroyed.

- Due to heavy sanctions imposed by the West, the Iraqi people continued to suffer from shortages of food, clean water and reduced access to welfare services. Oil sales were severely limited, causing a humanitarian crisis.
- Saddam survived and his dictatorship continued using terror and propaganda against the West.
- Many in the West began to consider whether Saddam's removal was a better option to protect their interests in the Gulf region.

Task

Study the cartoon below. Use the points next to the cartoon to draw a line to the relevant detail and add some notes.

SOURCE A A cartoon by Nicholas Garland, in the British newspaper, the *Independent*, 10 August 1990, six days after Iraqi forces invaded Kuwait. The leading figure represents the US President George Bush, followed in order by the French president, the British foreign secretary, the German Chancellor and the Russian foreign minister.

The figures on horses look like crusader knights which might suggest ...

The leading knight is carrying the Stars and Stripes flag which means ...

The knights on horseback represent different countries such as ...

Each knight has an oil barrel on his tunic which suggests ...

Tip

For interpretation questions that ask you to work out the cartoonist's message, make sure that you think about whether they are supporting, criticising or commenting on a particular event at a particular time. Use the provenance, the source details and your own knowledge to explain the message.

Practice question, Paper 2

What is the message of the cartoonist? Explain your answer using details of the source and your knowledge.

[8 marks]

Test yourself

1 Why did Saddam think that invading Iraq would solve his problems?
2 How did Saddam think a war with Iran could improve Iraq's economy?
3 Make a list of the different tactics used by the USA and its allies to defeat Iraq.
4 How far do you agree that the sanctions imposed on Iraq after the war were fair? Explain your answer.

Key terms

Make sure you know these terms, people or events and can use them or describe them confidently.

Arab nationalism Movement of Arab peoples in the Middle East to join together to resist outside influence and to oppose Israel in particular.

Ayatollah A senior Muslim cleric.

Baath Party Sunni Muslim political movement, most prominent in Iraq from the 1960s. Strongly opposed to external interference in the Arab world.

Chemical weapons Usually refers to weapons that employ poisonous gas to kill enemies.

Coup Revolution.

Martyr Person who dies for a cause they believe in.

Mullah A man or woman well educated in the Islamic religion, often a term used to describe Islamic clergy.

Sanctions Actions taken against states that break international law, most commonly economic sanctions, e.g. refusing to supply oil.

Shiite (Shia) One of the main branches of the Muslim faith.

Sunni One of the main branches of the Muslim faith.

Weapons of mass destruction (WMD) Missiles, bombs or shells that are armed with chemical, biological or nuclear weapons.

8.1.1 How well did the tsarist regime deal with the difficulties of ruling Russia up to 1914?

In 1900, the Russian Empire was huge, diverse and ruled by one man, the Tsar

- Russia was huge – nearly 5000 km wide!
- **Tsar** Nicholas II ruled the Russian Empire. He was a family man but not an effective ruler. He ignored calls for reform and placed family members and friends in government. He believed he was chosen by God and had a divine right to rule.
- Support of the army and navy were crucial to the Tsar's regime. **Cossack** regiments were used to put down any disturbances.
- The Orthodox Church promoted the **autocracy.** The secret police (**Okhrana**) removed opposition. There was heavy censorship of the press.
- The **peasants** belonged to a *mir* or village commune. District councils called *zemstva* elected officials who looked after local services.

> **Key point**
>
> The tsarist regime faced many pressures to reform and relied on repression and religion to maintain the autocracy.

> **Test yourself**
>
> 1 List the different reasons Russia was difficult to rule.
> 2 How far can Nicholas II be blamed for the poor government in Russia?
> 3 Which social group in Russia do you think would cause the most problems for the Tsar? Explain your answer.

Tsar Nicholas II faced many problems

People	Details	Problems
The nationalities	Over a dozen different nationalities, e.g. Russians, Poles and Jews. Only 40 per cent of the 130 million people were Russians.	Language and religious differences made communication difficult. Many disliked Russian rule and there were calls for independence.
The peasants	About 80 per cent of the population. Some richer peasants (**kulaks**). Mainly loyal and served in the army.	Backwards farming methods; no education; famine was common (nearly 400,000 died in the 1891 famine); many demanded more land.
The industrial workers	Less than 5 per cent of the population.	Poor living conditions in cities – cramped housing, no sanitation, disease, e.g. cholera. Poor working conditions – low pay and long hours. No trade unions.
The middle classes	A new class that emerged due to **industrialisation**, made up of professionals and **capitalists** (bankers and factory owners); made up less than 2 per cent of the population. Wealthy and had access to luxuries.	Many wanted a parliament and democracy.
Liberals	Mainly middle-class Russians who wanted greater democracy.	Demanded an elected Duma, civil rights and end to the tsarist autocracy.
Radicals	**Socialist Revolutionaries (SRs)** wanted to share the land; used propaganda and terror tactics; appealed to poorer peasants. The **Social Democratic Party** was a **Marxist** party that appealed to the workers, soldiers and sailors. It split in 1903: the **Bolsheviks** under **Lenin** wanted a revolution and the **Mensheviks** wanted to take power legally.	Both wanted to overthrow the tsarist system.

8.1.2 How did the Tsar survive the 1905 revolution?

REVISED

There were long-term and short-term causes of the 1905 revolution

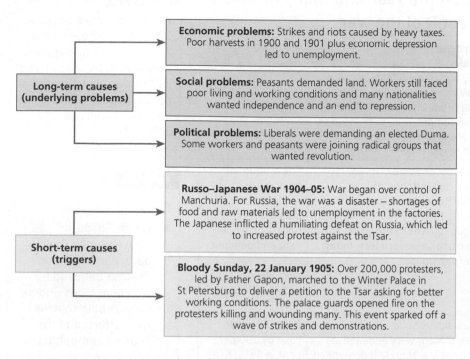

Long-term causes (underlying problems)

Economic problems: Strikes and riots caused by heavy taxes. Poor harvests in 1900 and 1901 plus economic depression led to unemployment.

Social problems: Peasants demanded land. Workers still faced poor living and working conditions and many nationalities wanted independence and an end to repression.

Political problems: Liberals were demanding an elected Duma. Some workers and peasants were joining radical groups that wanted revolution.

Short-term causes (triggers)

Russo–Japanese War 1904–05: War began over control of Manchuria. For Russia, the war was a disaster – shortages of food and raw materials led to unemployment in the factories. The Japanese inflicted a humiliating defeat on Russia, which led to increased protest against the Tsar.

Bloody Sunday, 22 January 1905: Over 200,000 protesters, led by Father Gapon, marched to the Winter Palace in St Petersburg to deliver a petition to the Tsar asking for better working conditions. The palace guards opened fire on the protesters killing and wounding many. This event sparked off a wave of strikes and demonstrations.

Tsar Nicholas II, however, survived the revolution

- The different groups failed to unite and the returning army was used to crush opposition. The Tsar appeased the middle class by announcing the October Manifesto, which promised a Duma and civil rights.

The Tsar used the carrot and stick to restore control

- The Tsar issued the Fundamental Laws (1906), giving him the power to dismiss the Duma at will.
- In 1907, the Tsar changed the voting rules so that less of his critics could be elected.
- The Tsar also appointed a new prime minister, Peter **Stolypin**.

Carrot

- Peasant Land Banks were set up to allow richer peasants (kulaks) to buy up land, increasing their loyalty, *but* poorer peasants became worse off.
- The middle class profited from industrial growth *but* many workers earned less than they did in 1903.

Stick

- The secret police (Okhrana) and army were used to remove opponents and stop riots.
- 'Stolypin's necktie': over 1000 hanged and 20,000 exiled; newspapers were heavily censored *but* there were still strikes such as in the Lena goldfields in 1912 over poor conditions.

Key point

The 1905 revolution had economic, social and political causes. The Tsar managed to survive using carrot-and-stick policies.

1905 revolution: timeline

Feb Strikes spread to other cities and workers demand an eight-hour day.

Mar–May Defeat in the Russo–Japanese War leads to demands for a change in government by Liberals.

June Sailors on Battleship *Potemkin* mutiny. Liberals demand a Duma and the Poles demand independence.

July Peasants riot and seize land. Workers' councils (Soviets) formed.

Sept Peace treaty with Japan signed. Tsar promises soldiers better pay. General strike spreads from Moscow to other cities; barricades on streets. St Petersburg Soviet formed.

30 Oct October Manifesto.

Dec Russian army returns from Japan and is used to reassert control.

Test yourself

1. Describe why each of the following groups wanted to end autocracy in Russia: peasants, workers, middle classes.
2. How did the war with Japan make the situation worse for the Tsar?
3. Create a summary diagram of the different methods used by the Tsar to help him survive the 1905 revolution.

It is illegal to photocopy this page

8.1.3 How far was the Tsar weakened by the First World War?

The relationship between the Tsar and many groups in society changed as a result of the war

Group	Impact of the war	Evidence
The army	The Russian army had many defeats (e.g. Tannenberg). They were badly led and there were shortages of rifles, ammunition, boots and clothing. In September 1915, the Tsar took personal control of the armed forces, which meant he became responsible for any defeats.	By 1917, 13 million soldiers had been mobilised; 9 million casualties by 1917.
The peasants and workers	Millions of peasants were conscripted, causing shortages and inflation of food prices. Trains prioritised sending supplies to the front, causing food and fuel shortages in the cities. Wages fell and unemployment grew. Widows and orphans were left, many without state war pensions.	The amount of food an average worker could afford dropped by about 500 per cent and peasant riots increased by over 150 per cent between 1914 and 1917.
The middle classes	The middle classes did not suffer like the peasants or workers. Many were appalled at conditions on the frontline. Many still demanded better representation. Factory owners complained about strikes, especially in 1916.	Price of goods rose by 300 per cent in 1916; over 1300 strikes by 1917.
The aristocracy	Peasant conscription meant less peasant farmers. Some nobles disliked the **Tsarina** and Rasputin being left in charge as she was German and made unwise political appointments (see Factfile). Newspapers and pamphlets spread around the cities criticising the Tsarina and Rasputin.	Over 13 million conscripts were mobilised, mainly from the peasantry.

> **Task**
>
> Study the table above. List each group affected by the war and give it a rating between one and five stars (1* = not very affected; 5*= extremely affected). Pick the two groups you have decided were the most affected by the war and write a paragraph for each justifying your choices.

> **Practice question, Paper 1**
>
> **Why did the First World War weaken the tsarist autocracy?** [6 marks]

> **Tip**
>
> Remember that six-mark questions require you to explain your reasons, rather than just describe or list them. Use examples to help support your explanation in full paragraphs.

8.1.4 Why was the revolution of March 1917 successful?

Key point

There were many short- and long-term causes of the March 1917 revolution that led to the abdication of Tsar Nicholas II.

On the 15 March 1917, Tsar Nicholas II abdicated – Russia had finished with tsars

Road to the March revolution

Jan–Feb 1917:	7–10 March 1917:	12 March 1917:	12 March 1917:	15 March 1917:
Strikes spread throughout Russia over food and fuel shortages, low pay and demands for the Tsar's abdication. Bread rationing introduced.	40,000 workers at the Putilov steelworks went on strike and joined thousands of women strikers on International Women's Day demanding an end to the poor conditions and a new government. By 10 March, 250,000 workers were on strike.	Duma prepared to take over government. The Tsar ordered Petrograd troops to put down the protests by force. They refused to fire on the crowds and instead joined the strikers. Some shot their officers.	Workers and soldiers marched to the Duma and demanded it take over the government. The Petrograd Soviet was set up again and took control of supplies.	Tsar Nicholas II tried to return to Petrograd, but railway workers refused him entry. He abdicated in favour of his brother Michael, but he refused the crown.

Tip

Paper 4 questions will always start with 'How important …' or 'How significant …'. You need to compare different causes or reasons to write a balanced answer using full paragraphs. It is always a good idea to plan the answer for a few minutes before you start writing, to collect your thoughts.

Practice question, Paper 4

How important was the First World War as a cause of the revolution in March 1917? [40 marks]

Task

Paper 4 questions, like the one here, want you to examine and compare several different factors. You *must* examine the factor in the question, but then compare the importance or significance of that factor with others to reach a conclusion. You will need to look back over the other focus points in this Depth Study to help you collect the information you need.

Use the table to help you plan and write your response. The whole process should take an hour.

(Note: You can use this writing frame for any other Paper 4 questions in this Depth Study.)

How important was the First World War as a cause of the revolution in March 1917?	
Plan	**Details to include**
Introduction	*Use this space to compare the different causes of the March revolution. Try to make a judgement about which cause was the most important/significant.*
Paragraph 1	*Examine one aspect of the factor/cause/reason stated in the question. Explain its relative importance/significance.*
Paragraphs 2–6	*Give balance to your answer by examining another factor/cause/reason. Explain its relative importance/significance.*
Conclusion	*Explain your overall judgement here. It should not have changed from the introduction if you made one. Was it short- or long-term factors? Is there a decisive or trigger individual, event or date? What links or connections are there between the different factors/causes/reasons?*

8.2.1 How effectively did the Provisional Government rule Russia in 1917?

REVISED

When the Tsar abdicated, the Duma set up a Provisional Government led by a 12-man executive

- The Provisional Government shared power with the Petrograd Soviet which represented the workers and soldiers. Both institutions agreed to work together and declared universal civil rights.
- This system was known as 'dual power'.
- On 14 March, the Petrograd Soviet issued Soviet Order No. 1. This gave the Petrograd Soviet control over the armed forces in Petrograd.
- A Kadet, Prince Lvov, became the first prime minister. His minister of justice, the SR Alexander **Kerensky**, was a member of both the Provisional Government and the Petrograd Soviet. He would become prime minister in July 1917.

> **Key point**
>
> After the March Revolution, power was shared between the **Provisional Government** and the Petrograd Soviet. The Provisional Government failed to solve many of the social and economic issues in Russia.

Factfile

Political parties, 1917

Kadets (Constitutional Democrats) The main liberal party that represented the middle classes. They wanted a representative democracy with civil rights.

Octobrists A middle-class liberal party that wanted a constitutional monarchy.

Progressive Party A moderate liberal party.

Socialist Revolutionary Party The largest socialist party, the SR Party was a populist peasant party that wanted land to be shared between the peasants. Committed to a democratic constitution.

Mensheviks A Marxist socialist party that wanted workers to control the country. Wanted to achieve **communism** gradually.

Bolsheviks A revolutionary Marxist socialist party that wanted to seize power for the workers to create a communist state.

The Provisional Government was welcomed initially and achieved several reforms

- The hated secret police (the Okhrana) was disbanded and the death penalty was abolished.
- Many political prisoners were released.
- Freedom of speech, universal suffrage and the right to strike were introduced.

However, the Provisional Government faced issues that undermined its effectiveness

Issue 1: The war

Some, like the Bolsheviks, demanded an end to the war. Over 2 million soldiers had deserted, and food and fuel shortages continued. The Provisional Government continued to fight with the Allies.

Issue 2: The land issue

The peasants demanded land, but the Provisional Government told them to wait for elections. By mid-1917 the peasants were tired of waiting for land redistribution and had begun to seize land in the countryside themselves.

Issue 3: The Petrograd Soviet

The Petrograd Soviet had power over the troops in the capital and the support of key workers such as railwaymen. Many, such as the Bolsheviks, began to undermine the Provisional Government.

Issue 4: Lenin's return

In April 1917, Lenin returned from exile. He set out the Bolshevik programme known as the April Theses. He demanded no co-operation with the Provisional Government, an end to the war, land to be given to the peasants and wanted the **Soviets** to take power. The famous Bolshevik slogans of 'Peace, bread, land' and 'All power to the Soviets' became very popular – by October 1917, the party had 500,000 members.

In the second half of 1917, the authority of the Provisional Government slowly collapsed

- In June, Kerensky became minister for war and began a summer offensive. It was a disaster and soldiers deserted in their thousands. It sparked off massive demonstrations in Petrograd in July, known as the July Days. Lenin chose not to support them.
- Kerensky blamed the Bolsheviks and arrested many of the leaders. Lenin fled to Finland.
- Kerensky appointed a monarchist, General Kornilov, as commander of the army. In September 1917, he attempted to seize power.
- Kerensky panicked and turned to the Bolsheviks for help. He released some Bolshevik leaders and armed their Red Guard (volunteer militias) with rifles. Kornilov's troops were stopped by railway workers and refused to fight the members of the Soviet. The Bolsheviks were the saviours of Petrograd and the Red Guard kept their rifles.
- By the end of September, the Bolsheviks had control of the Petrograd Soviet with **Trotsky** as its chairman.

> **Test yourself**
>
> 1 Describe the relationship between the Provisional Government and Petrograd Soviet.
> 2 Explain why the war was so significant in the downfall of the Provisional Government.
> 3 Describe the role of Kerensky in the problems faced by the Provisional Government.
> 4 Make a short timeline of the events from March to October 1917.

It is illegal to photocopy this page

8.2.2 Why were the Bolsheviks able to seize power in November 1917?

By October 1917, Lenin was convinced the time was right to seize power

- Lenin was able to convince other Bolshevik leaders to seize power. The Bolsheviks were in control of the soviets in Petrograd and Moscow.
- Trotsky oversaw organising the take-over. On 6 November, the Red Guard took control of the bridges, the main telegraph office and the railway and power stations. Later in the day they seized the State Bank.
- At 9 o'clock in the evening, the Battleship *Aurora* fired shots to signal the storming of the Winter Palace. The Red Guard met little resistance.

> **Key point**
>
> The failures of the Provisional Government and the ongoing issues from the war made Lenin's messages more appealing to many workers and soldiers. Lenin organised a seizure of power in the name of the Soviets.

Many factors ensured the Bolsheviks succeeded in seizing power in November 1917

Bolshevik leadership and tactics: The Bolsheviks were disciplined. Lenin was the undisputed leader and a good orator. Trotsky was chairman of the Petrograd Soviet and had organised the Red Guard. The Bolsheviks used effective propaganda to encourage workers to seize control of factories and peasants to seize land.

First World War: Continued shortages and bread rationing pushed people towards Lenin's message to end the war. Kerensky's disastrous offensive in the summer led to the July Days, showing there was popular support for ending the war, even though Lenin failed to support it.

Why were the Bolsheviks able to seize power in November 1917?

Failures of the Provisional Government: The Provisional Government failed to address the peasant land issue and continued to fight the war. The Petrograd Soviet seemed like a more representative institution in comparison. Kerensky lost influence after the Kornilov affair.

Bolshevik support: Moscow and Petrograd were controlled by the Bolsheviks. Their membership had risen to 800,000 by November, including many soldiers and sailors. Lenin's April Theses promised 'Peace, bread, land' and 'All power to the Soviets'.

> **Practice question, Paper 1**
>
> 'Bolshevik leadership and organisation was the main reason Lenin was able to seize power in November 1917.'
>
> **How far do you agree with this statement? Explain your answer.**
> [10 marks]

> **Task**
>
> Make your own copy of the table below to compare the different reasons Lenin was able to seize power. You may want to look back through the earlier focus points in this Depth Study. This will help you answer the practice question above.
>
> | Bolshevik leadership and organisation | Other factors |
> | --- | --- |
> | | |

> **Tip**
>
> Ten-mark questions need to be balanced. Spend a couple of minutes before you start to write your response to plan your answer by listing all the different reasons. You could use a table like the one in the Task to help you.

8.2.3 Why did the Bolsheviks win the Civil War?

The Bolsheviks moved quickly to consolidate power after November 1917

- Lenin strengthened his position and set up a new ruling council called the *Sovnarkom* (Council of People's Commissars) with himself as chairman.
- Constituent Assembly elections went ahead as promised in November 1917. The SRs won double the Bolshevik vote, so Lenin closed it down after a day.
- Lenin quickly issued several decrees: a decree on land abolished private ownership of the land and redistributed it among the peasants; a decree on workers' control gave control of the factories to workers' committees; a decree on women gave them equal rights with men; a decree on peace promised to end the war with Germany.
- Lenin banned other political parties and all non-Bolshevik newspapers and set up a new secret police force called the *Cheka* to remove political opponents.

By 1918, Lenin's enemies united against the Bolsheviks and a civil war broke out

- Trotsky met the Germans in March 1918 and negotiated the Treaty of Brest-Litovsk. It was a harsh treaty by which Russia lost much of its former empire.
- Anti-Bolshevik elements from many parties then joined forces – the Whites.
- By the summer, the Whites were fighting the Reds (Bolshevik forces). White forces were commanded by generals Yudenich and Denikin and Admiral Kolchak, partly supported by forces from Britain, the USA, France and Japan.

> **Key point**
>
> Lenin moved quickly to consolidate Bolshevik control, but a **civil war** broke out between the Reds (Bolsheviks) and the Whites (anti-Bolsheviks). The Reds' discipline, unity, leadership and propaganda meant they were able to be victorious.

> **Test yourself**
>
> 1 List the methods used by Lenin to strengthen Bolshevik rule.
> 2 List the advantages and disadvantages of both sides in the Civil War.

> **Practice question, Paper 1**
>
> **Why were the Bolsheviks victorious in the Russian Civil War?** [6 marks]

Reasons for Red success in the Civil War		
	Reds	**Whites**
Geography	Controlled the industry and railways in the centre including Moscow and St Petersburg so troops could be supplied and moved.	Spread around the centre making communication and organisation difficult.
Aims	United in their aim to stay in power and create a communist state.	Made up of SRs, Mensheviks, Liberals and monarchists with different ideologies.
Leadership	Led by Trotsky who created the Red Army of over 300,000. They were disciplined, and Trotsky travelled on his armoured train to inspire them. Political commissars watched over the troops with orders to shoot deserters. Lenin used the *Cheka* to terrorise the population (Red Terror) and requisition squads seized grain in the countryside.	The commanders often mistreated their troops causing some to swap sides. Poor co-ordination meant Trotsky was able to pick off each army one by one.
Propaganda	Lenin's propaganda campaign portrayed foreign troops as invaders and the Reds as defenders of the people. Peasants were told they would lose their land.	The Whites stirred anti-communist feelings, but their propaganda was less effective.

8.2.4 How far was the New Economic Policy a success?

During the Civil War, War Communism began

- War Communism kept the troops and workers fed, but:
  - all large industries were nationalised, and free enterprise banned
  - harsh discipline was introduced in factories
  - requisitioning squads took surplus food and arrested peasants who refused to hand it over
  - rationing was introduced.
- By 1921, aided by poor weather, an estimated 7 million Russians had died due to famine. Money was worthless and industrial output was lower than in 1913.

With the White forces defeated, a new opposition emerged within communist Russia

- The Red Terror and War Communism led some to call for a return to Soviet power.
- In March 1921, sailors at the naval base of Kronstadt passed a resolution calling for democracy and civil rights. They had been strong supporters of the Bolsheviks before the Civil War but were concerned over Lenin's dictatorship.
- Trotsky used 20,000 Red Army troops to crush the Kronstadt uprising. Lenin described the uprising as 'the flash that lit up reality'.

Lenin introduced a New Economic Policy in 1921

End of grain requisitioning: Grain requisitioning was replaced with a tax in kind. Peasants would give 50 per cent of what they grew to the state and could keep the rest and sell it at market. Grain production increased to pre-war levels by 1925.

Small-scale capitalism: Smaller factories were allowed back into private ownership. Consumer goods such as clothes could be sold for a profit. Traders (known as NEPmen) could buy and sell surplus goods and food – many communist leaders hated this aspect.

The main features of the NEP

Electrification: Increased electrification. Production increased by over 400 per cent between 1921 and 1925.

Large industries: Large industries, such as steel and coal, remained under state control.

The results of the NEP were mixed

- The NEP did improve production – it reached pre-war levels by 1926.
- Foreign trade with the West increased. An Anglo-Soviet trade agreement was signed in 1921.
- Lenin intended the NEP to be a temporary step backwards to capitalism – this was opposed by some communist leaders.
- Many communists hated the emergence of a capitalist class of kulaks and NEPmen.
- Unemployment remained high and crime and alcoholism rates rose.

Key point

War Communism and the Red Terror had won the Civil War for the Bolsheviks but the Kronstadt uprising forced Lenin to introduce the **New Economic Policy (NEP)** to improve conditions in Russia.

Test yourself

1. How did the policy of War Communism both help and hinder Lenin in consolidating his position?

2. Make a table of the successes and failures of the New Economic Policy.

8.3.1 Why did Stalin, and not Trotsky, emerge as Lenin's successor?

Lenin died in January 1924 and there were several candidates for his replacement

- Many leading Bolsheviks were possible contenders for the leadership of the USSR. On the left of the party and in favour of 'Permanent Revolution' were Trotsky, Kamenev and Zinoviev (although the latter two hated Trotsky). On the right, there was Bukharin, who favoured the NEP and a gradual move towards communism. Finally, there was Joseph Stalin, the General Secretary of the Party.

- The main struggle would be between Trotsky and Stalin.

- Trotsky was an able commander and speaker but he was arrogant and wanted to end the NEP and spread communism worldwide.

- Stalin used his position as General Secretary to appoint supporters and expel opponents. He wanted 'Socialism in One Country' – the position that communism should be set up in the USSR first.

By 1929, Stalin had emerged as absolute ruler

Lenin's funeral: Stalin told Trotsky the wrong date for the funeral, although Trotsky was ill with malaria at the time, which helped Stalin even more. Stalin made a big speech in support of Lenin and became the chief mourner.

Lenin's Testament: In his Testament, Lenin criticised Stalin for being too unruly and advised removing him from power. He both praised and criticised Trotsky. He also criticised other party leaders. The leaders collectively decided not to make it public.

First Party Congress: In 1924, Stalin sided with Zinoviev and Kamenev against Trotsky. Stalin used his position as General Secretary to ensure he had supporters. Trotsky was sacked as he might use his Red Army to create a dictatorship.

Siding with Bukharin: In 1926, Stalin joined with Bukharin to remove Kamenev and Zinoviev. He again packed the Congress with his supporters and announced his policy of 'Socialism in One Country'.

Expulsion from the party: In 1927, Trotsky, Zinoviev and Kamenev were all expelled.

Turning against Bukharin: Stalin turned against the NEP and its supporters including Bukharin. They were removed from their posts.

Key point

Stalin used political manoeuvring, cunning and his position as General Secretary to remove his opponents, particularly Trotsky. Trotsky's arrogance and bad luck saw him expelled from the party.

Test yourself

1. Make a list of all the actions used by Stalin to take power.

2. Explain why Trotsky could be blamed for allowing Stalin to come to power.

3. How did Stalin's position of General Secretary aid his rise to power? Give examples.

4. What were the main differences between Trotsky's 'Permanent Revolution' and Stalin's 'Socialism in One Country' ideologies? Why did Stalin's ideas have more appeal?

It is illegal to photocopy this page

Stalin needed to consolidate his position as leader to create a totalitarian state

- Stalin used the murder of a leading communist, Sergei Kirov, as an excuse to launch a series of **purges**.
- Kirov was a possible rival and wanted to reform the harsher aspects of Stalin's modernisation.
- Stalin now viewed anyone who was not a loyal supporter of his aims as a traitor.

Stalin launched the Great Purges in 1934 and targeted many different groups

- **The Communist Party:** Stalin arranged a series of **show trials** and focused on removing the 'Old Bolsheviks' such as Zinoviev and Kamenev in 1936. Bukharin followed in 1938. Over 500,000 Communist Party members were arrested and either executed or sent to labour camps known as **gulags**.
- **The armed forces:** Stalin feared the army could overthrow him. Over 25,000 officers including Supreme Commander Marshal Tukhachevsky were purged and 90 per cent of generals were removed.
- **The Soviet people:** Anyone who was suspected of opposing Stalin or his policies could be accused of counter-revolutionary activity and arrested by the secret police – the NKVD. Poets, writers, intellectuals and scientists were all targeted. Informers were often used by the NKVD to snoop on neighbours. NEPmen and kulaks were also targeted as class enemies. By 1937, an estimated 18 million people had been transported to labour camps and 10 million had died.
- **The NKVD:** By 1938, Stalin was blaming the NKVD for the excesses and purged them. He was concerned they would have knowledge of what happened. Even the head of the NKVD, Yagoda, was shot!
- By 1938, no one dared to challenge Stalin's rule in public. His position was now unchallengeable.
- However, Stalin had removed many able individuals such as military commanders, which would come to haunt him when the Germans invaded in 1941.

Test yourself

1 Make a list of the reasons why Stalin chose to purge the Soviet Union of its political enemies.
2 Explain how the purges helped Stalin secure his position and control of Soviet society.

8.3.3 What methods did Stalin use to control the Soviet Union?

Stalin used fear and terror to control the Soviet Union

- The NKVD (secret police) could arrest, imprison and execute people without a trial.
- Gulags (labour camps) housed NEPmen, kulaks and political enemies. Many died there through illness and starvation.
- Rules and harsh discipline in the factories and the countryside was enforced with fines, the fear of losing your job or even arrest.

> **Key point**
> Stalin wanted to create a totalitarian state where every aspect of Soviet society was controlled.

Stalin developed a cult of personality

- Stalin used propaganda to control ideas and information. Newspapers and other media were heavily censored and posters, pamphlets and public events showed the regime in a positive light.
- A god-like worship of Stalin emerged: processions were held in his honour; children were educated about his accomplishments; photographs and statues of Stalin were everywhere.
- History books were rewritten with images of Trotsky and others removed from photos and Lenin and Stalin presented as the heroes of the revolution.
- In 1936, Stalin created a new constitution that promised civil rights to the people. It had little basis in reality.

Stalin controlled the arts and culture

Religion: Churches were closed, and priests arrested – only one in 40 churches was active by 1939. Islamic practices and mosques were banned.

Education: Schools and the youth movement, the Young Pioneers, fed children with propaganda on Stalin's achievements, socialist values and the need to be loyal to Stalin.

Stalin's control of the arts and culture in the USSR

Music and arts: Music, poetry, literature and art were all heavily censored and monitored by the NKVD. Artists and writers were made to adopt a new style called Soviet Realism, which praised the workers and socialism.

Task

Copy and complete the table below. This could be used to help prepare you for six- or ten-mark questions in Paper 1 about Stalin's control of the Soviet Union.

Method of control	Details and examples	How this helped Stalin control the Soviet Union
Terror and the purges		
Propaganda and censorship		
Art and culture		

Test yourself

1. What similarities are there between Stalin's methods of control and a) Tsar Nicholas II's and b) Lenin's?
2. Explain how Stalin created his cult of personality. Give examples.
3. Why do you think some improved living conditions would have increased Stalin's control?

8.3.4 How complete was Stalin's control over the Soviet Union by 1941?

Stalin was the supreme leader of Soviet Russia, but was he in complete control?

Was Stalin in complete control of Soviet Russia?	
Yes	**No**
The Communist Party and the armed forces had been purged; those that remained were loyal to Stalin and his policies.	Bribery and corruption were widespread out of fear of missing targets in the factories. Figures were fiddled and sub-standard goods were produced in order to look like targets were being met.
The Soviet population was controlled by fear using the NKVD and gulags.	Stalin only had control around the centre of Soviet Russia – the outer regions were run by other party officials out of Stalin's direct control.
Stalin had complete control of the media and propaganda, which he used to create an image of himself as the best ruler for Russia.	Millions of peasants and workers were constantly relocating and could not be tracked properly.
Stalin cemented his control through a cult of personality and many, especially young people, worshipped him as god-like. Aspects of art and culture only gave pro-Soviet messages.	The purges removed some of the most able members of society leaving the Soviet Union without experts.
Collectivisation and the **Five-Year Plans** increased his control of the peasants and the workers.	Underground opposition groups did exist despite the terror – many young people would not conform. Criminal activity was rife.
Stalin was making the **Soviet Union** a strong, industrial nation.	

Key point

Stalin was clearly the unopposed leader, but his control was not absolute.

Practice question, Paper 4

How significant were the purges in increasing Stalin's control of the Soviet Union?

[40 marks]

Tip

Paper 4 questions require an essay-style response. You need to use in-depth contextual knowledge with plenty of examples to support your arguments. Make sure you use full paragraphs and explain clearly the importance/ significance of each factor/cause/reason.

Task

Look back at the advice on writing Paper 4 responses in 8.1.4 (page 69). Use this advice and the table below to model your answer for the practice question above.

How significant were the purges in increasing Stalin's control of the Soviet Union?	
Plan	**Details to include**
Introduction	*Use this space to compare the different methods used to increase Stalin's control. Try to make a judgement about which cause was the most important/significant.*
Paragraphs 1–2	*Examine one aspect of the method stated in the question in each paragraph. Explain its relative importance/significance.*
Paragraphs 3–6	*Examine other methods not stated in the question. Explain their relative importance/ significance. Try to cover four alternative methods in total, each in different paragraphs.*
Conclusion	*Explain your overall judgement here. It should not have changed from the introduction if you made one. What method do you think was the most significant? What links or connections are there between the different factors/causes/reasons?*

8.4.1 Why did Stalin introduce the Five-Year Plans?

Stalin wanted to modernise industry in the USSR for many reasons

- **Ideology:** Stalin needed control of the economy to build 'Socialism in One Country'. He wanted Soviet Russia to be self-sufficient, rather than relying on imported goods. He wanted the USSR to compete with the economies of the West and he wanted to improve standards of living in Russia.

- **Power and control:** By 1928, Stalin had allied himself to Bukharin and his supporters who believed in the NEP. He then switched to promoting large state-controlled projects, which undermined and ultimately removed Bukharin and his supporters. Industrialisation was then used to control the country as political prisoners could be used to work on these large projects.

- **Security:** Stalin feared invasions from the West. Heavy industry was vital for defence and developing a modern army. Stalin put many of the new industrial centres far to the east to protect them from invasion.

- **Personal reputation:** Stalin also wanted to be responsible for bringing about great change in Russia, and to be known as a great leader.

> **Key point**
>
> Stalin introduced the Five-Year Plans to rapidly modernise the USSR, demonstrate the superiority of communism to the West and improve Soviet defences in case of attack.

Stalin achieved industrial modernisation by using three Five-Year Plans

- The state planning organisation, Gosplan, was used to set ambitious but often unrealistic targets.

- Targets were then set for each region, each factory or mine, and even for each manager and worker.

- Stalin brought in foreign experts such as British engineers to help.

> **Test yourself**
>
> 1 Explain two reasons why Stalin wanted to modernise industry in the USSR.
>
> 2 Make a spider diagram to summarise the aims of the Five-Year Plans.

First Five-Year Plan

Date: 1928–32

Aims: To develop heavy industry such as coal, steel, iron and electricity to lay the foundations for further industrial development.

Achievements: Huge steel mills were built, for example Magnitogorsk; 1500 new industrial plants were built; coal and iron output doubled BUT targets were unrealistic and not met.

Second Five-Year Plan

Date: 1933–37

Aims: To further develop heavy industry and start to build secondary industries such as chemicals, metals, railways and communications.

Achievements: Moscow railway was built; heavy industry production more than doubled BUT targets were still too unrealistic.

Third Five-Year Plan

Date: 1938–41

Aims: Industrialisation was to focus on agriculture by building farm machinery like tractors, and on the production of some consumer goods.

Achievements: The plan was disrupted by the Second World War.

Stalin wanted to modernise agriculture in the USSR for many reasons

- **Ideology:** Stalin wanted to remove the richer kulaks. Collectivisation would bring socialism to the countryside by removing private farms and establishing collective farms.
- **Feeding the workers:** Stalin wanted to ensure that the workers were fed and famine would be avoided in the future as the USSR was still importing 2 million tons of food a year in 1928. Stalin wanted excess grain to be sold abroad to pay for the machinery and experts needed for the Five-Year Plans.
- **Personal reputation:** Stalin thought that modernising agriculture would also enhance his reputation and he used his propaganda machine to help convey this message and attack opponents.

Peasants were forced to collectivise their land

- Peasants were told to form collective farms (*kolkhoz*). They were allowed to keep a small plot for personal use. All animals, tools and machinery would be shared. Some state farms (*sovkhoz*) were made and peasants were paid a wage instead.
- The collective farms would then sell some of their produce to the state for a low price and in return they would receive new machinery like tractors to improve efficiency.
- Stalin hoped to avoid grain shortages and stop richer peasants from hoarding grain – it would be easier to collect grain from collective farms than from individual peasants.

> **Key point**
>
> Stalin needed control of the countryside to feed the workers and soldiers and end famine in the USSR. Many peasants opposed losing their land and were crushed by Stalin.

> **Task**
>
> The factors in the first column are reasons why collectivisation was introduced. Use the second column to explain why they were introduced, with supporting detail. An example has been given.
>
> | Factor | Explanation |
> | --- | --- |
> | Socialism in the countryside | Stalin wanted to ensure that all of the USSR was following communist ideas and wanted to end the NEP and capitalist practices. Removing private farms and kulaks would help achieve this. |
> | Feeding the workers | |
> | Personal reputation | |

> **Practice question, Paper 1**
>
> **Why did Stalin introduce the policy of collectivisation?**
>
> [6 marks]

> **Test yourself**
>
> 1. How are the reasons for collectivisation similar and different to the reasons for the Five-Year Plans?
> 2. What was the difference between the *kolkhoz* and the *sovkhoz*?

8.4.3 How successful were Stalin's economic changes?

There were many successes but also criticisms of the Five-Year Plans

- By 1940, the USSR produced 20 per cent of the world's manufacturing output (see Figure A).
- The Soviet military was stronger and without industrialisation it could have well lost the war with Germany after 1941.
- The Five-Year Plans led to massive urbanisation and some increase in the standards of living by the late 1930s as some consumer goods and farming machines were available.
- However, inefficiency and waste were common due to unrealistic targets. Managers focused on quantity, rather than quality.
- The human cost was high – thousands died working on building projects such as the Moscow Metro. Many in gulags were also used as slave labour. An estimated 10 million were deported as political opponents.

> **Key point**
>
> The USSR saw huge industrial and agricultural growth, but the human cost was very high.

FIGURE A Manufacturing output, 1928–37.

	1928	1933	1937
Coal (million tons)	35.4	64.3 (68)	128 (152.5)
Oil (million tons)	11.7	21.4 (19)	28.5 (46.8)
Steel (million tons)	4	5.9 (8.3)	17.7 (17)
Electricity (thousand million kilowatt hours)	5	13.4 (17)	36.2 (38)

*Figures in brackets = targets set by Five-Year Plans

Stalin achieved his aim of collectivising agriculture

- By 1941, almost all farming land had been collectivised. Grain production had increased from 73 million tons in 1928 to 95 million tons by 1940.
- New farming techniques and machinery such as tractors were brought to the countryside.
- Workers in the cities could now be fed without the fear of famine. Excess grain taken by the state could be sold abroad to hire experts and machinery for the Five-Year Plans. Between 1928 and 1933, grain exports rose from 0.03 million tons to 1.69 million tons.
- Stalin also achieved his aim of removing the kulaks as a class by 1934.
- However, collectivisation had to be forced on many peasants. Many rioted and burnt their crops and slaughtered their animals, rather than handing them over.
- This disruption, plus poor harvests in 1930–32, caused a horrendous famine in which nearly 13 million people died.
- Peasant farmers were paid very little for their grain by the state and only had one acre for private use compared to an average of 13.5 acres before 1917.

> **Test yourself**
>
> 1 Draw a table to compare the successes and failures of the Five-Year Plans and collectivisation. Which do you think was more successful in achieving its aims? Explain your answer.
>
> 2 What ways did the peasants resist collectivisation?
>
> 3 Why can the huge human cost be blamed on Stalin personally and his policies?

8.4.4 How were the Soviet people affected by these changes?

Stalin's modernisation policies had many positive and negative effects on the Soviet people

How were the Soviet people affected by Stalin's modernisation?		
	Five-Year Plans	**Collectivisation**
Positive	More housing in urban areas with improved access to healthcare and education.	New farming methods and access to new machinery.
	Improved access to training and better pay for good managers.	Collective farms had better access to education and healthcare.
	Unemployment nearly eradicated.	Famine eventually eradicated by the Second World War.
	Double the number of doctors per head than the UK by 1940.	
	Healthcare and education improved and were free.	
	In 1935, Alexei Stakhanov cut 102 tons of coal in one day, encouraging some to become **Stakhanovites** and earn bonuses.	
	A new ruling class or 'nomenclatura' emerged who had the top jobs in the Communist Party.	
	Women had paid holidays and childcare; by 1940 they made up 40 per cent of the workforce.	
Negative	Internal passports checked the movement of workers, especially non-Russians.	Collectivisation forced on the peasants who did not want to lose their private farms.
	Strict targets and constant propaganda.	Resistance led to heavy repression; propaganda campaign.
	Wages fell between 1928 and 1937; lack of consumer goods.	Removal of kulaks (dekulakisation) – the authorities set targets for the number to be found.
	Housing was expensive and hard to find.	
	Queuing to buy clothing and goods became commonplace.	Many so-called kulaks were denounced by neighbours and arrested or executed.
	Harsh punishments for not meeting targets – fines, dismissal or worse.	Famine killed nearly 13 million.
	Prisoners used as slave labour, e.g. Belomor Canal.	
	Many nationalities such as Jews continued to be persecuted by Stalin. At least nine different ethnic groups were deported by Stalin between 1935 and 1938.	

Key point

The Soviet people saw huge changes during Stalin's modernisation of industry and agriculture. Many suffered horribly, but there were some positive achievements.

Task

Ten-mark questions require an essay response so making a plan like the one below will help.

1   Add some details and examples to your own copy of the table (below), for each of the paragraphs.
2   For each of the ways people suffered or benefited, add a brief explanation.
3   Try to make a judgement about whether the suffering outweighed the benefits and explain your reasoning.

'The Soviet people suffered more than they benefited from Stalin's modernisation of the Soviet Union.' How far do you agree with this statement? Explain your answer.

Plan	Details to include
Introduction	Use this space to compare the different evidence as to whether people suffered or benefited from Stalin's modernisation of the Soviet Union.
Paragraph 1	Examine ways in which the Soviet people suffered due to the Five-Year Plans – you could look at the harsh discipline, repression, propaganda and low wages.
Paragraph 2	Examine ways in which the Soviet people suffered due to collectivisation – you could look at the removal of the kulaks and the famine.
Paragraph 3	Provide balance by examining ways in which the Soviet people benefited from the Five-Year Plans – you could look at women's opportunities, training and welfare.
Paragraph 4	Provide balance by examining ways in which the Soviet people benefited from the collectivisation – you could look at new machinery and methods and the end of famine.
Conclusion	Decide here what your overall judgement is. Did the Soviet people suffer more than they benefited? Were people in the towns and cities better off than those in the countryside? Explain your argument.

Practice question, Paper 1

'The Soviet people suffered more than they benefited from Stalin's modernisation of the Soviet Union.'

How far do you agree with this statement? Explain your answer.

[10 marks]

© Benjamin Harrison/Hodder & Stoughton

Key terms

Make sure you know these terms, people or events and can use them or describe them confidently.

Autocracy Rule by one individual with total power.

Bolshevik/Bolshevism Russian political movement led by Lenin and following communist ideas originally developed by Karl Marx and further developed by Lenin.

Capitalist/capitalism Political, social and economic system centred on democracy and individual freedoms such as free speech, political beliefs and freedom to do business.

Civil war War between two sides within the same nation or group – examples are Russia 1919–21 and Spain 1936–37.

Collectivisation Policy to modernise agriculture in the USSR 1928–40. It succeeded in modernising farming to some extent but with terrible human cost.

Communist/communism Political, economic and social system involving state control of economy and less emphasis on individual rights than capitalism.

Cossacks Elite troops of the Russian tsars.

Duma Russian Parliament established after 1905 revolution in Russia and a source of opposition to the tsar 1905–17.

Five-Year Plan Programme of economic development in the USSR from 1928 onwards. Achieved considerable progress in industry but with heavy human cost.

Gulag Prison camp in remote area where prisoners were put to work.

Industrialisation Building up factories, coal, electricity etc.

Kerensky Leader of the Provisional Government which governed Russia after first revolution in 1917.

Kolkhoz Large farms created by merging smaller farms under policy of collectivisation.

Kulak Prosperous peasant farmer.

Lenin Leader of the Bolshevik/Communist Party in Russia and a key figure in bringing them to power in 1917 and keeping power until his death in 1924.

Marxist Person who follows the ideas of Karl Marx, a political commentator who believed that societies would eventually become communist as workers overthrew bosses and took control of wealth and power.

Mensheviks Opposition party in Russia in early 1900s, part of the Social Democratic Party before it split into Bolsheviks and Mensheviks.

Nationalities Racial groups within larger states, e.g. Poles in the Russian Empire or Hungarians in the Austrian Empire.

New Economic Policy (NEP) Policy introduced by Lenin in the USSR after the Russian Civil War. Basically allowed limited amounts of private enterprise, which went against communist theory but was an emergency measure to help the economy recover from war.

NKVD Secret police in USSR, later becoming the KGB.

Okhrana Secret police force of the Russian tsars.

Peasants Poor farmers who worked their own small plots of land and usually had to work the lands of landlords as well.

Propaganda Method of winning over a population to a particular idea or set of beliefs. Also used in wartime to raise morale.

Provisional Government Government headed by Alexander Kerensky which took control of Russia after the March 1917 revolution overthrowing the Tsar.

Purges Policy pursued by Stalin in the USSR in the 1930s to remove potential opponents. Involved arrests, torture, show trials, deportations to labour camps and executions.

Show trials Trials of political opponents, which were given great publicity – most prominent in the USSR under Stalin in the 1930s.

Social Democratic Party A Marxist party that split into the Bolsheviks and Mensheviks in 1903.

Socialist Revolutionaries (SRs) Opposition group in tsarist Russia, the most well-supported as they had the support of the peasants.

Soviet Union The former Russian Empire after it became a communist state in the 1920s.

Soviets Councils of workers.

Stakhanovite A very hard-working and committed Soviet worker.

Stalin Leader of the USSR from 1929 to his death in 1953.

Stolypin Tsarist prime minister, 1906–11.

Trotsky Leading figure in the Bolshevik Party, especially in the Russian Civil War 1918–21.

Tsar Ruler of Russia up until revolution in 1917.

Tsarina Wife of tsar.

USSR The former Russian Empire after it became a communist state in the 1920s.

War Communism Policy pursued by communist leader Lenin 1918–21 to try to build communist society in Russia and also fight against his opponents. Caused major hardships and had to be temporarily replaced with New Economic Policy.

Zemstva Local councils in tsarist Russia.

9.1.1 How did Germany emerge from defeat at the end of the First World War?

In 1918, the Kaiser abdicated and Ebert signed an armistice with the Allies

- Politically, many felt that Germany had been stabbed in the back by the socialist politicians who had signed the armistice – known as the 'November Criminals'.
- Economically, Germany was in ruins after the war – national income was low, war debt was $40 billion and many died due to food and fuel shortages.
- Socially, there were 600,000 widows left due to the war, 1.5 million soldiers returned to Germany with few jobs available and there was anarchy on the streets.

Before Ebert could start solving problems, a communist uprising occurred in Berlin

- In January 1919, the **Spartacists** tried to set up a communist-style government like Bolshevik Russia.
- Led by Karl Liebknecht and Rosa Luxemburg, they seized newspaper offices in Berlin, barricaded the streets, organised a general strike and prepared for armed fighting.
- Ebert made a deal with the right-wing nationalist ex-soldiers, called *Freikorps*, and the German army to stop the uprising. Bitter fighting left 170 dead, including the leaders, who were brutally murdered.
- The Spartacist uprising showed how weak and unstable the new government was. It was forced to rely on the *Freikorps*. It also led to further communist uprisings in Bavaria (1919) and the **Ruhr** (1920).

On 19 January 1919, the first free elections were held in German history

- Ebert's Social Democrats emerged as the largest party. Ebert became the first president. He was forced to create a coalition government with the Centre Party and the Democratic Party.
- The new government met in **Weimar** (Berlin was too dangerous) to draw up a new constitution.

Key point

Germany was left weak after the First World War. The new Weimar **Republic** proved to be unpopular with some Germans and faced many challenges.

Creation of the Weimar Republic: timeline

Oct–Nov 1918:
Kiel mutiny and German revolution

9 November 1918:
Kaiser abdicates and Ebert becomes **Chancellor** and German Republic formed

11 November 1918:
Armistice signed and war ends

4–15 January 1919:
Spartacist uprising led by Karl Liebknecht and Rosa Luxemburg. *Freikorps* and the German army are used to stop the uprising

19 January 1919:
General election, Ebert becomes president

April 1919:
Communist uprising in Bavaria

28 June 1919:
Treaty of Versailles signed

11 August 1919:
Ebert signs in the new Weimar **Constitution**

The Weimar Constitution created a democratic system

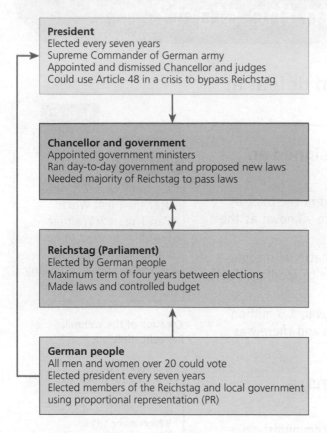

President
Elected every seven years
Supreme Commander of German army
Appointed and dismissed Chancellor and judges
Could use Article 48 in a crisis to bypass Reichstag

Chancellor and government
Appointed government ministers
Ran day-to-day government and proposed new laws
Needed majority of Reichstag to pass laws

Reichstag (Parliament)
Elected by German people
Maximum term of four years between elections
Made laws and controlled budget

German people
All men and women over 20 could vote
Elected president every seven years
Elected members of the Reichstag and local government
using proportional representation (PR)

The Constitution had both strengths and weaknesses

Strengths
- Very democratic – PR meant percentage of votes = the percentage of seats in the **Reichstag**.
- Article 48 meant in emergencies the Republic could be saved from threats or rebellions.
- The German people enjoyed universal civil rights.

Weaknesses
- PR allowed small, extremist parties to win seats in the Reichstag.
- It was very difficult for any one party to win over 50 per cent of the seats, which resulted in coalitions.
- The president appointed and dismissed the Chancellor. Article 48 was unclear on what constituted an emergency and gave the president massive power – Ebert used emergency decrees 136 times.

> **Tip**
>
> Make sure you understand the difference between the armistice and the Treaty of Versailles. The armistice was the ceasefire that ended the war and the Treaty of Versailles was the peace treaty signed the following year. Make sure you understand the difference between the Weimar Constitution (the document that set out the rules of government) and the Weimar Government itself! These are common misconceptions. Note as well that the Spartacist uprising was a left-wing, communist rebellion and it happened before the Weimar Constitution was signed.

> **Test yourself**
>
> 1 Make a list of all the problems Ebert faced after the First World War.
> 2 How much of a threat was the Spartacist uprising? Explain your answer.
> 3 Explain why the Weimar Constitution could be considered too democratic.
> 4 What were the strengths and weaknesses of Article 48?

9.1.2 What was the impact of the Treaty of Versailles on the Republic?

Many believed the Treaty was a 'stab in the back'

- Many Germans were expecting a fairer peace settlement based on Wilson's Fourteen Points.
- At the Paris Peace Conference Germany was not invited to the negotiations, which led many to refer to it as a '**diktat**' (dictated peace).
- Ebert was left with no choice but to sign the Treaty of Versailles in June 1919.

The Treaty punished Germany in many ways

- Article 231 (war guilt clause): Germany was to accept full blame for starting the war.
- Germany lost 10 per cent of its land and all its overseas colonies. In addition, 12.5 per cent of Germans would now live in other countries and 16 per cent of Germany's coal and 48 per cent of its iron industry were lost. Alsace-Lorraine went back to France and the Polish Corridor split Germany in two.
- **Reparations** were set at £6.6 billion in 1921. Coal from the Saarland went to France for 15 years.
- The German army was limited to 100,000 soldiers with no **conscription**, no tanks and no air force. The navy was reduced to six battleships, 15,000 sailors and no submarines.

Political instability followed

- In March 1920, Wolfgang Kapp attempted a rebellion using *Freikorps* units.
- The army refused to stop the *Freikorps,* but workers organised a general strike which brought the putsch to an end. The Weimar Government saw it could not rely on the army.
- The rebels went unpunished.
- In 1922, the foreign minister Walther Rathenau was assassinated and in 1923, the Nazis, led by Adolf Hitler, attempted the **Munich Putsch**. It failed, but Hitler and other Nazi leaders received short sentences and increased publicity.

The reparations also led to economic instability

- In 1922, the Government failed to pay the second reparations instalment. France and Belgium invaded the Ruhr in January 1923.
- Ebert ordered passive resistance – workers went on strike. French soldiers reacted by killing 130 Germans and expelling over 100,000.
- This halted industrial production, so Ebert authorised the printing of money to pay debts. This led to **hyperinflation**.
- The German mark became worthless. People had to barter. The middle classes and pensioners lost their savings.

Only a few people benefited from the hyperinflation

- Industrialists paid off their debts from banks using worthless marks.
- Some big businesses were able to easily buy out smaller businesses.
- People with mortgages paid them off at a fraction of the cost.

Key point

The Treaty punished Germany harshly and led to social, economic and political problems for the new Weimar Government.

Practice question, Paper 1

Why did the Treaty of Versailles lead to instability in the Weimar Republic? [6 marks]

Tip

For a six-mark question, a good answer will explain at least two different factors. Think about how the Treaty was damaging to the German people, the German economy and Weimar's reputation.

Test yourself

1 Why did most Germans resent Article 231?

2 Draw a chart of the main terms of the Treaty. Explain why each term would anger the German people.

3 Was the Kapp Putsch more of a threat than the Spartacist uprising?

4 What were the causes and consequences of the Ruhr invasion in 1923?

5 Briefly describe those that were worse off and those that were better off due to hyperinflation.

9.1.3 To what extent did the Republic recover after 1923?

Stresemann led Germany through economic recovery in the 1920s

- A new government under Stresemann was formed in August 1923. He only served as Chancellor for 102 days and then became foreign minister, but continued to dominate German politics until 1929.
- Stresemann tackled each of the problems facing the Weimar Republic to help bring stability.
- Throughout Europe, during the 1920s, many countries were gradually recovering from their post-war depression.

> **Key point**
>
> Stresemann helped solve many of the issues caused by the crises of 1923, which led to economic and political stability, but Germany was heavily reliant on loans from the USA.

Issue	Stresemann's achievements	Weaknesses
Industry and economy	1923: worthless marks were burned, and the hyperinflation ended. A new currency (Rentenmark) was introduced so businesses could trade again. 1924: **Dawes Plan** – US loans worth 800 million marks. Investment in industry and public facilities; production exceeded pre-war levels by 1928. Reparation payments were lowered and renegotiated again in the 1929 Young Plan.	German economy depended on US loans that could be called back. Employment remained at over a million and continued to rise. Further divide between rich and poor. Farmers, in particular, suffered from low prices and farming income was half the national average.
Politics	Passive resistance called off and the French left the Ruhr. Politics stabilised and moderate parties received more of the vote. By 1928, pro-Weimar parties had 136 more seats than anti-Weimar parties.	Nationalists saw this as giving in to the Allies. The Nazis launched the Munich Putsch on 9 November 1923 to try to seize power. Extremist parties still captured 13 per cent of the vote and were building up their party organisations. In 1925, the nationalist war hero, Hindenburg, was elected president.
Foreign policy	1925: Locarno Treaties guaranteed Germany's western borders and improved foreign relations with the Western powers. 1926: Germany joined the League of Nations and was given a seat on the Council. 1929: Young Plan – reduced reparations and removed British, French and Belgian troops from Rhineland.	Nationalists criticised the Locarno Treaties and membership of the League because it meant Germany accepted the Treaty of Versailles.

Practice question, Paper 1

'Germany was stable due to Stresemann's policies from 1923 to 1929.'

How far do you agree with this statement? Explain your answer.

[10 marks]

> **Tip**
>
> Ten-mark questions can often be argued in two ways. In the case of this practice question you could question whether Germany was stable or not. You could also argue whether stability was down to Stresemann's policies or other factors. Either approach is fine as long as your response is balanced.

Task

Study the table above. Write out each issue and give it a success rating of one to five stars (1* = not very successful; 5* = extremely successful). Write a paragraph for each issue, justifying your choice.

9.1.4 What were the achievements of the Weimar period?

Under Stresemann, the Weimar Republic stabilised

- Stresemann's policies stabilised the German economy and saw reparation payments lowered.
- Moderate parties in the Reichstag began to co-operate with each other and form more stable coalitions. Votes for extremist parties declined – the Nazis won only 2.6 per cent of the vote in 1928.
- The Weimar Constitution brought an end to censorship.

> **Key point**
>
> The period 1924–29 has sometimes been called the 'Golden Years' as Weimar Germany prospered, stabilised and a new Weimar culture developed in the cities. But some Germans resented these changes.

The increased stability and prosperity saw the growth of a Weimar culture

Art and literature: Writers and poets flourished with the end of strict censorship, e.g. Bertolt Brecht (*The Threepenny Opera*, 1928) and Thomas Mann (*The Magic Mountain*, 1924). Artists were free to criticise politics, big business, the war and the Church. A new artistic style called 'new objectivity' developed with artists such as George Grosz (*Grey Day*, 1921) and Otto Dix (*Big City*, 1928).

Cinema: The 1920s were a golden age for cinema. Epic science-fiction films like *Metropolis* (1927) by Fritz Lang became popular. German actress Marlene Dietrich became an international star in Josef von Sternberg's *The Blue Angel* (1930).

Weimar culture

Architecture: A new style of architecture emerged called the **Bauhaus** with its slogan 'Art and Technology – a new unity'. Walter Gropius and Paul Klee designed furniture, apartments and town halls from the Bauhaus design college in Dessau.

Nightlife: Theatres, nightclubs and cabarets became popular in towns and cities, especially Berlin. Modern forms of dancing, songs about sex and open criticism of political leaders flourished – in 1927, there were 900 dance bands in Berlin alone.

There was a backlash against these new liberal attitudes by some Germans

- Rural, conservative and elderly Germans were shocked by the decadent behaviour in the cities.
- The Wandervogel movement called for a return to traditional German culture.
- The Nazis also criticised Weimar culture as liberal and Jewish.

> **Test yourself**
>
> 1 Describe some of the achievements made in Weimar Germany under Stresemann.
> 2 How different were attitudes towards Weimar culture in rural and urban areas? Give examples.

9.2.1 What did the Nazi Party stand for in the 1920s?

The Nazi Party was an extremist party with a nationalist agenda

- Hitler was an excellent public speaker (he spoke publicly 31 times in his first year), attracting large crowds in the Munich beer halls. Nazi Party membership grew from 2000 to 20,000 between 1920 and 1923.
- The Nazis said their emblem, the swastika, represented the victory of the Aryan man.
- The Twenty-Five Point Programme tried to appeal to all classes.

> **Key point**
>
> The Nazis were an extremist, right-wing racist party that wanted to seize power in Germany and destroy Weimar **democracy** to establish a dictatorship under Hitler.

Nationalism:
Abolish the Treaty of Versailles and destroy the Weimar Republic.
Anti-democratic and anti-communist (Marxist).
A union between Germany and Austria.
A strong central government.
Appealed to nationalists, the army and business.

Socialism:
Nationalise large industries.
Educate gifted children using taxes.
Increase old-age pensions.
Appealed to working-class Germans.

Aims of the Nazi Party

Militarism:
Rearm Germany.
Take back lost German land.
Conquer living space (*Lebensraum*) in the East.
Appealed to the German army and ex-soldiers.

Anti-Semitism:
Only Aryan Germans could be citizens.
No Jew could be a citizen.
Appealed to racist and anti-Semitic Germans.

- By 1923, the **SA** had over 2000 members and was organised like the military with different ranks.

Although a failure, the Munich Putsch was also an opportunity for Hitler

- In 1923, Hitler believed the Nazis should try to topple the Weimar Government by force.
- He hijacked a beer hall meeting and announced he was taking over the Bavarian government.
- He used 600 SA (Stormtroopers) to lead the rebellion organised by Röhm.
- The rebellion failed, 16 Nazis were killed, and Hitler was arrested. Hitler received a lot of media attention during his trial and was given a very light prison sentence.
- During his time in prison, Hitler wrote ***Mein Kampf.*** In it he wrote about the way the Nazi Party would work within the democratic system in order to take power.

> **Test yourself**
>
> 1 Describe how Hitler helped the early Nazi Party develop.
>
> 2 How did the Twenty-Five Point Programme appeal to many different types of Germans? Give examples.
>
> 3 Explain why the Munich Putsch was both a failure and a success for Hitler.

9.2.2 Why did the Nazis have little success before 1930?

The Nazis remained a small, extremist party 1924–29, but membership slowly grew

- The Nazis won 32 seats in the Reichstag in 1924, probably due to the coverage of Hitler's trial following the Munich Putsch. But their electoral support had declined to only 12 seats by 1928. They were still a fringe, minority party.
- Many Germans were uninterested in extreme politics during the Stresemann years, which were more prosperous and peaceful.
- Hitler focused on winning over new members:
  - He reorganised the party by setting up local branches and creating the **Hitler Youth** in 1926.
  - At the Bamberg Conference (1926) he established the leadership principle (*führerprinzip*).
  - He appealed to the unemployed through the SA. People could join (for a membership fee) and were given a uniform, food and a place to sleep.
  - *Mein Kampf* sold a few thousand copies in the mid-1920s; it was not a bestseller until the 1930s. But, it became the political manifesto of the Nazis and gave Hitler a small income.
  - Hitler had his Nazi leaders trained by professionals to speak publicly.
  - Hitler changed unpopular policies to win over farmers and the lower middle class – groups who were not thriving under the Weimar Government.
  - Hitler ordered the SA to calm down their violent activity and hold parades and give out pamphlets instead to show discipline and strength.
- By 1928, Nazi membership had swollen to over 100,000. Farmers and the lower middle classes like shopkeepers were attracted to their anti-communist messages. The Nazis promised farmers higher prices for their food during their suffering in the 1920s.
- Annual rallies at Nuremberg from 1923 gradually attracted more spectators.
- The **SS** (*Schutzstaffel* or protection squad) was created out of loyal SA men to protect Nazi leaders.

> **Key point**
>
> The Nazis remained a fringe party for most of the 1920s attracting few votes, but their membership grew as Hitler changed tactics.

Test yourself

1. Why did support for the Nazi Party remain low between 1924 and 1929?
2. How did Hitler increase his personal control over the Nazi Party?
3. How did Hitler change the role of the SA in this period? Explain why.
4. Make a list of the different tactics used by Hitler to increase Nazi support.

9.2.3 Why was Hitler able to become Chancellor by 1933?

The Nazis won 18.3 per cent of the vote in 1930 and 37 per cent of the vote by July 1932

● There were many reasons for their electoral success.

Depression

The Depression led to economic collapse in Germany and 6 million unemployed by 1932.

Many Germans turned to extremist parties like the Nazis and the Communists.

Hitler promised jobs and **rearmament**.

Nazi campaigning

Hitler was a good public speaker. He used rallies, marches and speeches to promote his ideas. The Nazis used radio, films, posters etc. to spread their message.

They relied on generalised slogans rather than specific pledges.

They took action such as setting up soup kitchens.

'Negative cohesion'

The Nazis brought people together by their common fears rather than their common views.

Democracy

Many were disillusioned with Weimar democracy and its inability to solve the economic crisis.

Communist threat

The Nazis promised to protect farmers and business leaders from the communist threat.
The disciplined SA and SS looked much more organised than the communist gangs.

Decadence

The Nazis promised a return to old-fashioned values, rather than the Weimar decadence.

Weak opposition

The Nazis' rival parties underestimated the Nazis and failed to work together to prevent them getting into power.

The Nazis still did not have a majority of seats in the Reichstag by July 1932

● Hitler, as leader of the largest party, demanded Hindenburg appoint him Chancellor. Hindenburg declined Hitler's request.

● Hitler ordered his SA and SS to cause more chaos on the streets and Nazi members of the Reichstag to always vote against the Government. Hindenburg kept the current Chancellor, Franz von Papen (a conservative member of the Centre Party), as Chancellor.

Through political scheming, Hitler became Chancellor

How did Hitler become Chancellor?

Von Papen: Hoped to form a right-wing coalition with the Nazis in order to control them. He failed and did not have support in the Reichstag. After the November elections, the Nazi vote dropped slightly, but they remained the largest party. Hindenburg then decided to appoint a different Chancellor. ➡ **General von Schleicher:** Von Schleicher was an opponent of von Papen but had the same problem. He could not get the support of the Reichstag. Von Papen, keen on revenge, privately agreed to work with Hitler to remove von Schleicher. ➡ **The plan:** Von Papen agreed to allow Hitler the Chancellorship if he was Vice-Chancellor. Von Papen met with Hindenburg, army leaders and industrialists and persuaded them that he could control Hitler as part of a Nazi–Conservative coalition. ➡ **Hitler is appointed Chancellor:** General von Schleicher resigns and with the threat of a Nazi revolt and possible civil war, Hindenburg appoints Hitler as Chancellor on 30 January 1933.

Practice question, Paper 1

'The threat of communism was the most important reason for the increase in Nazi support.'

How far do you agree with this statement? Explain your answer. [10 marks]

Task

Create a spider diagram entitled 'How did the Nazis become the largest party in the Reichstag?' Use the material above to explain each of the reasons.

9.2.4 How did Hitler consolidate his power in 1933–34?

On 30 January 1933, Hitler became Chancellor, but he was in a weak position

- Hitler was Chancellor of a conservative coalition with von Papen as Vice-Chancellor. There were only two other Nazis in the Cabinet.
- Hindenburg and von Papen hoped that the coalition could hold off the Nazis' more extreme ideas.
- Hindenburg was still president and could still use his power to sideline Hitler.
- The German army also opposed the violent SA and its leader Ernst Röhm. By 1934, there were nearly 4 million Stormtroopers compared to just 100,000 in the German army, the *Reichswehr*.

> **Key point**
>
> When Hitler was appointed Chancellor in January 1933, his hold on power was far from complete. By the end of 1934, after a series of clever legal and more dubious methods, Hitler was in complete control as **Führer** of Germany.

Hitler needed a majority in the Reichstag to become dictator

Event	How it helped Hitler consolidate power
Reichstag Fire, 27 February 1933 The Reichstag building burnt down, and a Dutch communist was arrested. Hitler declared it the start of a communist uprising.	Hitler demanded emergency powers to suspend personal freedoms and increase police powers. Hitler used the SA and the SS to arrest over 4000 communists and other opponents. The communists were effectively banned.
Reichstag elections, 5 March 1933 Hitler used the fire, government control of the radio, and the SA and SS to intimidate opponents and voters.	The Nazis received nearly 44 per cent of the vote, but still lacked a majority.
Enabling Act, 24 March 1933 Hitler got the two-thirds majority support he needed from the Nationalists and Centre Party using both promises and intimidation from the SA and SS.	Hitler could now pass laws without consulting the Reichstag – democracy had been destroyed and Hitler was a virtual dictator. Political parties and trade unions were banned. But Hindenburg could still dismiss him and the army could have removed him by force.
Concordat, 20 July 1933 Hitler signed a **Concordat** (agreement) with the Catholic Church to stay out of religious issues if the Catholic Church stopped all political activity.	Hitler could now ensure that anti-Nazi messages were not preached by the Catholic Church.

Hitler still needed the president and the German army on his side

- The SA under Ernst Röhm was a problem for Hitler. Röhm controlled these 4 million undisciplined men and sought to make the SA into a second Germany army.
- The army was also suspicious of Röhm and the SA.
- On 29–30 June 1934, Hitler used the SS to arrest leaders of the SA in a purge. Around 400 SA leaders, including Röhm, were murdered in the **Night of the Long Knives**.
- Hindenburg congratulated Hitler for his actions and the German army now believed Hitler's loyalty was with it and not the SA.
- Hindenburg died on 2 August 1934. Hitler used the **Enabling Act** to make himself Chancellor and Führer of Germany. The German army swore an oath of loyalty to Hitler. Hitler was now the undisputed leader of Germany.

How significant was the Enabling Act in allowing Hitler to create a one-party state? Explain your answer. [40 marks]

Tip

Paper 4 questions will always start with 'How important ...' or 'How significant ...'. You need to compare different causes or reasons to write a balanced answer using full paragraphs. It is always a good idea to plan the answer for a few minutes to collect your thoughts, before you start writing.

Task

Paper 4 questions, like the one in the practice question, want you to examine and compare several different factors. You *must* examine the factor in the question, but then compare the importance or significance of that factor with others to reach a conclusion. You will need to look back over the other focus points in this Depth Study to help you collect the information you need.

Use the table below to help you plan and write your response. The whole process should take an hour. Note: You can use this writing frame for all the Paper 4 questions in this Depth Study.

How significant was the Enabling Act in allowing Hitler to create a one-party state? Explain your answer.	
Plan	**Details to include**
Introduction	*Use this space to compare the different ways Hitler created a one-party state. Try to make a judgement about which cause was the most important/significant.*
Paragraph 1	*Examine one aspect of the factor/cause/reason stated in the question. Explain its relative importance/ significance.*
Paragraph 2	*Examine another aspect of the factor/cause/reason stated in the question. Explain its relative importance/significance.*
Paragraphs 3–6	*Give balance to your answer by examining other factors/causes/reasons. Explain the relative importance/significance of each.*
Conclusion	*Explain your overall judgement here. It should not have changed from the introduction if you made one. Is there a decisive factor? Why is it more significant than the other factors/causes/reasons? What links or connections are there between the different factors/causes/reasons?*

Test yourself

1 Make a list of all the problems Hitler faced when he became Chancellor in January 1933.

2 Draw a timeline of Hitler's **consolidation** of power. Circle the event that you think was the most important. Explain your choice.

3 Why did Hitler launch the Night of the Long Knives?

9.3.a.1 How much opposition was there to the Nazi regime?

The Nazis never had a majority in the Reichstag, so anti-Nazi opposition always existed

- Hitler used the Enabling Act to ban political parties and trade unions. He also used the SA, SS and **Gestapo** to root out opponents and often send them to **concentration camps**.

> **Key point**
>
> The Nazis wanted to create a **totalitarian** state. But the Nazis had to deal with opposition to Nazi rule from many different groups in German society.

Opposition	Methods	Effectiveness
Left-wing parties and trade unions	Communists and Social Democrats met in secret and issued pamphlets, slogans and anti-Nazi jokes. Some printed anti-Nazi newspapers and encouraged strikes.	The Enabling Act had banned these groups, forcing them underground. The SS and Gestapo tried to stop these groups and broke up over 1000 opposition meetings in 1936. They never effectively challenged the regime.
Conservative groups	Some army officers, industrialists and aristocrats met in secret to plan the overthrow of the Nazis on moral grounds, most famously the Kreisau Circle.	Their leader was arrested by the Gestapo for treason and they never sanctioned a violent overthrow of the Nazis.
The army	General Beck and other army leaders became disillusioned with the Nazis, especially when the war turned against them in 1942. Beck and other army leaders planned to assassinate Hitler in the 20 July 1944 Bomb Plot – Operation Valkyrie.	The bomb plot failed when the case carrying the bomb was moved. Hitler enacted a harsh revenge and 5000 were executed.
The churches	The Catholic Church spoke out against the Nazi T-4 euthanasia programme in 1941. Protestant Pastor Niemöller organised a Confessing Church that opposed the Nazi take-over of the Churches. Many also helped Jews and others escape Germany.	The Nazis publicly changed the euthanasia policy (but carried on in secret). Many outspoken priests, including Niemöller, were sent to concentration camps or executed.
Youth groups	Anti-Nazi teenagers who did not want to join the Hitler Youth formed a Swing movement and listened to jazz music, which was banned. The **Edelweiss Pirates** put anti-Nazi messages on walls and fought the Hitler Youth. The White Rose movement printed anti-Nazi pamphlets.	Depending on the threat, the Gestapo and SS sometimes successfully broke up meetings and even arrested and executed some members, but it was difficult to stop them.
Ordinary Germans	Many Germans were fed up with constant Nazi **propaganda**. The Gestapo reported public grumbling against the Nazis. Some refused to give the Hitler salute or say 'Heil Hitler'. Anti-Nazi jokes were common.	Many only complained in private, out of fear of the concentration camps.

> **Test yourself**
>
> 1 Give a rating out of ten for each opposition group based on how much of a threat to the Nazis you think it was. Justify your choices.
>
> 2 Do you think the lack of an effective opposition proves the Nazis were popular or simply had control? Explain your answer.

9.3.a.2 How effectively did the Nazis deal with their political opponents?

The Nazi police state was run by the SS

- The SS, led by Himmler and his deputy Reinhard Heydrich, grew to a force of over 1 million by 1944.
- It was used to crush opponents and by 1936 had its own courts.
- The SS was violent and could arrest and detain opponents without charge or a trial.
- The Death's Head units ran the concentration camps for political enemies and undesirables, and later the extermination camps.
- The SD (Security Services) investigated disloyalty within the Nazi Party and the armed forces.
- The Waffen-SS was made up of fighting troops that fought alongside the regular army.

The Gestapo was used to keep tabs on ordinary Germans

- The Gestapo (secret state police) was set up by Hermann Goering in Prussia in 1933. It was feared by the German population.
- By 1934, under Reinhard Heydrich, the Gestapo became a feared organisation. It used networks of informers to spy on the German population and tap phone lines to hunt out enemies of the Nazis.
- It had unlimited powers of arrest and could send people to concentration camps without trial.

Informers were used everywhere

- There were not enough Gestapo agents to spy on every German. Local Nazi officials used loyal residents to inform the Gestapo of suspicious behaviour or treasonous activities.
- Some informers, to get back at neighbours they disliked, settled scores and fabricated stories. Children sometimes reported on their parents.

The Nazis controlled the courts and legal system

- All magistrates and judges had to take an oath of loyalty to Hitler. Hitler used them to ensure opponents were punished harshly.
- By 1943, there was a total of 43 capital (death penalty) offences, including telling anti-Nazi jokes.
- Top jobs in local police forces were given to high-ranking Nazis.

Political opponents were sent to concentration camps

- The first concentration camp was opened near Dachau in 1933. Many communists, Social Democrats and other political opponents were sent there after the Enabling Act.
- Run by the SS, conditions were harsh, and many died of disease, beatings or executions.
- Many prisoners were used as slave labour, especially during the war.
- Hitler also used camps to imprison undesirables including beggars, prostitutes, alcoholics, and later homosexuals, Jews and Gypsies.
- Between 1933 and 1939, over 1.3 million Germans had spent some time in a concentration camp.

Key point

The Nazis used a range of ways to control the German people. The terror machine, controlled by Himmler's SS, was seen everywhere.

Profile

Heinrich Himmler

- Joined the Nazi Party in 1923 and the SS in 1925.
- Became head of the SS in 1929.
- Helped Hitler remove Röhm.
- By 1936, was chief of all German police and security forces.
- Himmler's SS ran the concentration camps and carried out the **Final Solution** in the extermination camps.

Practice question, Paper 1

'The SS was the most important aspect of the Nazi police state after 1933.'

How far do you agree with this statement? Explain your answer.

[10 marks]

Task

Make a copy of the table below to compare the importance of the SS and other factors that led to the creation of a police state after 1933. This will help you answer the practice question.

SS	Other factors

9.3.a.3 How did the Nazis use culture and the mass media to control the people?

The Nazis used propaganda to try to control German hearts and minds

- In 1933, Joseph Goebbels was made Minister for Propaganda and Enlightenment (see Profile).
- He used control of the arts, media and culture to inform the German people of Nazi achievements, demonise the enemies of Nazi Germany and ensure Hitler was portrayed as a saviour.
- Propaganda did help indoctrinate some people, especially younger Germans. However, many Germans saw through the lies but did not dare criticise the Nazis due to the police state.

Goebbels used many methods to keep people loyal to Hitler and the Nazis

- The annual **Nuremberg rallies** were watched by hundreds of thousands. Uniformed SS, swastikas, bands and flying displays were all used to create a sense of belonging to the Nazi movement. They emphasised order over chaos and celebrated Hitler as leader.
- Goebbels shut down all anti-Nazi newspapers and sacked Jewish and left-wing journalists. Editors were told to print pro-Nazi messages.
- The Nazis saw Weimar culture as decadent. Expressionist art was removed from galleries and new buildings were built in a more classical style, like the new Reich Chancellery.
- Jazz music was banned and classical music (e.g. Wagner) was promoted along with folk songs.
- Movies carried pro-Nazi and anti-Semitic messages and foreign films were heavily censored.
- All books had to be approved by Goebbels. *Mein Kampf* became a bestseller. Between April and May 1933, Goebbels organised a book burning of Marxist and Jewish authors.
- Posters were posted all over Germany and bombarded the people with Nazi messages.
- Goebbels used radios and loudspeakers on the streets to air Hitler's speeches daily. A cheap radio – the 'People's Receiver' – was in over 70 per cent of households by 1939. Foreign broadcasts were banned, and all radio stations were controlled by the Nazis. Listening to an anti-Nazi radio station like the BBC could result in the death penalty.

In 1936, Goebbels saw the Olympics in Berlin as a propaganda opportunity

- The Berlin Olympics was used to showcase Nazi achievements to Germany and the rest of the world. A new stadium for over 100,000 people was built with modern electric lighting and television cameras.
- Germany topped the medal table, although the black American Jesse Owens stole the show by breaking 11 Olympic records in defiance of Nazi racial theory.
- Many visitors were in awe of the scale of the spectacle, but also shocked at the military presence.

Key point

Joseph Goebbels used propaganda, censorship and control of the media to spread Nazi messages and promote Hitler as the saviour of Germany.

Profile

Joseph Goebbels
- Joined the Nazi Party in 1924 and was made regional leader of Berlin in 1926.
- Hitler put him in charge of propaganda in 1930 and he became Minister for Propaganda in 1933.
- Goebbels was fiercely loyal to Hitler and used the media to portray Hitler as the saviour of Germany.
- In 1945, he and his family committed suicide just before Hitler did.

Test yourself

1 Make a list of all the different types of propaganda used by Goebbels.
2 Why do you think propaganda was effective at controlling the German people?
3 Why do you think the propaganda was disliked by some Germans?
4 How far was the Berlin Olympics a significant achievement for Goebbels? Explain your answer.

9.3.a.4 Why did the Nazis persecute many groups in German society?

- The Nazis wanted to create an Aryan 'master race'.

- Hitler and the Nazis believed that the Germans were an Aryan race, superior to all other races. They believed Germany would be powerful again if the Aryan race was pure and free of racial undesirables (*Untermenschen*).

- In *Mein Kampf*, Hitler blamed the loss of the First World War and Germany's economic problems on the pollution of Aryan blood in Germany.

- Fear and hatred were particularly directed towards the Jews who were demonised as parasites – **anti-Semitism**.

- The Nazis also believed other races such as Gypsies and blacks were inferior.

- The Nazis believed that groups such as homosexuals, the mentally handicapped and 'asocials' like alcoholics, prostitutes, beggars and habitual criminals were a drain on society and the economy.

- There was little opposition to the actions against Gypsies, Jews and 'asocials'.

> **Key point**
>
> The Nazis aimed to remove Jews and other 'undesirables' from German life in order to create a pure Aryan race, which they believed was superior to all other races.

Racial minorities
- Propaganda against Jews and Gypsies
- Banned from citizenship
- Many sent to concentration camps, where from 1942, many were killed

Homosexuals
- Gay and lesbian organisations were shut down
- Over 100,000 homosexuals were arrested
- Around 10,000 were sent to concentration camps where they were forced to wear a pink triangle

How did the Nazis persecute minorities?

Mentally handicapped
- Sterilisation Law 1933 left over 700,000 with certain 'illnesses' unable to have children
- In 1939 the T-4 'euthanasia programme' killed over 70,000 mentally ill patients using carbon monoxide gas
- Around 5000 babies with mental handicaps were killed by 1945 using injection or starvation
- Following a public outcry about the gassing of the mentally handicapped, this extermination ended

'Asocials'
- Many were rounded up and arrested by the SS
- Many died from hard labour, beatings and random executions

The Jews were seen as the biggest threat to the Aryan race

- Jews had experienced discrimination for hundreds of years. They had been blamed for the death of Christ and were seen as a prosperous and well-educated minority.

- This idea threatened Hitler's notion of the superiority of Aryans. Once in power, he therefore took immediate action against them.

Nazi persecution of the Jews

Boycotts and bans: 1933 – Jews banned from the civil service, teaching and news broadcasting; boycott of Jewish shops and businesses by SA and SS; stores marked with a Star of David. ▶

Propaganda: Anti-Semitic messages dominated in the media and throughout the school curriculum. ▶

Nuremberg Laws, 1935: Removed German citizenship from Jews and Gypsies and banned them from marrying Aryan Germans; Jews also banned from public facilities and many were refused passports. ▶

Kristallnacht (Night of the Broken Glass), 1938: Goebbels organised a pogrom (violent attack) on Jewish homes and businesses after a Jew killed a German diplomat in Paris; SS troops murdered 91 Jews and 20,000 were sent to concentration camps. ▶

Second World War: Jews were evicted from their homes in 1939 and by 1940 did not receive ration cards; 1941 – were forced to wear a yellow Star of David and forbidden to leave the country; 1942 Wannsee Conference, the Final Solution agreed upon; as a result, 6 million Jews were murdered in specially built extermination camps.

- Many historians see the events of *Kristallnacht* as a turning point in Nazi anti-Semitic policy.
- Before 1938, Jews faced discrimination and segregation. *Kristallnacht* saw the first organised violence against the Jews with mass arrests, murders and imprisonment in concentration camps.

Test yourself

1 Make a list of the different groups in Germany that the Nazis labelled as undesirables.
2 For each group in your list, explain a) how they were persecuted; b) why they were persecuted.
3 Draw your own timeline of the persecution of the Jews in Germany. Explain how each event worsened the position of Jews in Germany.

9.3.b.1 How did young people react to the Nazi regime?

The Nazis used schools to try to indoctrinate young Germans

- The Nazis wanted to ensure young Germans formed part of the new *Volksgemeinschaft* or **national community** – they were the future.
- Biology lessons focused on racial theory and taught that Aryans were superior to other races.
- History lessons instilled nationalism and anti-Semitism by teaching students about the 'November Criminals' who signed the armistice and the Treaty of Versailles.
- Geography lessons taught about the need for *Lebensraum* (living space) in the East and the need to reclaim lost territory.
- Physical education was given 15 per cent of school time – boys were prepared for the military and girls for bearing children.
- Religious studies was voluntary after 1937 – Hitler did not want Christian ideas contradicting Nazi ideas.
- Girls were taught domestic studies so they could be future wives and mothers. Eugenics taught girls how to choose a husband and have healthy Aryan children.

Youth were encouraged, and then forced, to join youth organisations

- **Hitler Youth** was set up in 1926. Boys joined at age 14 until 18. It focused on sports, camping, map-reading, marching, physical fitness and firing rifles, and aimed to produce future soldiers who were loyal to Hitler.
- **League of German Maidens** was set up in 1930. It focused on physical fitness for child-bearing purposes and domestic skills like cooking, cleaning and managing a home. It aimed to produce future child-bearers for the Reich.
- In 1936, all other youth groups in Germany were banned. In 1939, membership of a Nazi youth organisation became compulsory.
- Many young people joined because it looked exciting – boys were promised a uniform, camping trips, singing and sports. However, by 1939, nearly 1 million young Germans still had not joined. Many rebelled against the Nazi discipline and rules and joined the Swing movement or Edelweiss Pirates.

Nazism also affected family life

- Parents expected children's first loyalty to be to their family, but the Hitler Youth leaders told the youth it was to Hitler.
- Divisions were created within the family – for German youth, Nazi propaganda and ideology was the norm, and they could not understand any criticism of **Nazism** made by their parents' generation.

> **Key point**
>
> The Nazis wanted to ensure that young people grew up to become loyal Nazis. Boys were needed for the German army and girls as future mothers to the Aryan race.

> **Test yourself**
>
> 1 Why do you think Hitler saw young people as the future of Germany's greatness?
> 2 Make a chart to show how the different subjects in the school curriculum helped indoctrinate young people with Nazi ideas.
> 3 What evidence is there that the Hitler Youth was and was not a success for the Nazis?

> **Practice question, Paper 1**
>
> **Explain why young people were important to the Nazi regime.**
> [6 marks]

> **Task**
>
> Draw a table to help you answer the practice question. In the first column include the following factors: Future soldiers; Future mothers; Nazi ideas. In the second column explain why each factor was important to the Nazi regime.

9.3.b.2 How successful were Nazi policies towards women and the family?

The Nazis held many traditional views about women and the family

- Hitler's aim was to increase the declining birth rate.
- During the Weimar period, many women had careers. Hitler needed women to return to their traditional roles as wives and mothers and husbands to be breadwinners, in order to increase the birth rate.
- Many rural Germans supported this idea; women in urban areas resented losing their freedoms.

> **Key point**
>
> The main role for women was to bring up healthy Aryan children for the Reich. The Nazis gave incentives for women to have lots of children, but the war forced them to change direction.

The Nazis introduced many incentives for women to marry and have more children

- Goebbels' propaganda showed the ideal family as blonde-haired and blue-eyed Aryan parents with lots of children. Women were portrayed as caring mothers and fathers as soldiers or workers. Women were encouraged to stop smoking, stop wearing make-up and stay fit.
- From 1933, loans of 1000 marks were offered to newlyweds if women gave up work to raise a family. Marriage to an Aryan husband was promoted at school and in other Nazi organisations.
- The Honour Cross of the German Mother was introduced in 1938: a bronze cross was awarded for four children, a silver cross for six and a gold cross for eight or more.

Repressive measures were also used to increase the birth rate

- Women were forced out of their political roles.
- Women were gradually banned from the professions such as medicine, law and the civil service.
- The Nazis promoted the '3Ks': *'Kinder, Kirche, Küche'* ('children, church, kitchen').

The Nazis had some success in increasing the birth rate

- The number of marriages increased from 500,000 in 1932 to 750,000 by 1934.
- The birth rate increased from 15 per 1000 in 1933 to 20 per 1000 in 1939.

The war forced the Nazis to reverse some of their policies

- Hitler reintroduced conscription and announced rearmament in 1935 – many men left their factory jobs and farms to join the new *Wehrmacht* (armed forces).
- By 1937, there was a national shortage of workers in the war industries. The Nazis encouraged women to fill the shortages in the factories. The number of women in work increased by 1939, but this was still less than it had been in 1930. Some resisted going back to work due to the low wages.
- By 1939 and the outbreak of war, Nazi policies towards women were confused. However, over half a million served in the *Wehrmacht* as auxiliaries with roles in nursing and other non-combatant work.

> **Test yourself**
>
> 1 Make a list of all the methods used by the Nazis to increase the birth rate in Germany.
>
> 2 Draw a chart to show the successes and failures of Nazi policies towards women and the family.
>
> 3 How significant was the Second World War in changing Nazi policies towards women?

9.3.b.3 Did most people in Germany benefit from Nazi rule?

When Hitler took power, he promised to end the Depression and provide work

- By late 1933 there were still over 5 million unemployed.
- Dr Hjalmer Schacht introduced the New Plan to help solve the economic crisis in 1934.
- Government spending increased and was channelled into work-creation programmes. A National Labour Service (RAD) was set up to employ men (18–25 years old) for six months before they were conscripted. They built new *autobahns* (motorways) and other facilities.
- The Government took control of foreign trade to focus on raw materials for the war industry.
- Jews and political opponents were removed from their jobs and replaced with Aryan Germans.
- By 1936, unemployment had dropped to under 2 million and by 1938 it was less than half a million. This was sometimes called the Nazi 'economic miracle', but there was huge government debt.
- Schacht was replaced by Goering in 1937 who introduced a Four-Year Plan to prepare Germany for war. Wages and prices were closely controlled, and industries were forced to produce war materials rather than consumer goods. Public debt rose rapidly, and rationing was introduced (e.g. butter).

> **Key point**
>
> The Nazis seemingly solved the unemployment problem caused by the Depression, which increased their support, but some Germans prospered more than others under Nazi rule.

> **Task**
>
> Study the table below. List the groups in the order in which you think they benefited from Nazi policies. Then write a paragraph justifying your decision.

> **Practice question, Paper 1**
>
> 'The German workers benefited the most from Nazi rule.'
>
> How far do you agree with this statement? Explain your answer.
>
> [10 marks]

Some Germans were better off but others were worse off under Nazi rule

Group	Better off	Worse off
Workers	Unemployment fell to 2 million by 1936; **Strength Through Joy** (KDF) organisation gave workers cheap holidays, sports events and cinema tickets; Volkswagen (people's car) scheme introduced; **Beauty of Labour** scheme introduced better working conditions.	Wages remained low and discipline was harsh; trade unions banned and replaced by the German Workers' Front (DAF); striking was illegal; no worker ever received their Volkswagen.
Farmers	Reich Food Estate guaranteed German farmers better prices; Reich Entailed Farm Law stopped banks seizing land if they did not pay their debts; 'Blood and Soil' campaign portrayed the German peasant as the backbone of the Aryan race.	Farmers forced to grow what the Nazis wanted; only the eldest child could inherit the farm, leaving younger children without an income; this led to increased rural depopulation.
Business	The Nazis had removed communist threat; small shopkeepers were told that large department stores would be restricted; industry benefited from rearmament; trade unions and strikes banned; huge government contracts for industries that produced war goods like explosives and chemicals.	Despite Nazi promises, small businesses still had to compete against department stores; big business increasingly under state control; lack of consumer goods to sell.

9.3.b.4 How did the coming of war change life in Nazi Germany?

Key point

Nazi support grew in the early years of the Second World War, especially after the successful invasion of France. But defeat at Stalingrad and increased Allied bombings saw life worsen for most Germans. The war also intensified Nazi terror, propaganda and helped lead to the Final Solution.

The war progressed in different stages and conditions for ordinary Germans deteriorated

Stage 1 (1939–41):
Successful conquest of western Europe. New goods and raw materials taken (e.g. wine, perfumes); France defeated, and Nazi support was high; two-fifths of workers ate better on rations than before the war. BUT rationing extended over most foods and clothing; black markets appeared in cities.

Stage 2 (1941–43):
Operation Barbarossa (1941) – invasion of the USSR. German advance halted by 'Russian' winter; army defeated at Stalingrad (1942). British bombing campaign of German cities – huge civilian casualties and industries destroyed. Quality of life decreased.

Stage 3 (1943–44):
All Germans ordered to provide for the war effort – 'Total War'. Goebbels used propaganda to keep Germans focused on the war effort. Entertainment and luxuries removed as non-essential; women drafted into war work due to labour shortages. British bombing campaign intensified. SS became a profitable business empire using slave labour in concentration and labour camps.

Stage 4 (1944–45):
Hitler created the Home Guard made up of elderly and children. Bombing raids flattened cities like Dresden – 150,000 civilians were killed in two days in 1945. Hitler committed suicide.

The war affected some groups more than others

Young people:
- Increased rebel activity, e.g. Edelweiss Pirates.
- Members disrupted supplies and sheltered escaped prisoners.
- The Nazis publicly executed 12 leaders.

Women:
- 1944: severe labour shortages so women drafted into the labour force.
- Women suffered the most due to rationing.
- Many killed by the bombing campaigns.

How did the war affect different groups in the Third Reich?

Polish:
- Nazis aimed to 'Germanise' the region.
- Germans were given confiscated Polish property.
- Poles reduced to second-class citizens.
- Many were sent to labour camps for slave labour and one in five had died by 1945 due to the occupation.

Jews:
- Millions more Jews came under Nazi control, especially in Poland and eastern Europe.
- SS set up special killing squads called *Einsatzgruppen* which shot over 1.3 million Jews by 1945.
- Jews were forced into ghettos in Poland – thousands died of starvation and forced labour.
- 1942: 'Final Solution' to the 'Jewish Question' decided at the Wannsee Conference.
- In the extermination camps (e.g. Treblinka, Auschwitz), 6 million Jews, Gypsies and homosexuals were murdered then burned.
- The SS ran the camps – civil servants, local police, industry and the army helped with transportation and logistics.

Test yourself

1 List positive and the negative effects of the war on German civilians.
2 What was the turning point for Germany in the Second World War? Explain your answer.

Key terms

Make sure you know these terms, people or events and can use them or describe them confidently.

Anti-Semitism Prejudice against Jews.

Autobahns High-speed motorways built by the Nazis in Germany in the 1930s to create jobs.

Bauhaus German design movement incorporating sleek lines and modern materials.

Beauty of Labour Nazi movement to improve conditions for industrial workers to try to win their support.

Chancellor Head of the government.

Communist/communism Political, economic and social system involving state control of economy and less emphasis on individual rights than capitalism.

Concentration camps Camps used by Nazis to hold political opponents in Germany.

Concordat A deal between the state and the Catholic Church.

Conscription Compulsory service in the armed forces.

Consolidation Making a position more secure, usually when a political party has just taken power.

Constitution A system of government.

Dawes Plan Financial aid package provided by the USA to Germany in 1924.

Democracy Political system in which the population votes for its government in elections held on a regular basis.

Diktat Term used in Germany to describe the Treaty of Versailles because Germany had no say in the terms of the Treaty.

Edelweiss Pirates Youth groups in Germany who opposed the Nazis, especially in the war years.

Enabling Act Law passed in 1933 which gave the government powers to arrest opponents.

Final Solution Nazi plan to exterminate the Jews and other races in Europe. Generally thought to have begun in 1942.

Freikorps Ex-soldiers in Germany after the First World War.

Führer Leader (German).

Gestapo Secret police in Nazi Germany.

Hitler Youth Youth organisation in Nazi Germany designed to prepare young people for war and make them loyal Nazis.

Hyperinflation Process of money becoming worthless, most notably in Germany in 1923.

Kaiser Ruler of Germany.

Kristallnacht Night of Broken Glass – attack on Jewish properties across Germany in November 1938.

League of German Maidens Organisation in Nazi Germany for girls to encourage them to embrace Nazi beliefs and values.

Mein Kampf 'My Struggle': the autobiography of Adolf Hitler in which he set out his theories about power and racial superiority.

Munich Putsch Attempted revolt by Hitler and Nazis in 1923, aiming to overthrow the Government.

National community (*Volksgemeinschaft*) Key idea of Nazis in Germany in the 1930s – they wanted people to become part of and promote a 'national community'.

Nazism National Socialism, the political belief of Adolf Hitler and the Nazi Party, based on aggressive expansion of German lands and the superiority of the Aryan race.

Negative cohesion Term coined by historian Gordon Craig to describe the way different groups in Germany supported the Nazis because they feared the Nazis' opponents (particularly the communists).

Night of the Long Knives Attack on Ernst Röhm and other leading figures in the SA in June 1934.

Nuremberg Laws Series of laws passed in Germany in 1935 discriminating against Jews and other racial groups in Germany.

Nuremberg rally Huge Nazi political meeting held every June from 1923 to 1938.

Propaganda Method of winning over a population to a particular idea or set of beliefs. Also used in wartime to raise morale.

Rearmament Building up arms and armed forces, used as a means to fight unemployment by many states in the 1930s, including Nazi Germany and Britain.

Reichstag German parliament.

Reparations Compensation to be paid by Germany to France, Belgium, Britain and other states as a result of the First World War.

Republic System of government which does not have a monarch.

Ruhr Main industrial area of Germany.

SA The Brownshirts – Stormtroopers of the Nazi Party.

Spartacists Communists in Germany in 1919 who wanted a revolution in Germany similar to the 1917 revolution in Russia.

SS Organisation within the Nazi Party which began as Hitler's bodyguard but expanded to become a state within a state.

Strength Through Joy Leisure programme run by the Nazis in Germany to improve the lives of ordinary people.

Totalitarian Complete control.

Treaty of Versailles Treaty that officially ended war between the Allies and Germany in 1919. It was controversial because of the terms, which Germany claimed to be excessively harsh.

Weimar Small town in Germany, home of the German government in the 1920s.

10.1.1 On what factors was the economic boom based?

Key point

The USA emerged as the richest nation in the world after the First World War. Business-friendly government policies, new innovations, **mass production** and confidence allowed the US economy to boom in the 1920s.

By the end of the First World War, the USA had the strongest economy in the world

Factors that led to a boom in the US economy		
Factor	Details	Explanation
Natural resources	Plentiful natural resources and raw materials such as iron, coal and oil.	The USA could expand rapidly without relying on imports.
The First World War	The USA only entered the war in 1917. It provided loans, food and war supplies for the Allies.	Before 1917, the Allies were buying raw materials, food and munitions from the USA. The USA took over European markets and gave loans to the Allies that had to be repaid.
New technology and innovations	Electricity widely available; new appliances (e.g. radios, refrigerators, vacuum cleaners). New plastics, e.g. Bakelite; new textiles, e.g. rayon.	Factories could now power assembly lines. Increased demand for household appliances leading to increased profits for industries.
Mass production	Henry Ford's (see Profile on page 106) **assembly line** allowed mass production of cars and other goods.	Consumer goods produced quickly and cheaply. Prices dropped rapidly, increasing domestic market for new goods.
Advertising	Commercials in cinemas and on the radio; billboards on highways. Magazines and catalogues – by 1928, 30 per cent of Americans bought goods via **mail-order** catalogues.	Mass marketing led to increased awareness of new consumer goods; boosted sales and company profits – telephone sales doubled by 1930.
Credit	**Hire-purchase** schemes: 'Buy now pay later'; accounted for 60 per cent of car sales by 1928.	Availability of **credit** meant Americans did not have to save to buy; interest paid back saw companies make huge profits. Lower earners could buy new goods.
Republican policies	Low taxes, **tariffs** on imports, **trusts**, and low government interference (**laissez-faire**).	Low taxes: businesses could invest more, and consumers had more expendable income. Tariffs: (e.g. 1922 Fordney-McCumber tariff) protected US industry against foreign **competition**. Laissez-faire (Hoover called it 'rugged individualism'): government did not interfere and let business get rich. Powerful trusts dominated industry such as Rockefeller oil.
Confidence	Created a consumer society; banks allowed Americans to speculate by 'buying on the margin' – a 10 per cent deposit was laid down and the rest of the money for the **shares** was lent by the bank. By 1929, there were 20 million shareholders out of a population of 120 million.	Share prices rose rapidly. Businesses paid huge dividends to shareholders.

Profile

Henry Ford

- Created the Ford Motor Company in 1903.
- Model T car for the ordinary man – 10,000 were sold in the first year.
- Ford used an assembly line to increase efficiency and lower costs.
- In 1911, the Model T cost $1100 and by 1928 it was just $200.
- By 1929, the motor industry employed hundreds of thousands of Americans.
- The motor industry stimulated other industries – it used 75 per cent of US glass, 90 per cent of petrol and 80 per cent of rubber production by the late 1920s.
- The motor car also led to the growth of suburbs, new roads and gas stations and allowed the film industry to grow as cinemas were now accessible.

Tip

Paper 4 questions will always start with 'How important ...' or 'How significant ...'. You need to compare different causes or reasons to write a balanced answer using full paragraphs. It is always a good idea to plan the answer for a few minutes before you start writing, to collect your thoughts.

Practice question, Paper 4

How significant was mass production in allowing the US economy to prosper in the 1920s? Explain your answer.

[40 marks]

Task

Paper 4 questions like the one here want you to examine and compare several different factors. You *must* examine the factor in the question, but then compare the importance or significance of that factor with others to reach a conclusion.

Use the table to plan and write your response. The whole process should take one hour.

Note: You can use this writing frame for any other Paper 4 questions in this Depth Study.

How significant was mass production in allowing the US economy to prosper in the 1920s? Explain your answer.	
Plan	**Details to include**
Introduction	*Use this space to compare the different factors that led to prosperity in the USA in the 1920s. Try to make a judgement about which cause was the most important/significant.*
Paragraph 1	*Examine one aspect of the factor/cause/reason stated in the question. Explain its relative importance/significance.*
Paragraph 2	*Examine another aspect of the factor/cause/reason stated in the question. Explain its relative importance/significance.*
Paragraphs 3–6	*Give balance to your answer by examining other factors/causes/reasons. Explain the relative importance/significance of each.*
Conclusion	*Explain your overall judgement here. It should not have changed from the introduction if you made one. Is there a decisive factor? Why is it more significant than the other factors/causes/reasons? What links or connections are there between the different factors/causes/reasons?*

Test yourself

1 Why was the First World War an important factor in the economic boom in the 1920s?

2 What is meant by Republican policies?

3 Draw a spider diagram or flow chart showing how the motor industry helped stimulate other industries in the USA.

10.1.2 Why did some industries prosper while others did not?

New industries were the main winners in the 1920s

- The motor car industry boomed with companies like Ford and Chrysler making huge profits – over 26 million cars had been made by 1929. Workers' wages tended to be high.

- The motor industry stimulated other secondary industries like glass and rubber (see Profile on page 106).

- Some older industries like steel and oil continued to grow, partly due to the motor industry – 20 per cent of steel production could be attributed to the motor industry by the mid-1920s.

- The construction industry was successful as new homes, factories and schools were built. New skyscrapers like the Empire State Building were built by the early 1930s.

- Oil and gas also prospered as they were used as fuel for electrical power stations.

Key point

High demand for new consumer goods allowed new industries to boom in the 1920s at the expense of **traditional industries** and farming, which struggled to make a profit.

Traditional industries did not share in the prosperity

- Coal, tin and copper were **overproduced** after the end of the war and prices dropped rapidly and wages fell. Coal was replaced by newer industries such as gas and oil.

- Pit closures and redundancies led to strikes – in 1928 there was a strike in the coal mines of North Carolina where men were only paid $18 and women just $9 for a 70-hour week.

- Textiles like cotton and wool struggled to compete with synthetic fibres like rayon.

- New machines and processes meant fewer workers were needed in many industries.

- By the end of the 1920s, about 42 per cent of the population were living below the poverty line. Immigrants who arrived after the war were especially affected as they often had the lowest paid jobs.

Test yourself

1 Why was the motor industry so important to the prosperity of the 1920s?

2 Make a list of industries that did not share in the boom of the 1920s.

10.1.3 Why did agriculture not share in the prosperity?

The farming industry faced many problems

- After the war, Europe imported less food from the USA due to poverty in Europe and US tariffs.

- US farmers faced new competition from Canadian wheat growers.

- From 1900 to 1920 new machinery and improved fertilisers meant more land was being farmed – by 1920, they were overproducing wheat.

- Prices them plummeted as desperate farmers tried to sell their produce.

- Problems in farming affected more than 60 million Americans. African Americans were particularly badly hit with over three-quarters of a million unemployed.

Test yourself

1 Make a chart or spider diagram showing all the different reasons farming suffered in the 1920s.

2 Which members of the rural population were worst hit by the decline in the farming industry?

There was a wide gap between the rich and poor in the USA in the 1920s

- In 1925, 32 per cent of national income went to the richest 5 per cent and only 10 per cent of national income went to the poorest 42 per cent. While dividends and company profits rose by over 160 per cent between 1920 and 1929, nearly 60 per cent of Americans earned less than $2000 a year – many of these worked in the older industries and farming.

> **Key point**
>
> Industrialists, investors and urban Americans largely benefited from the economic boom while rural America remained impoverished, especially black and native Americans.

Winners during the boom	Losers during the boom
New industries: Company profits rose due to the increasing demand for consumer goods, e.g. car industry and household appliances. Workers in the new industries had better wages and more disposable income to spend on leisure and entertainment.	**Farmers:** Small farmers were not able to sell their surplus produce after the war and government tariffs and foreign competition drove down their profits forcing them to sell their farms or face eviction.
Trusts: Men such as Carnegie in the steel industry and Rockefeller in the oil industry became 'captains of industry', making billions of dollars.	**Old industries:** Workers in older industries like textiles faced competition from new fibres such as rayon. Company profits fell and many faced lower wages or unemployment. Coal was also replaced by oil and gas as the preferred fuel for many.
Urban middle class: Bankers, professionals, small business owners and some skilled workers were able to afford the new consumer goods and speculate by buying shares on the margin and selling them when prices rose. Many bought goods such as cars, radios and vacuum cleaners using hire-purchase schemes.	**Immigrants:** Many new immigrants were poorly educated and given the lowest-paid jobs. Many lived below the poverty line.
Large landowners: They were able to diversify their crops to meet the demand for fresh fruit and vegetables in the cities.	**Black Americans:** Black Americans in the South were mainly farm labourers and were hardest hit by the collapse of the farming industry. Those who moved to the North faced discrimination with low-paid jobs as domestic servants and poor housing.
Construction: The motor car led to the need for more roads, growing suburbs, hospitals and schools. Large companies built skyscrapers in the cities.	**Native Americans:** Native Americans were given the poorest farming land on **reservations**, earned very low incomes and fell into poverty.
Entertainment: Sports, music, cabarets, nightclubs and the cinema became popular leisure activities for many Americans in the cities and the suburbs. The car allowed them easy transport to venues.	

Practice question, Paper 1

'The economic boom led to great prosperity in the USA in the 1920s.'

How far do you agree with this statement? Explain your answer.

[10 marks]

Tip

Remember that the six- and ten-mark questions in Paper 1, and 40-mark questions in Paper 4, require you to explain your reasons, rather than just describe what happened. Make sure you address the question and use solid facts to back up your explanations.

Task

Ten-mark questions require an essay response so making a plan like the one below will help.

1 Add some details and examples for each of the paragraphs.
2 Add a brief explanation for each of the factors.
3 Try to make a judgement about which factor/s is/are the most important and explain your reasoning.

'The economic boom led to great prosperity in the USA in the 1920s.' **How far do you agree with this statement? Explain your answer.**	
Plan	**Details to include**
Introduction	*Compare the different evidence as to whether people prospered or not during the economic boom.*
Paragraph 1	*Examine ways in which some people prospered during the boom – you could look at new industries or trusts.*
Paragraph 2	*Examine another way in which some people prospered during the boom – you could look at people in the cities, the entertainment industry or construction.*
Paragraph 3	*Provide balance by examining ways in which some people did not prosper – you could look at workers in older industries and farmers.*
Paragraph 4	*Examine another group that did not prosper from the boom – you could look at black Americans, immigrants and Native Americans.*
Conclusion	*Decide here what your overall judgement is. Did people in the USA prosper more than they suffered? What is your clinching argument for this? Can it be supported by evidence?*

10.2.1 What were the 'Roaring Twenties'?

Prosperity changed lifestyles and entertainment

- The '**Roaring Twenties**' refers to the bustling and glamorous lifestyle lived by some in the towns and cities.

- The term conjures up images of nightclubs, music, dancing, partying and young people enjoying themselves. For wealthier, young Americans this was true, but for many rural Americans who faced poverty, this lifestyle was viewed as decadent and immoral.

The motor car enabled this new lifestyle

- People could now drive to work and new suburbs appeared as a result.

- People could drive to shops, restaurants and cinemas.

- Many people could now visit friends, take holidays at beach resorts or go to sporting events.

- Young Americans could now go out without their parents, which gave a sense of freedom for many.

New forms of entertainment appeared

- By 1930, 40 per cent of homes in the USA owned a radio and there was a growing choice of radio stations to listen to with the first national network set up in 1926 – NBC.

- Some stations exposed people to new music such as **jazz** and allowed families to listen to sporting events such as baseball. This changed people's tastes and became a habit across the USA.

- Jazz music captured the imagination of young Americans – the 1920s became known as the Jazz Age.

- Jazz was played in the nightclubs (e.g. Cotton Club of Harlem) and on the radio. New dances like the Charleston influenced a generation of young, urban women known as '**flappers**' who wore short dresses, smoked and drank alcohol in public and went out without chaperones.

- Conservative Americans viewed jazz music and the 'flapper' as a threat to the American way of life.

- New big money sports such as baseball and boxing became popular. Millions visited stadiums or tuned in on their radios. Sports stars like Babe Ruth became household names.

- In **Hollywood**, the film industry rapidly developed. Movie stars such as Clara Bow and Rudolf Valentino influenced people's fashions, hairstyles, make-up and mannerisms.

- The first 'talkies' were introduced in 1927, and by 1929 cinema audiences reached nearly 100 million each week.

- Young Americans were exposed to sex appeal at the cinema. Some Americans criticised its influence and new censorship legislation was introduced in some states.

> **Key point**
>
> Americans in the cities and suburbs enjoyed a change in lifestyle and culture thanks to the motor car, which gave them access to cinemas, stadiums and nightlife. Many people in rural America, who faced poverty, did not experience the same changes.

> **Test yourself**
>
> 1 Make a summary diagram of the different factors that changed life for Americans in the 1920s.
>
> 2 Why did some Americans oppose the changes taking place in US society in the 1920s?

10.2.2 How widespread was intolerance in US society?

Immigration numbers were reduced in the 1920s

- Over 8 million immigrants came to the USA, 1901–10, creating competition for jobs and housing.
- The National Origins Act (1924) reduced **immigration** to 150,000, banned Asian immigration and reduced immigrants from eastern and southern Europe.

Many feared immigrants brought radical ideas

- The Bolsheviks seized power in Russia in 1917. Many Americans feared that new immigrants would spread radical ideas like anarchism and **communism** – the **Red Scare**.
- In 1919, strikes involving over 400,000 workers convinced many that communists were to blame.
- Attorney-General Mitchell Palmer's house was bombed.
- Palmer drew up a list of 60,000 suspected communists and nearly 600 were deported as illegal 'aliens' in the Palmer Raids.
- Two Italian anarchists, Sacco and Vanzetti, were charged with murder after an armed robbery. The evidence against them was flimsy and the trial focused more on their radical ideas and stirring up racial intolerance. They were executed in 1927.

Racism was widespread, especially in the South

- The Jim Crow Laws segregated black Americans and prevented many from voting.
- The **Ku Klux Klan (KKK)** aimed to protect white, Protestant America from blacks, Jews, Catholics, communists and immigrants. It organised parades and used intimidation such as beatings and **lynchings**.
- The KKK was popular in the Midwest and the rural South.
- Many black Americans fled to the North. There was still discrimination, but some found opportunities as jazz musicians and had access to higher education.
- Organisations to help black Americans were set up such as the **National Association for the Advancement of Colored People (NAACP)**.

In the 'Bible Belt', fundamentalism led to intolerance

- Christian fundamentalism was strong in the Midwest and the South. Fundamentalists believed that everything in the Bible was literal truth and opposed the theory of evolution.
- Many Southern states passed laws against the teaching of evolution in schools. When John Scopes challenged these laws (the '**Monkey Trial**'), he was convicted of breaking the law, but had successfully challenged the anti-evolution lobby.

Key point

Intolerance was widespread in the USA in the 1920s, especially in the South and Midwest. Racism, religious fundamentalism and the fear of **radical** ideas brought over by immigrants, led to many wanting to preserve the American way of life.

Practice question, Paper 4

How significant was immigration as a cause of growing intolerance in US society in the 1920s? Explain your answer. [40 marks]

Task

Look back at the advice on writing Paper 4 responses on page 106. You can use this to model your answer for the question above.

10.2.3 Why was Prohibition introduced, and then later repealed?

The Volstead Act introduced national Prohibition in 1920

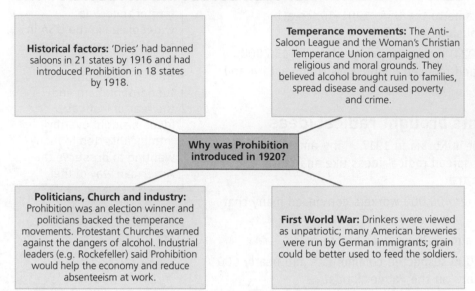

Historical factors: 'Dries' had banned saloons in 21 states by 1916 and had introduced Prohibition in 18 states by 1918.

Temperance movements: The Anti-Saloon League and the Woman's Christian Temperance Union campaigned on religious and moral grounds. They believed alcohol brought ruin to families, spread disease and caused poverty and crime.

Why was Prohibition introduced in 1920?

Politicians, Church and industry: Prohibition was an election winner and politicians backed the temperance movements. Protestant Churches warned against the dangers of alcohol. Industrial leaders (e.g. Rockefeller) said Prohibition would help the economy and reduce absenteeism at work.

First World War: Drinkers were viewed as unpatriotic; many American breweries were run by German immigrants; grain could be better used to feed the soldiers.

> **Key point**
>
> **Prohibition**, the 'noble experiment', was introduced in 1920 with support from **temperance** movements, the Churches and some politicians. Many in the cities ignored the new law as criminal gangs took over the illegal alcohol trade. It was repealed in 1933 after it became impossible to enforce.

Prohibition led to a huge change in US society

- Alcohol consumption fell by about 30 per cent in the early 1920s.
- Prohibition agents arrested offenders and those smuggling in illegal 'liquor'. They made 66,000 arrests in 1929 alone.
- Illegal bars called 'speakeasies' flourished and by 1929, there were over 30,000 in New York alone.
- Normal Americans became law-breakers and some brewed 'moonshine', which was dangerously high in alcohol.
- Bootleggers supplied illegal 'booze' to the cities – rum from the West Indies and beer from Canada.

Gangster crime emerged

- **Gangsters** often ran the illegal alcohol trade – it was worth over $2 billion a year! The most infamous was Chicago boss Al Capone.
- During the St Valentine's Day Massacre in 1929, seven people were gunned down on the orders of Capone.
- Gangsters bribed the police, the judges and courts and even Prohibition agents. One in 12 Prohibition agents was dismissed for corruption.

Prohibition ended and the law was repealed in 1933

- Prohibition was difficult and expensive to enforce.
- Bribery and corruption were rife and street gun violence was common.
- The **Depression** of the 1930s saw some politicians argue that tax from alcohol could be used to help those in poverty and the unemployed.
- Farmers would be able to sell their grain if breweries reopened.
- Roosevelt ended Prohibition in 1933.

> **Practice question, Paper 1**
>
> **Why was the Volstead Act repealed in 1933?**
> [6 marks]

> **Task**
>
> Create a table to explain why the Volstead Act was repealed in 1933. In the first column list the factors that led to its repeal: Gangsters; Depression; Bribery and corruption. In the second column write an explanation of each factor.

10.2.4 How far did the roles of women change during the 1920s?

REVISED

Before the First World War, women's lives were restricted in many ways

- Working-class women in urban areas worked in factories, as secretaries or as domestic servants. In poor rural areas, women mainly helped on the farm.
- Middle-class women were expected to behave like ladies and not wear make-up, drink or smoke, or go out in public without a chaperone. They were expected to be housewives.
- In rural areas, the churches preached traditional roles for women as mothers and wives.

> **Key point**
>
> The 1920s brought new freedoms for some women, especially in the cities. However, many in rural areas disapproved of these changes.

The end of the First World War brought positive changes for some women

- In 1920, women gained the vote in all states.
- Many middle-class women worked in factories during the war and spent their wages on enjoying themselves.
- In the 1920s, many women embraced these new freedoms especially in the cities. They continued to seek employment. There was a 25 per cent increase in women in paid employment by 1930, mainly in manufacturing industries, the radio stations and as assistants.
- Women benefited from the liberty of the car and from new electrical goods such as washing machines and vacuum cleaners.
- Some women, influenced by movie stars at the cinemas and the new clothes in the mail-order catalogues, adopted different fashions. They wore make-up, wore shorter dresses and had bobbed hair – they were known as 'flappers'.
- Changing attitudes meant marriages broke down more easily as women were less likely to stay in unhappy relationships. Divorce rates doubled between 1914 and 1929.

However, there were limitations and some women did not enjoy these changes

- Middle-class women in the cities benefited the most from changing attitudes and lifestyles.
- Women in rural and conservative areas of the USA were still expected to fill the traditional role of mother and wife. The Protestant Church helped reinforce this value.
- Many rural Americans opposed the decadent lifestyle of young women in the cities. They were horrified by the exposure of women to sex in films and the corrupting influence of jazz music.
- Women still earned less than men, even for doing the same job.
- Women still had little political power – less than 1 per cent of Congress was made up of women in the 1920s.

> **Test yourself**
>
> 1 Describe the different experiences of working-class and middle-class women in the 1920s.
> 2 Why did the end of the First World War impact some women's lives so much in the 1920s?
> 3 How did life for women in the city differ to life in rural America?
> 4 Draw a chart to compare how far life for women changed in the 1920s.

What were the causes and consequences of the Wall Street Crash?

10.3.1 How far was speculation responsible for the Wall Street Crash?

Speculation seemed like an easy way to get rich quickly to many Americans

- Big investors bought shares and made money through dividends as share prices rose. Speculators gambled by risking their money to make a quick profit by selling their shares when price rose. **Speculation** is a gamble – you can make money quickly or lose everything.

- Banks were willing to allow speculators to buy shares 'on the margin'. A 10 per cent deposit was paid and the rest of the money for the shares was lent by the bank.

- By 1929, there were over 20 million speculators and 1.5 million big investors. Many believed that prices would keep rising.

> **Key point**
>
> In 1929, the economic **boom** came to a dramatic end when **Wall Street crashed**. The confidence of the 1920s disappeared as investors panicked and sold their shares as the economy slowed down.

In 1929, Wall Street crashed …

| **1928:** Confidence at an all-time high. Share prices rose by 300 per cent, 1928–29. | **Summer 1929:** Factory output began to decline. Overproduction and falling profits. Some big investors began to sell their shares. | **Autumn 1929:** Small investors followed suit and sold their shares. Many were ruined as prices collapsed. Black Thursday, 24 October – stock market lost 11 per cent of its value. Banks tried to restore confidence by buying up shares. | **Black Tuesday, 29 October:** Banks stopped supporting the stock market. In one day, 16 million shares were sold and the market lost $14 billion. |

Other factors also caused the Crash

- Banks lent money 'on the margin' and consumers bought goods on credit – debt was rising again.

- The USA was saturated with consumer goods that could not be sold, leading to overproduction.

- Tariffs meant that companies could not sell their surplus goods overseas as foreign countries put up tariffs on US goods making them too expensive to buy.

- The economy had been slowing down since 1927 and big investors were losing confidence.

- There was inequality in the distribution of wealth – over 50 per cent of the population earned less than $2000 a year. Low earners (farmers, immigrant workers) had not shared in the boom.

> **Test yourself**
>
> 1 What is the difference between a big investor and a speculator?
>
> 2 Why were so many Americans attracted to the idea of owning shares?
>
> 3 Why can speculation be seen as a form of gambling?
>
> 4 Why are the banks partly responsible for the Wall Street Crash?
>
> 5 Draw a summary diagram of the different factors that led to the Wall Street Crash.

10.3.2 What impact did the Crash have on the economy?

The Wall Street Crash helped lead to the Great Depression

- The Wall Street Crash was not the only cause of the Depression – weaknesses in the economy had been building up for many years beforehand.

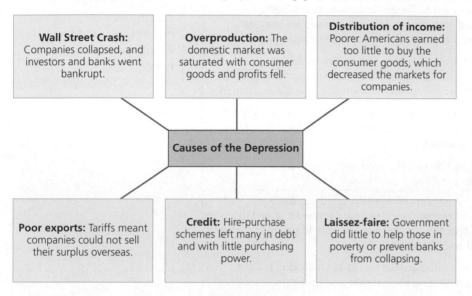

Wall Street Crash: Companies collapsed, and investors and banks went bankrupt.

Overproduction: The domestic market was saturated with consumer goods and profits fell.

Distribution of income: Poorer Americans earned too little to buy the consumer goods, which decreased the markets for companies.

Causes of the Depression

Poor exports: Tariffs meant companies could not sell their surplus overseas.

Credit: Hire-purchase schemes left many in debt and with little purchasing power.

Laissez-faire: Government did little to help those in poverty or prevent banks from collapsing.

> **Key point**
>
> The Wall Street Crash led to a worldwide economic depression: banks closed, income dropped and rich investors lost millions.

The rich were hit hardest at first

- Large investors lost the most. Some survived and some were ruined: Rockefeller lost 80 per cent of his wealth and Winston Churchill lost over $500,000 after the Crash.
- The rich were the big spenders. Demand for consumer goods dropped further.
- Those who had borrowed money 'on the margin' now had worthless shares. They could not pay the banks back and went bankrupt.

The Crash meant that confidence had been lost

- In 1929, 659 banks failed as loans remained unpaid and people stopped saving or withdrew their money.
- The banks that survived stopped giving out loans to businesses and mortgages to homebuyers.
- Industry began to reduce wages or lay off workers. By 1933, there were 14 million unemployed.
- Food income dropped to $5 billion by 1933 as prices fell rapidly.
- International trade suffered. Tariffs made the situation worse and the USA's exports dropped from $10 billion in 1929 to $3 billion in 1932.

> **Tip**
>
> Make sure you understand the difference between the Wall Street Crash and the Depression. The Wall Street Crash was the period of panic selling in the US stock market in October 1929. The Depression was the period in the 1930s where there was a sustained, long-term downturn in economic activity, which led to social problems as well.

Test yourself

1 Explain how the Wall Street Crash helped lead to the Great Depression in the 1930s.
2 List the other factors that contributed to the Depression.
3 Explain why bank failures were common during the Depression.
4 Why did the failures in the banks lead to unemployment in the USA during the Depression?

10.3.3 What were the social consequences of the Crash?

The Depression affected nearly every section of US society in the 1930s

US society	Effects of the depression
Towns and cities	By 1933, 25 per cent of the workforce were unemployed. Companies laid off workers or reduced their wages. Many lost their homes as they could not pay their mortgages.
	Thousands of families lived in shanty towns called **'Hoovervilles'** – named after US President Herbert Hoover. People begged for food; malnutrition and disease increased.
	There was no social security. People relied on charity and queued in breadlines for food, but there were not enough to help the huge numbers.
	As many as 2 million unemployed men travelled by train looking for work in 1932.
Countryside	Farming was hit hardest. Prices dropped rapidly. Farm income was so low that farmers could not even afford to harvest their crops. Farmers were unable to pay mortgages and loans and went bankrupt.
	Some farmers formed armed bands to try to stop the authorities from seizing their farms and property.
	In the South and Midwest, over-farming and drought had caused a 'dustbowl' which left 20 million hectares of farmland like desert.
	Many farmers left their farms and went to the cities in California to look for work, but there was very little available.
Immigrants and black Americans	Immigrants often had the lowest paid jobs and were first to be laid off. Poverty, crime and malnutrition were common.
	Black American sharecroppers were often worse off than their white neighbours. They lost their land and income first and many moved northwards.

> **Key point**
>
> Unemployment was the biggest problem caused by the Depression. Farmers and low-income workers such as immigrants and black Americans were hit hardest.

Practice question, Paper 1

'Farmers were the worst affected by the Depression in the 1930s in the USA.'

How far do you agree with this statement? Explain your answer.

[10 marks]

Task

You could use the essay plan task on page 109 to help you answer the above practice question.

Test yourself

1 Explain how unemployment led to other social problems for Americans in the cities and the countryside.

2 Why were non-white Americans hit particularly hard by the effects of the Depression?

10.3.4 Why did Roosevelt win the election of 1932?

Hoover was regarded as a 'do-nothing' president

- Hoover believed in 'rugged individualism' or self-help. There was no welfare state to help the millions of unemployed.
- Hoover insisted that 'prosperity was just around the corner', but this seemed like a fantasy to the 13 million unemployed, and there was resentment towards Hoover and the Republican Government.

Hoover's actions to deal with the Depression were ineffective

- The tax cuts did little to improve confidence and public spending. Tariffs only made the situation worse for farmers and industry as they now found it more difficult to sell their surpluses overseas.
- Public works programmes had little impact on the millions of unemployed.
- Hoover encouraged charities to help and asked businesses to make voluntary arrangements with their workers to maintain wages, but this was impossible.
- In June 1932, thousands of ex-servicemen marched on Washington demanding their war bonuses early. These 'Bonus Marchers' camped outside the White House and sang patriotic songs. Hoover asked General MacArthur to deal with them. MacArthur, convinced they were communists, sent in troops and used tear gas to disperse them and even burned their camps. Hoover's reputation was further damaged.

Roosevelt promised the Government would take action to deal with the Depression

- Roosevelt was in the Democratic Party – it believed that the government should use public money to help those worst affected by the Depression.
- Roosevelt had been Governor of New York and had proved that spending public money on job creation schemes could help the unemployed. This was known as 'pump priming'.
- He promised a '**New Deal**' for the American people using the '3Rs': Relief, Recovery and Reform.
- Roosevelt led a massive 20,800-km campaign in which he publicly criticised the Republicans and Hoover for doing nothing. He was a charismatic speaker and inspired confidence in the crowds.
- Roosevelt won the election with a landslide victory, winning 7 million more votes than Hoover.

> **Key point**
>
> President Hoover's actions were seen as too little too late whereas the American public believed Roosevelt's promise of an active government would help reverse the effects of the Depression.

> **Task**
>
> Draw a table to help you answer the practice question. In the first column list the factors that enabled Roosevelt to beat Hoover: Hoover's actions; Effects of the Depression; Roosevelt's campaign. Use the second column to add an explanation and supporting detail.

> **Practice question, Paper 1**
>
> **Why was Roosevelt able to beat Hoover in the 1932 presidential election?**
>
> [6 marks]

10.4.1 What was the New Deal as introduced in 1933?

Roosevelt introduced a series of reforms in his first Hundred Days as president called the First New Deal

- Roosevelt and his advisers (the 'Brains Trust') introduced 15 new pieces of legislation in the first **Hundred Days**.

- Many of these reforms set up 'alphabet agencies'.

- Roosevelt broadcast 'fireside chats' every Sunday to the American nation to explain his actions.

> **Key point**
>
> Roosevelt's First New Deal aimed to tackle many of the worst effects of the Depression using public money to fund government agencies.

Who was helped	Alphabet agencies/reforms	Actions taken
Banks	Emergency Banking Act (EBA), 1933; Securities Exchange Commission (SEC), 1934	EBA: all banks were closed for a four-day holiday and only well-run ones could reopen, with loans to support them. Over $1 billion was redeposited by customers in 1933 as confidence was restored. SEC: tightened up regulations to stop reckless speculation and to prevent another crash.
The poor	Federal Emergency Relief Administration (FERA), 1933; Home Owners Loan Corporation (HOLC), 1933	FERA: $500 million was spent on soup kitchens, clothing and employment schemes. It provided work for over 20 million people, 1933–35. HOLC: over 1 million people received loans to prevent them losing their homes.
The unemployed	Civilian Conservation Corps (CCC), 1933; Civil Works Administration (CWA), 1933; Public Works Administration (PWA), 1933	CCC: unemployed men 18–25 were given low paid work ($30 per month) on environmental projects. By 1941, 2.5 million were employed, including 15,000 Native Americans. CWA: provided short-term work for nearly 4 million, 1933–34. PWA: used public money to build roads, schools, bridges and airports. $7 billion spent building 70 per cent of US schools and 35 per cent of its hospitals.
Farmers	Agricultural Adjustment Administration (AAA), 1933; Farm Credit Administration (FCA), 1933	AAA: quotas on food production – income rose by 50 per cent, 1932–35. Land taken out of production. About 99 per cent of farmers helped, but not sharecroppers or tenant farmers. FCA: loans to 20 per cent of all farmers so they did not lose their farms. Prohibition was repealed, legalising the sale of alcohol again; this helped farmers by increasing sales to breweries.
Industry	National Recovery Administration (NRA), 1933	Codes of fair competition introduced which helped improve wages, working conditions and increase prices. Industries that took part could fly the NRA blue eagle symbol. By 1935, industrial production was 22 per cent higher than in 1933.
Farmers, unemployed and industry	**Tennessee Valley Authority (TVA)**, 1933	Built 33 dams, improved farmland with new irrigation, planted new forests and built hydroelectric power stations in dustbowl states such as Tennessee, Alabama and North Carolina. New industries created thousands of jobs and helped farmers. The land was improved and health and welfare facilities were developed.

Practice question, Paper 1

'The First New Deal benefited farmers the most.'
How far do you agree with this statement? Explain your answer.   [10 marks]

10.4.2 How far did the character of the New Deal change after 1933?

Roosevelt was persuaded to take more radical action in the Second New Deal

- Roosevelt had been criticised for not helping ordinary Americans, so between 1935 and 1937 he persuaded Congress to introduce a range of far-reaching reforms known as the Second New Deal.

> **Key point**
>
> The **Second New Deal** aimed to help ordinary Americans through a set of radical reforms and targeted the poorest sections of society.

Trade unions: Wagner Act, 1935 – employers forced to recognise trade unions so they could negotiate better conditions and pay. Workers could not be sacked for trade union membership.

Welfare: Social Securities Act, 1935 – state pensions for the elderly and widows; insurance for the sick and unemployed using contributions from government, employer and employee.

Second New Deal

Unemployed: Works Progress Administration (WPA), 1935 – united the work creation agencies. Created jobs building roads, schools, bridges and tunnels; 7 per cent of the budget provided work for unemployed actors, photographers, artists and musicians. By 1943, 8.5 million jobs had been created.

Tenant farmers and sharecroppers: Resettlement Administration (RA), 1935 – half a million poorer farming families moved to new land. Replaced in 1937 by the Farm Security Administration (FSA) – loans for sharecroppers and tenant farmers to buy their own land; labour camps for migrant workers – nearly $1 billion spent to help the poorest farmers.

Test yourself

1 Which groups in US society did the Second New Deal focus on helping?

2 Did the Second New Deal help those working in agriculture more than the First New Deal? Explain your answer.

3 Were ordinary Americans better off under the Second New Deal than they were under the First New Deal? Give examples.

Practice question

What were the main reforms introduced as part of the Second New Deal?

[4 marks]

10.4.3 Why did the New Deal encounter opposition?

Conservative opposition argued that the New Deal went too far

- Republicans, business leaders and the wealthy saw the New Deal as interfering with businesses and other core American values.
- Roosevelt was accused of being a socialist or communist and acting like a dictator.
- Republicans criticised the New Deal for using public money to pay for reforms.
- In 1934, business leaders formed the Liberty League and accused Roosevelt of destroying free enterprise and creating unfair competition with agencies such as the TVA.
- Richer Americans resented the increase in taxation to pay for the New Deal reforms – they believed high taxes discouraged people from working hard.

Radical critics believed the New Deal did not go far enough

- Huey Long (former Governor of Louisiana) taxed big corporations and businesses and spent the money building roads, schools and hospitals. He promised a minimum wage, pensions and free education. He employed African Americans on the same terms as whites. He had 7.5 million supporters and had ambitions to run for president before his assassination in 1935.
- Dr Francis Townsend set up Townsend Clubs and campaigned for the radical Townsend Plan – higher pensions of $200 per month for over-60s provided they spent it that month to stimulate the economy. There were over 7000 Townsend Clubs across the USA.
- Father Coughlin and his National Union for Social Justice criticised the New Deal for not doing enough to help the poorest. Coughlin's organisation had over 7 million members and his radio broadcasts were heard by over 40 million Americans every Sunday.

The US Supreme Court declared some New Deal agencies unconstitutional

- The Supreme Court was dominated by Republicans. In 1935, they declared the NRA unconstitutional because the president was interfering with business illegally. In 1936, the AAA was also declared unconstitutional on the grounds that it interfered with states' rights.
- Roosevelt tried to 'pack' the Supreme Court with five new, more moderate justices. Congress refused and even members of his own party revolted, thinking it would give the president too much power.
- Although the plan failed, the Supreme Court was shaken and some justices retired. New justices were less hostile to reform and the Social Security Act and Wagner Act were declared constitutional in 1937.

> **Key point**
>
> The New Deal was criticised for being un-American by the Republicans and business and for being not radical enough by others. The **Supreme Court** argued that some of the agencies were unconstitutional.

> **Test yourself**
>
> 1 What were the main arguments against the New Deal from conservative opponents?
>
> 2 What were the main arguments against the New Deal from radical critics?
>
> 3 Describe how Roosevelt tried to deal with opposition from the Supreme Court.

> **Task**
>
> Draw a spider diagram to help you with the practice question. Write 'Why did the New Deal face opposition?' in the centre and add the following branches: Conservative opposition; Radical opposition; Supreme Court opposition. Then add details and examples.

Practice question, Paper 1

Why did Roosevelt face opposition to the New Deal? [6 marks]

10.4.4 Why did unemployment persist despite the New Deal?

REVISED

The New Deal was limited in its scope

- The New Deal never nationalised industries or took complete control of the economy. It dealt with the symptoms rather than the causes of the Depression.
- When the economy seemed to be recovering by 1937, Roosevelt cut back on public spending. This resulted in another recession and unemployment rose to 19 per cent in 1938.
- Some Americans lost confidence in Roosevelt after this and the Republicans improved their vote in Congressional elections making it harder for Roosevelt to pass new reforms.

> **Key point**
> The New Deal never solved the problems caused by the Depression and high unemployment continued until the outbreak of war in 1939.

Consumer spending never returned to pre-1933 levels

- Unemployment never fell below 5 million so many Americans could not afford to buy new goods.
- Farming prices did rise considerably, but sectors such as meat, cotton and wheat stayed below their 1929 levels throughout the 1930s leaving many still in poverty.
- Foreign markets were still weak, and exporting was still difficult due to tariffs reducing profit from overseas trade. Industry continued to pay poor wages and many remained on low incomes.

Only the outbreak of the Second World War brought the Depression to an end

- War broke out again in Europe in 1939. The USA did not enter the war directly until 1941, but there was a huge demand from Europe for US goods, war supplies, raw materials and food.
- Rearmament in the USA began by 1940 and defence spending increased providing many jobs; unemployment dropped to below 5 million for the first time in 1942.

Test yourself

1 Draw a spider diagram giving all the reasons for continued high unemployment in the 1930s.
2 Why did confidence not fully return to the US economy during the life of the New Deal?
3 Describe the impact of the Second World War on the US economy.

10.4.5 Did the fact that the New Deal did not solve unemployment mean that it was a failure?

The success of the New Deal has split opinion among historians

- Some historians believe that the New Deal, despite failing to solve unemployment, was largely successful at relieving the worst effects of the Depression.
- Other historians view the New Deal as failing to target women and to improve the lives of the poorest, such as black Americans and Native Americans.
- Right-wing critics tend to characterise the New Deal era as a time of 'big government' when American values like individualism, self-help and laissez-faire were eroded.

> **Key point**
>
> The New Deal did successfully ease the suffering of those worst affected by the Depression and was supported by most Americans. However, it did not end the Depression, nor did it help everyone in the USA.

	Evidence of success	Evidence of failure
Unemployment and the economy	Unemployment fell by over 30 per cent, 1930–39. The banking system stabilised, and confidence was restored. Deprived areas such as the Tennessee Valley were helped. The poorest benefited from FERA's emergency help.	Unemployment never fell below 14 per cent. Tax increases and public spending were in billions of dollars. Industry faced greater regulation. Consumer spending and investor confidence remained low. Budget cuts in 1937 triggered further recession. Only entry into the war ended unemployment.
Workers	Trade union membership was nearly 7 million by 1939. Pay and conditions generally improved. Alphabet agencies found jobs for millions.	Some companies treated unions with suspicion and many strikes were broken up with violence. Big business remained powerful. Many lived below the poverty line with temporary or poorly paid jobs.
Farmers	Large farmers benefited from higher food prices and government loans. Some tenant farmers and sharecroppers were helped by government investment.	Tariffs meant overseas markets were limited. Tenant farmers and sharecroppers were not helped until the Second New Deal – many were forced off their land by the AAA and TVA.
Women	Some women gained access to the political system. Eleanor Roosevelt became a campaigner and Frances Perkins was Secretary of Labor.	Many New Deal reforms were aimed at men – only about 8000 women were involved in the CCC. Social security payments were often not paid to women.
African Americans	Sharecroppers helped in the Second New Deal. Some African Americans found work in the CCC.	Agencies like the CCC segregated black Americans. Domestic workers were not included as part of the Social Security Act. No civil rights laws were passed by Roosevelt in fear of angering Southern **Democrats**. More black workers were unemployed.
Native Americans	Indian Reorganisation Act, 1934 gave money to preserve Native American land and culture.	Native Americans remained a poor and excluded group of society.

- But ... the New Deal created a more compassionate society and Roosevelt remained hugely popular. Many Americans were content with the fact that the Depression had not led to revolution or extremism.

> **Practice question, Paper 1**
>
> 'The New Deal was largely a failure in solving the effects of the Depression.'
>
> How far do you agree with this statement? Explain your answer.
>
> [10 marks]

> **Task**
>
> Use the essay plan task on page 109 to help you answer the practice question.

Key terms

Make sure you know these terms, people or events and can use them or describe them confidently.

Assembly line System of producing cars in which each worker had only one job.

Boom Period of high economic prosperity.

Communism/communist Political, economic and social system involving state control of economy and less emphasis on individual rights than capitalism.

Competition Pressure from rivals, usually in business and often in other countries.

Credit Borrowing money, usually from a bank.

Democrat Member of one of the main US political parties.

Depression Period of economic hardship in which trade is poor and usually leading to problems such as unemployment and possibly political unrest.

Flappers Young women in the 1920s, especially in the USA, who had greater freedom than previously because of job opportunities and changing attitudes.

Gangster A criminal.

Hire purchase System of paying for goods in instalments so they could be enjoyed straight away.

Hollywood Suburb of Los Angeles, home of the US film industry.

Hooverville Shanty town made up of temporary shacks, common in the economic depression of the 1930s in the USA and named after President Hoover.

Hundred Days The initial period of F.D. Roosevelt's presidency in 1933 in which he passed a huge range of measures to help bring economic recovery.

Immigration Entry into a country with the purpose of settling.

Jazz Type of music which became extremely popular from the 1920s, generally associated with African American musicians.

Ku Klux Klan (KKK) Secret society in USA which aimed to keep white supremacy in USA and terrorised African Americans and other groups.

Laissez-faire Philosophy based on the idea that governments should not get involved in economy, business or people's lives.

Lynching A murder, usually by a mob and carried out on African Americans.

Mail order Popular type of shopping in the USA in the 1920s in which customers ordered from catalogues.

Mass production System of producing goods in factories using production lines in which workers specialised in one task. Made production quick, efficient and relatively cheap.

Monkey Trial Trial of teacher John Scopes for teaching about evolution in Tennessee in 1925.

National Association for the Advancement of Colored People (NAACP) Organisation whose aim was to promote and support the cause of African Americans in the USA in the 1920s and 1930s.

New Deal Policies introduced by US President Roosevelt from 1933 onwards to try to tackle US economic problems.

Overproduction Usually in agriculture – growing too much food so that demand is filled and prices fall.

Prohibition Amendment to US Constitution passed in 1919 (Volstead Act) to ban production and sale of alcohol.

Radical Term used to describe extreme political views.

Red Scare Wave of fear about communist infiltration of American political and social

life to undermine it. Seen in the 1920s and also the 1940s and 1950s.

Republican One of the two main political parties in the USA.

Reservation (native American) Area of land set aside for Native Americans.

Roaring Twenties Refers to the 1920s in the USA, a period of major social and economic change for many Americans.

Second New Deal Set of policies introduced by US President Roosevelt in 1935–36.

Shares System that allows large or small investors to own part of a company and get a share of its profits.

Speculation Buying shares in the hope that their price will rise and they can be sold at a profit.

Stock market Trading arena where investors can buy and sell shares in companies.

Supreme Court Highest court in the USA, whose job was to rule if laws passed by the government were challenged as being unconstitutional.

Tariff Taxes on imported goods which made them more expensive – often designed to protect makers of home-produced goods.

Temperance Movement that opposed alcohol.

Tennessee Valley Authority (TVA) Organisation set up by President Roosevelt to help provide economic development in the Tennessee Valley. Most famous projects were giant hydroelectric dams.

Traditional industries Well-established industries such as textiles, coal, agriculture.

Trusts Groups of businesses working together illegally to reduce competition.

Wall Street Crash Collapse in value of US companies in October 1929 which led to widespread economic distress.

Answers

The following are sample answers to the practice questions in this book, along with an examiner's comment on the answer in the margin.

1 Were the peace treaties of 1919–23 fair?

Practice question, Paper 2 (page 2)
Study Source A.
What is the message of the cartoonist? Explain your answer using source details and your own knowledge. [8 marks]

The message of the cartoonist is that the peace settlement was a compromise. In the cartoon, the Big Three can be seen adding ingredients to the 'Melting Pot', which has the words 'Peace Soup' written on it. This suggests that the peace settlement in 1919 contained terms from all the different countries at the Paris Peace Conference. The buckets also have the words 'National Sentiment' written on them which tells us that the leaders, like Lloyd George and Clemenceau, had to consider public opinion at the end of the war, which was to punish Germany. The cartoon was made in 1919 and is referring to the Paris Peace Conference where the Big Three decided on the terms of the Treaty of Versailles. There were lots of disagreements over how harshly Germany should be punished. For example, Lloyd George wanted to punish Germany but not too harshly whereas Clemenceau wanted to cripple Germany's economy and military. The cartoonist seems to be criticising the fact that the peace treaty was such a mixture of terms.

The student begins well by explaining the main message of the cartoonist.

The student explains the details in the cartoon well, which develops the answer further.

The response links the date of the cartoon to suitable contextual knowledge to support this.

The response identifies the cartoonist's attitude towards the Treaty, which develops the main message further.

Practice question, Paper 1 (page 4)
What aims did Clemenceau achieve in the Treaty of Versailles? [4 marks]

Clemenceau managed to achieve several aims in the Treaty of Versailles such as a massive reduction in the German military. For example, as part of the Treaty terms, Germany was only allowed an army of 100,000 soldiers and conscription was banned. He also managed to secure the return of Alsace-Lorraine to France which would help protect the German–French border. Clemenceau was determined to blame the Germans for the start of the war and this was achieved with the war guilt clause, Article 231.

The response is short and to the point and identifies an adequate range of examples to answer the question.

Practice question, Paper 1 (page 6)
Why did the Treaty of Versailles make Weimar Germany unstable up to 1923? [6 marks]

One reason the Treaty of Versailles made Germany unstable by 1923 was the reparation payments. These were set at £6.6 billion in 1921, and Germany failed to pay the second instalment, which resulted in France and Belgium invading the Ruhr in 1923. The Ruhr was the industrial heartland of Germany and the occupation disrupted normal trade. It also led to hyperinflation when the German Government chose to print more money to pay the striking workers. This created massive economic instability as people were unable to buy and sell goods as prices rose so rapidly and many Germans, especially pensioners, lost all their savings.

The Treaty also caused political instability. Many right-wing nationalists viewed the Treaty as a betrayal by the socialist-led Government. They believed that the Government was made up of the same leaders who had signed the armistice in 1918 and stabbed Germany in the back. This led

The first paragraph clearly explains one of the reasons the Treaty led to instability in Germany. It uses well-selected evidence to support the explanation in the last sentence.

A second reason is also explained here and there is good development of the knowledge to address the question.

Cambridge IGCSE and O Level History Study and Revision Guide

to uprisings and rebellions in Germany such as the Kapp Putsch in 1920 where groups of *Freikorps* attempted to seize power in Berlin, causing the government to flee the city. There were also political assassinations carried out by right-wing extremists such as the murder of Walther Rathenau in 1922. Much of this was due to the harsh military terms of the Treaty and the bitterness caused by the war guilt clause.

Practice question, Paper 1 (page 8)
**'Germany suffered the most in the peace settlements after the war.'
How far do you agree with this statement? Explain your answer.** [10 marks]

Germany suffered greatly due to the Treaty of Versailles. Many Germans particularly resented the war guilt clause, known as Article 231. This blamed Germany for the start of the First World War and meant that Germany had to pay reparations for the war damage, which were set at £6.6 billion in 1921. Many people in Germany believed that blame for the war should have been shared. Huge war debt and high unemployment after the war meant that the reparation payments severely weakened the Germany economy. Germany's inability to pay the second instalment in 1922 led to a French and Belgian invasion of the Ruhr in 1923, which caused a crisis for normal trade. This was made worse when the German Government ordered the printing of more money to pay the workers on passive resistance and led to hyperinflation. The loss of German territories also led to suffering as 10 per cent of its land was given to other countries, such as France and Poland. This meant nearly 13 per cent of its population was living in a foreign country and half of its iron and steel industry was lost, which weakened the economy further. The huge reduction in Germany's military meant that Germany was left defenceless – it only had an army of 100,000 soldiers and no air force. The German army had been a source of pride in Germany and led to huge numbers of unemployed ex-soldiers roaming the streets, some of which joined the *Freikorps* and engaged in political violence.

However, Germany's allies also suffered when they were forced to sign their peace treaties. The Austro–Hungarian Empire was broken up by the Treaty of St Germain and the Treaty of Trianon, leaving millions of people living in different states. Furthermore, the transfer of territory to new states like Czechoslovakia meant that Austria's economy was severely weakened as much of Austria's industry was in those territories. Likewise, over 3 million Hungarians along with much of Hungary's raw materials were lost to countries like Romania.

Furthermore, Turkey lost a substantial amount of its territory in the Treaty of Sèvres in 1920. The old Ottoman Empire was split into zones where countries like Britain, France and Italy controlled the economy, leading to great economic instability and resentment as Turkey had once been a proud and strong empire. Turkey's military was also reduced to only 50,000 troops and it was not allowed an air force. This caused further problems and the growth of nationalism, leading to the Treaty of Lausanne in 1923 to help solve the problems by fixing the borders.

Overall, Germany did suffer the most due to its peace settlement. Austria and Hungary were left in such an economic state that they never paid reparations and Bulgaria was treated less harshly by the Allies in the Treaty of Neuilly. Turkey, although harshly punished at first, saw the Treaty overturned in 1923. Germany, however, was invaded by France and Belgium when it failed to pay its reparations and saw constant threats to its political stability by 1923. France in particular wanted to ensure that Germany was not a threat to its national security in the future.

The student begins by addressing the factor explicitly in the question – a focused start to the response.

The economic hardship caused by the Treaty is dealt with first and the explanation is well developed with precise factual evidence to support.

A second effect of the Treaty is examined here – the territorial losses. This explanation is partially developed and more could have been made of how economic hardship led to suffering.

Military restrictions are examined in the last part of the first paragraph. Detailed evidence is used to explain their impact on Germany.

The student provides balance in the response by examining the peace treaties for Austria and Hungary. Solid factual evidence is used to explain their impact.

Further range is added to the response by examining the peace treaties for Turkey. The explanations are supported and well focused.

The conclusion gives a clinching argument to address the 'How far …?' aspect of the question. The judgement is clearly explained with convincing evidence to support.

2 To what extent was the League of Nations a success?

Practice question, Paper 2 (page 11)
Study Sources A and B.
How similar are these two sources? Explain your answer using
details of the sources and your knowledge. [8 marks]

Sources A and B are similar as they both view the League's initial actions as positive when dealing with the Corfu incident in 1923. Source A says the League 'acted promptly and fairly' and similarly Source B says the League 'upheld the principles on which it was based'. Both sources also suggest that the League's actions were not a victory. Source A differs slightly to Source B, however, as it suggests that the League failed when it dealt with Italy, when it says 'a great power had once again got away with using force'. Source A ultimately praises the League for its quick response to the Corfu incident but also suggests it failed to have any impact whereas Source B suggests that the League responded as it should have, even if it was 'not strictly a League victory'. These sources are referring to the fact that Mussolini was able to force the League to reverse its ruling and instead of condemning Mussolini's actions, Greece was made to apologise and pay compensation.

A valid comparison is made that directly compares the content and overall view of the two sources to show they are similar.

This answer is well balanced and explains how the two sources also differ in their views of the League's actions in the Corfu incident.

Valid knowledge is used here to put the details of the sources into context by explaining what event the authors are referring to in 1923.

Practice question, Paper 1 (page 13)
Describe the main features of the organisation and structure
of the League of Nations. [4 marks]

The League had an Assembly which met once a year and was very democratic as every member had a vote. There was also the League's Council, which was a smaller group and met up to five times a year and in emergencies. It had the power to condemn aggressive nations and place sanctions on them. The Secretariat was the collection of administrators who carried out the League's work and the League's agencies and committees focused on improving living and working conditions around the world.

The response is focused and to the point. A variety of features of the League's organisation and structure have been identified with some supporting detail added, which develops the response well.

Practice question, Paper 1 (page 14)
Explain why the Depression led to problems for the League
of Nations. [6 marks]

The Depression led to many countries, such as Britain and France, ignoring their responsibilities in the League of Nations. The Depression caused mass unemployment in countries around the world that were linked to the USA as trade declined rapidly. Leading League members, like Britain and France, concentrated on solving their own economic problems instead of more actively addressing aggressive actions by other great powers, such as Japan and Italy, when they invaded Manchuria and Abyssinia.

The effects of the Depression were felt especially hard in Germany where unemployment reached nearly 6 million by 1932. This economic downturn caused many Germans to turn to extremist political parties such as the Nazis and Communists. In 1933, the Nazi leader, Adolf Hitler, was appointed Chancellor of Germany. He left the Disarmament Conference set up by the League and began reversing the terms of the Treaty of Versailles, which the League was supposed to prevent. This made the League look increasingly weak in the face of aggressive nations.

The first paragraph focuses on the effects of unemployment caused by the Depression. The paragraph lacks some detailed knowledge, but suggests a general context is understood. The explanation could be explicitly developed further to improve the answer.

The second paragraph examines the effect of the Depression in Germany and the increase in extremism. The evidence is stronger here and the explanation is well developed and focused, although an example of how Hitler reversed the Treaty would add extra detail to the answer.

Practice question, Paper 1 (page 16)
'The weak leadership of France and Britain was the main reason the League failed in Manchuria and Abyssinia.'
How far do you agree with this statement? Explain your answer. [10 marks]

I agree that France and Britain's weak leadership was a major reason the League failed in Manchuria and Abyssinia, but it was not the only reason. The League lacked the military and economic might of the USA among its member states, which meant that it was very difficult to stop aggressive nations when they threatened world peace. The League also had a weak structure and organisation which led to inaction when peace was threatened.

Britain and France failed to act quickly enough in the Manchurian crisis. Both countries had colonies in the Far East and did not want to lose them by being pushed into a conflict with Japan. Japan ignored the Lytton Report and left the League when it realised that Britain and France were not willing to get involved in a conflict on the other side of the world, especially when they would have to donate the forces to stop Japan. Even more damaging to the League's reputation was when Britain and France decided to make a secret pact with Italy over Abyssinia. The Hoare–Laval Pact in 1935 promised to give Mussolini two-thirds of Abyssinia in return for stopping the war, because both Britain and France wanted to retain Italy as an ally in the future against Germany. This pact was leaked to the press and totally discredited the League and its leading members.

However, the weak leadership of the League was not the only reason it failed in Manchuria and Abyssinia. The League's membership was inherently weak without the USA or the USSR as a member. The Council of the League did have the power to use force to stop aggressive nations when they threatened world peace, as was the case in Manchuria and Abyssinia. But, without the economic and military resources of the USA this was impossible as neither Britain nor France were prepared to commit their military or their financial resources to stop aggressive countries. Therefore, in many ways the absence of the USA helped lead to the weak leadership of Britain and France, as they were not economically strong enough to fulfil the aims of the League.

Furthermore, the League's structure and organisation were too weak to cope with the powerful nations when they acted in an aggressive way and this led to failure. The Assembly only met once per year and was too slow to react to international situations that threatened world peace, such as in Manchuria. For example, it took a whole year after the Mukden incident before the Lytton Report was published. The Council was also weakened by the fact that each permanent member had a veto. As Japan and Italy were both permanent members of the Council it meant they could delay the League further, even if the other members of the League all agreed to act.

To conclude, the League was too weak an organisation without powerful members such as the USA and the USSR (until 1934). It lacked the military might to intimidate or stop aggressive powers like Japan and Italy. While both Britain and France were willing to bypass the League's authority, especially during the hardship caused by the Depression, both countries did not have the military or economic power to fight multiple conflicts around the globe, without the USA.

The introductory paragraph suggests that the response will be well balanced and examine alternative factors that led to the failure of the League.

The next section focuses clearly on the factor in the question and gives two solid examples of how Britain's and France's weak leadership led to the League's failure.

The next paragraph provides balance to the answer. The student examines the impact the lack of US and Soviet membership had on the League's ability to deal with aggressive nations and makes a valid link between this factor and the weak leadership of Britain and France.

The student then examines the League's organisation and structure and uses well-selected evidence to support the explanation.

The conclusion clearly makes a judgement and explains how the League failed primarily due to the lack of the USA as a member.

3 Why had international peace collapsed by 1939?

Practice question, Paper 1 (page 18)

Describe how Hitler destroyed the terms of the Treaty of Versailles. [4 marks]

Hitler destroyed many of the terms of the Treaty of Versailles when he came to power in 1933. In 1933, Hitler began to secretly rearm and build an air force, which was prohibited by the peace settlement. In 1936, Hitler went further and publicly announced conscription and invaded the demilitarised Rhineland. Both actions reversed the terms in the Treaty. In 1938, Hitler invaded Austria and formed an *Anschluss* or union which went against the territorial terms of the Treaty.

The response is well focused on addressing the demands of the question and gives a good range of examples of how Hitler destroyed the terms of the Treaty.

Practice question, Paper 1 (page 19)

Explain why the League of Nations' failures encouraged Hitler's aggressive foreign policy. [6 marks]

One of the aims of the League was to enforce the terms of the Treaty of Versailles. This included making sure that Germany did not increase the size of its army to above 100,000, build an air force, introduce conscription or reoccupy the Rhineland. However, the League failed to prevent Hitler from carrying out any of these actions between 1933 and 1936. This encouraged Hitler to make further aggressive foreign policy demands, such as the *Anschluss* with Austria and the annexation of the Sudetenland in 1938.

The first reason is well explained and supported by a good range of well-selected evidence.

The League also failed to stop the aggressive actions of Japan and Italy in the Manchurian and Abyssinian invasions. Japan invaded Manchuria in 1931, and the League reacted slowly to Japan's aggressive moves. Britain and France were not prepared to commit their military to stop a powerful nation. This encouraged Hitler to follow Japan's example as he saw that the League was powerless to stop Japan and that Japan simply left the League. Furthermore, Hitler took advantage of the League's failure over the Abyssinian crisis in 1936 and reoccupied the Rhineland when he saw that Britain and France were not willing to commit troops against Mussolini.

The student examines both invasions here and deals with their impact on Hitler's foreign policy. Explanations are explicitly addressing the question and supported by key knowledge.

Practice question, Paper 2 (page 21)

Why was this photo published in 1937? Explain your answer using details of the source and your knowledge. [7 marks]

This photo was published in France to try to persuade the French to stand up against Hitler's aggression in the Spanish Civil War. When civil war broke out in Spain in 1936, Mussolini and Hitler declared their support for Franco and the Nationalists. Hitler sent his new air force to aid Franco and it carried out massive bombing raids on civilian populations like the one in the photo as it says, 'The Basque people murdered by German planes'. Britain and France did not intervene, and this photo is trying to show the French that innocent people have been killed by the Germans and it is trying to encourage them to stop Hitler.

The student begins the response by explaining the purpose of the source – what the intended impact of the photo was on its French audience.

The response is then put into the context of 1937 as part of the Spanish Civil War. This helps explain the purpose of the photo.

Details from the source are used here to help develop the answer further.

The student then explains the message of the photo – what it was trying to show the people of France. This then helps explain the purpose of the source in more detail.

Practice question, Paper 1 (page 23)
'Appeasement was a necessary policy that could be justified at the time.'
How far do you agree with this statement? Explain your answer.   [10 marks]

I agree that Appeasement was a necessary policy and it could be justified at the time. Britain was not ready to fight a war against Hitler in the mid-1930s. Hitler had been secretly rearming since 1933 and was also building a huge air force (the *Luftwaffe*) which had been put to the test in 1936–37 during the Spanish Civil War. Chamberlain knew that Britain would not be able to successfully stop German armed forces in a war so needed time to rearm. After 1936, Chamberlain ordered a massive increase in spending on the British armed forces, particularly the Royal Air Force, so that it could wage a more successful war in the future if necessary.

Furthermore, Britain was still dealing with the memory of the First World War. Britain had suffered nearly a million casualties in the First World War and its civilians had been attacked by German battleships, zeppelins and bomber aircraft, killing over a thousand innocent people. This meant that many in Britain wanted to avoid another conflict at all costs and did not want to be plunged into another European war. Appeasement was the right policy at the time as most people in Britain wanted a peaceful solution. This was further justified by the fact that many in Britain, including many politicians, viewed the Treaty of Versailles as too harsh on Germany. Some Britons believed that Hitler was just taking back what was rightfully the territory of Germany when it reoccupied the Rhineland in 1936, for example.

However, some historians suggest that Appeasement was not justified and only encouraged Hitler's aggressive foreign policy even more as Britain and France met his demands. Churchill, for example, favoured a more aggressive foreign policy against Hitler, but was ignored by many until war broke out in 1939. Churchill believed Hitler could not be trusted, aimed to conquer territory in the East and was quickly rearming so should be stopped before the German military got too powerful. This would have avoided a full-scale war in the future and lessened his foreign policy demands when he saw that Britain and France would stand against him.

Appeasement could be justified at the time and was necessary. Many in Europe feared another world war involving Germany after the huge loss of life in the First World War. Moreover, as many had predicted, Germany was reacting to the harsh terms of the post-war peace settlement, which overly punished Germany and had partially led to Hitler's rise to power in the first place.

Practice question, Paper 1 (page 24)
Explain why Stalin signed the Nazi–Soviet Pact in 1939.   [6 marks]

Stalin needed time to rearm the Soviet Union and prepare for a future invasion by Germany. The Nazi–Soviet Pact guaranteed Stalin that time as Germany would now be able to wage war in the West against Britain and France. Stalin could now concentrate Soviet industry on building up tanks, planes and the war materials necessary to fight Germany in the future as he knew that Hitler intended to wage war in the East to create *Lebensraum*. The territory that Stalin would gain in Poland from the Nazi–Soviet Pact meant that the Soviet Union would have a bigger defensive border to protect its war industry.

Furthermore, Stalin signed the Pact because he did not trust Britain and France. Stalin had been left out of the negotiations over the future of Czechoslovakia at the Munich Conference in 1938, and had seen that Britain and France were not willing to commit their forces to stopping Hitler in the Spanish Civil War. This led Stalin to turn his back on Britain and France, even though he knew that Hitler was just trying to avoid a war on two fronts rather than creating an alliance with the Soviet Union as they were common enemies.

The first paragraph clearly states the line of argument taken by the student and explains one of the reasons why Appeasement could be justified. Good supporting knowledge is used in the argument.

The student then adds extra range and depth to the response by examining other arguments for the policy of Appeasement. These well-explained and well-selected examples are cited in support.

The student then provides an alternative viewpoint to provide balance to the answer. A strong argument against the policy of Appeasement is presented here with good supporting evidence in the explanation.

The student finishes by reasserting their judgement from the first paragraph, but it is mainly a summary of their previous material. A more clinching argument is needed here to develop the conclusion.

The first paragraph clearly explains one of the main reasons why Stalin signed the Pact and develops the explanation convincingly with accurate contextual knowledge.

The second factor is also well explained, and the paragraph is well structured for a six-mark question.

Practice question, Paper 1 (page 25)

'Long-term factors were the main cause of the outbreak of war in 1939.'
How far do you agree with this statement? Explain your answer.

[10 marks]

Long-term factors were important in causing the outbreak of war in 1939. The impact of the Treaty of Versailles had left Germany resentful and defenceless. The war guilt clause meant many people in Germany despised the Treaty and the Weimar politicians who signed it. This left an undercurrent of nationalism with political groups such as the Nazis promising to destroy the Treaty by rearming Germany and reclaiming the lost territory such as the Polish Corridor. The German army had been a source of pride and its forced reduction to just 100,000 soldiers, no tanks or air force meant that Hitler's promise to rearm was a popular policy to many in Germany, especially when the effects of the Depression made extremism and militarism all the more appealing to the German voter. Hitler's aggressive foreign policy was based on overturning the injustices of Versailles and played a major part in the outbreak of the Second World War.

Another long-term factor that caused the outbreak of war was the failure of the League of Nations. The League was supposed to promote international peace and co-operation and stop potentially aggressive nations from invading weaker ones. The 1930s saw the League fail to stop both Japan and Italy from successfully invading Manchuria and Abyssinia. This was made worse by the fact that the Depression had led to militaristic foreign policies being adopted in Japan, Italy and Germany. The League was powerless to stop the invasions and did nothing to prevent Hitler from reoccupying the Rhineland in 1936. This gave Hitler the encouragement to demand more territory and take Europe to the brink of war when he invaded Czechoslovakia in 1939.

However, there were short-term factors that also led to the outbreak of war in 1939. The policy of Appeasement is often blamed for the outbreak of war as it saw Britain and France giving in to Hitler's ever-increasing demands for restoring lost German territory. Britain and France did little to stop Hitler reoccupying the Rhineland in 1936. Britain even saw this as rightfully German territory even though it broke the terms of the Treaty of Versailles. Furthermore, Britain, France and Italy signed the Munich Agreement with Germany in 1938, which gave Hitler the Sudetenland without a shot being fired. This encouraged Hitler to invade the rest of Czechoslovakia and Poland as he believed Britain and France were not willing to go to war.

Finally, it was short-term factors that mainly caused the outbreak of war in 1939 and most importantly the Nazi–Soviet Pact because it allowed Hitler to avoid a war on two fronts. Hitler's main aim was to invade the East to create *Lebensraum* and destroy communism, but he needed to defeat the West first. The Pact shared Poland between the Soviet Union and Germany and allowed Hitler to invade without the fear of facing a Soviet force as well as the possibility of declaration of war from Britain and France.

4 Who was to blame for the Cold War?

Practice question, Paper 1 (page 29)

Why did the alliance between the Big Three begin to break down
at the Potsdam Conference in July 1945?

[6 marks]

The Grand Alliance began to break down between the Big Three at the Potsdam Conference in 1945 because of the replacement of Roosevelt with Truman as US president. Harry Truman was much more aggressively anti-communist in his approach than Roosevelt, who had been willing to work with Stalin towards a post-war settlement. Truman was willing to stand up against Soviet expansionism and announced that the USA had an atomic bomb that would end the war against Japan without the need for Soviet help. This created distrust between the two leaders and forced Stalin to begin developing his own nuclear weapons.

The response begins well and focuses on addressing the long-term causes by examining the lasting effects of the Treaty of Versailles. This paragraph is well structured which helps it clearly explain how the Treaty helped lead to the outbreak of war in 1939.

The student then looks at the League's failures as another long-term cause and cites two strong examples to support their argument.

This paragraph provides balance by offering a counter-argument that short-term factors were the most important cause. Various valid evidence is cited to support the argument.

The conclusion reaches a convincing judgement and specifically picks out an event that the student thinks is the most important. The explanation supports the judgement.

The student clearly explains how Truman was a cause of the breakdown of the alliance at Potsdam. Secure knowledge is used to support the argument.

Another factor that led to the breakdown in the Grand Alliance was that the Red Army now occupied most of the eastern European states where Germany was defeated. Germany had been a common enemy for both sides, but now Stalin had his forces in most eastern European countries and refused to remove them. Truman viewed this as an act of aggression that went against the agreements made at Yalta, and believed Stalin would try to create Soviet-friendly communist governments rather than allow free elections as promised, especially in Poland.

A valid second factor is explained and the addition of the example of Poland adds a solid example to support the explanation.

Practice question, Paper 2 (page 31)
Study Sources A and B.
How far do these two sources agree? Explain your answer using details of the sources. [7 marks]

Sources A and B agree on the fact that a division was occurring between the democracies of the West and the communist-controlled East in Europe. Both sources refer to the emergence of an iron curtain that will split Europe. However, Source A disagrees with Source B because Source A suggests that the iron curtain has appeared due to the Soviet take-over of eastern European states whereas Source B suggests that it was Churchill who is threatening an iron curtain. Both sources disagree because they pin the blame for the divisions in Europe on different people – Source A on Stalin and Source B on Churchill and the West's aggressive history of invasion of the Soviet Union. They disagree because Source A was a British cartoon made to persuade the audience that Stalin was the aggressor whereas the purpose of Source B was to persuade Soviet citizens that Churchill, like Hitler and the Nazis in the Second World War, wanted to attack the Soviet Union, which must be defended from Western aggression.

The student begins by making a valid comparison of how the content of the two sources agree.

The response shows balance by examining how the content and overall views of the two sources disagree.

The contrast between the two sources is developed further by examining why they disagree. This is done well by explaining the purpose and motives of the authors.

Practice question, Paper 1 (page 33)
Why did the USA introduce Marshall Aid in 1948? [6 marks]

The USA introduced Marshall Aid in 1948 to try to prevent the further spread of communism in Europe. Truman and Marshall both believed that communism appealed to people in countries where the economy was weak. The end of the Second World War meant that the countries in Europe owed $11.5 billion to the USA and this debt would mean that communist ideas would sound attractive to many if they were not lifted out of poverty. Marshall Aid would help rebuild prosperity and therefore help stop the Soviet Union spreading communism across all of Europe.

The first paragraph is well structured and uses a specific example to develop the explanation. It is well focused on addressing the question.

Marshall Aid also helped the USA gain European markets. The Depression of the 1930s was still in the memories of many Americans and the US Government wanted to prevent it from happening again. To achieve this, the USA wanted to flood European markets with US goods and make countries that accepted Marshall Aid use US dollars as currency. This would ensure that the USA did not face another economic disaster in the future.

The second paragraph clearly explains a second reason for Marshall Aid and uses general contextual knowledge, but lacks a specific example.

Practice question, Paper 1 (page 35)

'The Cold War began with the crisis in Berlin in 1948.'
How far do you agree with this statement? Explain your answer.   [10 marks]

The Cold War could be said to have begun because of the Berlin Blockade. By 1948, both the USA and the USSR had poor diplomatic relations, were stockpiling weapons and increasing their use of propaganda. When Stalin blocked the routes into Berlin in an attempt to force the Western Allies to relinquish the city, he believed it would be a substantial propaganda victory. Instead, Truman ordered planes in West Germany to drop supplies to West Berlin, in what was known as the Berlin airlift. If Truman had tried to force his way through the Soviet blockades or if Stalin had shot down a single aircraft, it would have been a declaration of war. However, neither side took the aggressive option; instead Stalin eventually lifted the Blockade when he realised the USA would not back down. This was the first sign of a Cold War emerging as neither side was willing to start a direct conflict, but would instead try to win a propaganda victory or humiliate the opposing side. The Berlin Blockade helped lead to the creation of West Germany in 1949, after the three Allied zones were combined in 1946, and led to the formation of a defensive alliance known as NATO. This was followed quickly by the creation of East Germany, which showed the world that the divisions in Europe were permanent. Germany, and Berlin in particular, became a focal point of Cold War tensions between the two superpowers until 1989.

However, some historians suggest that the Cold War began earlier. Some point to the ideological differences between the USA and the USSR as the starting point. Russia became a communist state in 1917, and the USA was swept with the Red Scare in the 1920s, after the Russian Civil War when Britain, the USA and Japan all sent troops and supplies to aid the anti-communist forces. However, the USA and the USSR had been allies during the Second World War, which suggests that this is too early a starting point.

Instead, some have suggested that the Cold War began at the Potsdam Conference with the breakdown of the Grand Alliance, especially the relationship between Truman and Stalin. Truman was openly aggressive towards communism and Soviet expansion in eastern Europe. He also boasted of the USA's new atomic bomb that helped begin an arms race between the two superpowers, which would become a defining feature of much of the Cold War. Equally, Stalin's expansion into eastern Europe and his refusal to remove the Red Army from occupied countries and hold free elections as agreed at Yalta can also be blamed for beginning the Cold War. The West viewed communism as a threat to Western democracy and its freedoms, especially when Stalin placed a pro-communist regime in Poland, which was supposed to remain neutral. This idea was further enhanced by Churchill's 'iron curtain' speech in 1946. This helped cause the Cold War as it claimed that Europe was now divided between Soviet-controlled countries in the East and capitalist democracies in the West.

Overall, I believe that the Cold War began when Stalin took over most of the countries in eastern Europe and imposed communist regimes friendly to the USSR in them. Stalin even set up Cominform and Comecon to co-ordinate the parties and the economies so they would aid in the defence of the USSR. This was a clear sign of expansionism that went against the agreements at Yalta and Potsdam and led to a distrust between the two superpowers that could not be repaired.

The response clearly focuses on the factor in the question. There is good knowledge of the Berlin crisis used here.

The student then gives a well-developed and detailed explanation of how this factor helped cause the Cold War between the superpowers.

The response is balanced here by analysing the ideological origins of the Cold War back in 1917. It lacks sufficient depth to be a fully developed explanation.

The first part of the paragraph explains Truman's role in the breakdown of the alliance and why it helped create the nuclear arms race.

The student then examines Stalin's role in the breakdown of the alliance and adds details about Churchill's 'iron curtain' speech to help develop the material. This is then all linked to a clear and direct explanation.

Good examples are used here to support the final judgement and address the question of 'How far ... ?'

Practice question, Paper 2 (page 36)
Study all the sources.
How far do these sources provide convincing evidence that the Soviet Union was to blame for the start of the Cold War? Use the sources to explain your answer. [12 marks]

Source G, written by Churchill, supports the statement that the Soviet Union was to blame for the start of the Cold War. In the source Churchill says that the 'Soviet Union has become a danger to the free world', which suggests that Churchill viewed communism as a threat to democracy. Churchill believes that the USSR will try to take over eastern Europe as part of 'her onward sweep'. Likewise, Source D, which is a British cartoon commenting on the creation of the iron curtain, also supports the statement that the Soviet Union is to blame for creating the divisions in Europe. In the source the iron curtain is shown to say 'No admittance by order of Joe', suggesting that it was Stalin's actions in eastern Europe and the take-over of eastern European governments in countries such as Poland, Romania and Bulgaria by communist parties friendly to the Soviet Union, that has created this division. The cartoon is clearly criticising Stalin's methods and objectives, but the source is one-sided as it has been made for the *Daily Mail*, which was a conservative newspaper with strong anti-communist and patriotic values. The cartoonist is clearly trying to persuade British readers that Stalin is the aggressor in Europe and is a danger to peace.

Source E also supports the statement. This is an American cartoon showing the Soviet Union represented by a giant bear trying to take over eastern Europe. This suggests that the Soviet Union was to blame for the start of the Cold War, as the message of the cartoonist is that the Soviet Union was the aggressor and trying to extend its control in Europe to spread communism. This cartoon is also one-sided, as the purpose of the source is to try to persuade US citizens to oppose the threat posed by communism and to take a tougher stance against Stalin, a view that President Truman took at the Potsdam Conference and in his policy of containment.

However, Source B opposes the statement and suggests that both the USA and the Soviet Union are to blame for the Cold War divisions in Europe. Stalin says that 'Everyone imposes his own system as far as his army has power to do so', which suggests that both superpowers will naturally try to spread their ideology, be it capitalism or communism. Source C is a Soviet cartoon from 1947. The message of the cartoonist is that it is the Western powers that are the aggressors who broke the promises made at the Yalta and Potsdam conferences. The source shows the USA, Britain and France all trying to smash through a pillar representing the agreements made at the conferences. The stick they are holding is tied together, representing the fact that in 1946, the USA, France and Britain combined their zones, and eventually this became West Germany in 1949. This act would force the Soviet Union to create East Germany. This opposes the statement that the Soviet Union was to blame for the start of the Cold War as it portrays the Western powers as the ones causing the conflict and divisions over Germany.

The student has clearly read the question carefully and uses two of the sources to explain how the details of Sources G and D support the statement. Well-selected source details are used to develop the explanation.

The student evaluates the purpose of Source D, which adds depth to the argument.

The student adds range to their argument by examining Source E and explaining the source details.

The evaluation of the purpose of the cartoon adds extra weight to the overall argument.

The student balances their argument by explaining how the details of Sources B and C disagree with the statement in the question.

5 How effectively did the USA contain the spread of communism?

Practice question, Paper 1 (page 40)
Describe the consequences of the Korean War. [4 marks]

One consequence of the Korean War was that it showed the world that the USA was serious about Truman's policy of containment and would stand up to communist expansion in Asia. The Korean War also demonstrated that the USA could not push the communists back or remove them from power in North Korea and had to accept a ceasefire in 1953, which left the country divided between a pro-American South Korea and communist-controlled North Korea. It also showed the USA that China would also help support communist governments in Asia. The Korean War demonstrated that the USA would not be able to easily defeat the spread of communism in Asia.

The student offers a wide range of consequences that fully address the question. Some of these have additional detail which adds greater depth to the response.

Practice question, Paper 1 (page 42)

**'The Cuban Missile Crisis was a success for the US policy of containment.'
How far do you agree with this statement? Explain your answer.** [10 marks]

To an extent the Cuban Missile Crisis was a success for the US policy of containment. Kennedy had successfully removed the nuclear threat from Cuba by setting up a blockade and preventing further nuclear warheads and missiles from reaching Cuba, which would have directly threatened the USA and given the Soviet Union first-strike capability. Kennedy had managed to avoid a nuclear confrontation with the Soviet Union and Cuba and prevent the Soviet Union from closing the missile gap with the USA by putting nuclear warheads in 'Uncle Sam's backyard'.

However, it could be argued that the Cuban Missile Crisis was not a success for containment. Kennedy was forced to accept the fact that Cuba would remain a communist state in America's backyard. Part of the deal struck between the two superpowers was that the USA would promise not to invade Cuba or try to overthrow Castro again. This meant that Castro was safe from another US invasion. Furthermore, Kennedy also secretly agreed to remove US nuclear missiles from Turkey. These missiles had helped give the USA first-strike capability against the Soviet Union. By removing them it had now helped close the missile gap slightly, although the USA still had the technological advantage in the nuclear arms race.

Overall, the Cuban Missile Crisis was more of a failure for the policy of containment than a success. Castro and communist Cuba remained, and the Soviet Union still had an ally on the border of the USA that could also support communist groups in South America, which was at the very least a significant propaganda victory for Khrushchev. Kennedy even came under heavy criticism from military commanders and NATO for trading the missiles in Turkey. To many, it looked like the USSR had managed to push back the USA rather than the other way around.

The response is well focused on the factor in the question and clearly explains why the Cuban Missile Crisis was a success for the USA, with a good use of key terminology.

The response shows balance by explaining how the crisis was also a success for Cuba.

This is developed further with a valid explanation of the Soviet success in closing the missile gap between the two superpowers. Key knowledge is used here to support the response.

The conclusion shows an understanding of the wider context of the Cold War and contains a clinching argument that is clearly explained and supported by additional evidence.

Practice question, Paper 2 (page 45)

**Study Source A.
Are you surprised by this source? Explain your answer using details of the source and your knowledge.** [7 marks]

I am surprised by this source as it was written in an influential American news magazine. It suggests that the Vietnam War was a huge mistake that had cost the USA dearly in terms of casualties and finances when it says it was 'a quicksandy war that had plagued four Presidents' and 'a tragic mistake'. I would have expected a US magazine to have been more patriotic and supportive of the US policy of containment in Vietnam as it tried to stop the spread of communism and prevent the domino theory from becoming a reality.

However, the source is not really that surprising given the huge loss of life on both sides. The source was made in 1973, when Nixon had signed a peace settlement with North Vietnam and pulled out the USA's last troops. Public sentiment had turned against the war since the late 1960s as more US casualties returned home and the horrors of the war became a reality, such as the My Lai massacre of 1968. The US media reported more and more negatively on US involvement in Vietnam as the war continued and many started to view it as a waste of life and resources. Huge peace demonstrations were held opposing the war, such as the one in Washington DC in 1969. This is suggested in the source when it says 'a war that produced no famous victories, no national heroes and no strong patriotic songs'.

The student begins by explaining why the source is surprising and explains some of the details in the source to support their explanation.

This is balanced by an explanation of why the source is not surprising. Good contextual knowledge is used to support this argument.

The use of source details here further develops the argument.

6 How secure was the USSR's control over eastern Europe, 1948–c.1989?

Practice question, Paper 2 (page 48)
Study Sources A and B.
How far does Source A prove Source B is wrong? Explain your answer using details of the sources and your knowledge. [8 marks]

Source A does prove that Source B is wrong. Source A suggests that the Soviet Union was acting aggressively and invading Czechoslovakia when the two countries were supposed to be communist allies when it says 'contrary to the basic principles of good relations between socialist states'. This refers to the fact that in 1968, Brezhnev ordered Soviet troops and tanks to move into Czechoslovakia to stop the Prague Spring reforms from spreading under Dubček. This proves Source B wrong as it suggests that the Czech communists had asked for military assistance from the Soviet Union to crush 'counter revolutionary forces'. Source A was taken from a Prague radio station which was reporting on the invasion directly. It proves that the communist-controlled Soviet news agency report in Source B is wrong as B was more likely to be biased in favour of Soviet actions and part of the propaganda used to justify the actions to Soviet citizens and other communist states in eastern Europe. It was trying to persuade people that the action was necessary to save communism in Czechoslovakia and encourage them to support the Soviet assistance.

Practice question, Paper 1 (page 50)
'The Hungarian and Czechoslovakian uprisings had very different causes and consequences.'
How far do you agree with this statement? Explain your answer. [10 marks]

I agree to an extent with the statement. One main cause of the Hungarian uprising was Khrushchev's promises of a different approach to communist rule in eastern Europe, which would allow a certain amount of reform to the old Stalinist system. In Poland in 1956, this had led to some concessions and reforms, which spurred reformers and rebels in Hungary to force the appointment of a new leader, Nagy. Nagy promoted far-reaching changes, which would essentially abolish the old communist system and allow free elections, demand the removal of Soviet interference and even withdrawal from the Warsaw Pact. This is different from Czechoslovakia where the reformist leader Dubček wanted to maintain the communist system and remain in the Warsaw Pact, but create a socialist government with 'a human face'. This included decreasing censorship and repression rather than allowing a democratic system to emerge.

Furthermore, the responses to the invasions were very different. In Hungary, the rebels were prepared to fight the Soviet forces – 3000 rebels were killed in the street fighting and about 300,000 fled the country to escape the repression. Nagy was even executed when the Soviets restored control. This was different to Czechoslovakia where the Soviet and Warsaw Pact troops met with little resistance. The Soviets did remove the reformist leader Dubček, but he was not executed like Nagy. Instead, the Soviet leadership issued the Brezhnev Doctrine that stated the Soviet Union had a right to prevent communist states from leaving the Warsaw Pact by force if necessary, which strengthened their hold over eastern Europe.

However, I disagree to a degree with the statement and think there were many significant similarities in the causes and consequences of the Hungarian and Czechoslovakian uprisings. Both countries resented the presence of Soviet troops and the repression of the communist system. This led to Stalinist leaders in both countries being replaced by reformers (Nagy in Hungary and Dubček in Czechoslovakia) who tried to change the communist system and move towards a less authoritarian style of government.

Likewise, both Hungary and Czechoslovakia faced invasions by the Soviet and Warsaw Pact troops. In Hungary, troops and tanks were sent in to remove the rebels and in Czechoslovakia the Warsaw Pact countries also decided that military intervention was required to prevent the reforms from spreading. There was concern among Warsaw Pact leaders and the Soviet Union that if the reformers succeeding in changing the communist system then the ideas might spread to other Warsaw Pact countries. This in turn might even break the defensive alliance apart, which would weaken Soviet control of eastern Europe and give the USA and its defensive alliance, NATO, the upper hand in any future conflict. In both cases, the West publicly denounced the Soviet invasions, but did not directly intervene and accepted the fact that these uprisings were in the Soviet 'sphere of influence'.

Overall, I believe the uprisings were more different than similar, even if the Soviet response was the same. There was every intention in Hungary to leave the defensive alliance of the Warsaw Pact and leave the Soviet Union at a disadvantage in the Cold War as it may have caused other states to follow suit, whereas in Czechoslovakia the main intention was not to leave the alliance, but instead end corruption by questioning the more repressive elements of communist rule.

Once again, the student displays a good essay structure by then explaining how the consequences of the two uprisings were similar and uses good evidence to support their argument.

A clear and concise judgement is reached in the conclusion and the student demonstrates an excellent understanding of the demands of the question.

Practice question, Paper 1 (page 51)
Why did East Germany build the Berlin Wall in 1961? [6 marks]

One reason the Berlin Wall was built in 1961 was because East Germany needed to prevent the mass exodus of East Germans to the West through Berlin. The borders in Berlin had remained open since 1948 and hundreds of thousands of East Germans had escaped the communist system in East Germany through Berlin in the 1950s and early 1960s. In 1961 alone, over 150,000 people had crossed the border from East to West Berlin. Many of them were skilled engineers, professionals and intellectuals, and the East German Government could not allow this 'brain drain' to continue as it was affecting the economy. In response, the East German leader was given permission by Khrushchev to build the wall.

The first factor is explained in a good amount of detail. Strong supporting evidence adds weight to the explanation.

Another reason the Berlin Wall was built was to prevent the spread of capitalist ideas in East Germany. Those in East Berlin could see the freedoms, luxuries and better standards of living enjoyed by their West Berlin counterparts. West Berlin had cafés and shops full of goods on display so East Germans were tempted to defect to the West. The wall was built to stop the influence of capitalism spreading in East Berlin as it would undermine the communist system.

The second paragraph follows a similar structure and demonstrates a strong contextual knowledge of the situation in Berlin at the time to explain the argument.

Practice question, Paper 1 (page 53)
Why was martial law introduced in Poland in 1981? [6 marks]

One of the main reasons for the introduction of martial law in Poland in 1981 was the growing popularity and influence of Solidarity. Solidarity was a trade union whose membership had grown to over 8 million by 1981 and had been officially recognised by the Government. It demanded an end to censorship, improved welfare and for Catholic services to take place. These ideas threatened Soviet control in Poland. In 1981 the leader of the army in Poland introduced martial law and crushed Solidarity and arrested its leaders.

A well-structured explanation shows that the student has good knowledge and understanding of the role played by Solidarity in Poland in 1981.

Another reason for the introduction of martial law in Poland was the fact that Solidarity had gained support in the West, in fact more so than the uprisings in Hungary or Czechoslovakia ever had. Solidarity's leader, Walesa, was well-liked by the Western media and people in the West bought Solidarity badges to show their support for the reforms and the movement. This threatened Soviet control in eastern Europe as strikes and protests became more commonplace in Poland as they were encouraged by the West. Martial law was introduced to reassert Soviet dominance in Poland and ensure that Solidarity would not try to take over the government.

The second factor also looks at Solidarity, but demonstrates a wider knowledge of its impact in Poland by examining its international appeal and support.

Practice question, Paper 1 (page 55)
'Gorbachev's reforms were the main cause of the collapse of communism in eastern Europe.'
How far do you agree with this statement? Explain your answer. [10 marks]

Gorbachev's reforms were very important in causing the collapse of communism in eastern Europe. Gorbachev intended to save the communist systems in eastern Europe by forcing them to change in order to survive. He wanted the communist governments to reform their economic systems and improve standards of living for people so it could match capitalism and make the people loyal to the communist system.

Gorbachev introduced the policy of *perestroika* in 1987 to allow market forces to be introduced into the Soviet economy so businesses could make a profit. This meant that a limited form of capitalism was now allowed in the Soviet Union and this idea could be taken on board by other eastern European communist leaders.

Furthermore, Gorbachev introduced the policy of *glasnost*, which allowed open debate and criticism of the communist government. This opened the way for a reduction in censorship, which saw more and more people openly oppose the communist system and even promote democratic reforms across eastern Europe. It encouraged people power to rise up and demand change. This was helped by the fact that Gorbachev ordered the removal of Soviet troops in 1989, which meant they could no longer enforce the Brezhnev Doctrine and keep countries in the Warsaw Pact.

However, it was not only Gorbachev's reforms that signalled the collapse of communism in eastern Europe. The Soviet Union had been fighting an expensive war in Afghanistan since 1979, and it seemed unwinnable. It had cost the Soviet Union a huge amount of money and resources to fight and this meant that standards of living had dropped not only in the Soviet Union, but in eastern Europe as well where the economies were dependent on the health of Soviet finances.

Furthermore, the Soviet Union was also locked in a new arms race with the USA since the election of President Reagan, who took a tough line against the Soviet 'evil empire'. He wanted to bankrupt the Soviet Union and see an end to Soviet control of eastern Europe by forcing it to build up its weapons and spend huge amounts of money. This added to the financial strain in the USSR and forced Gorbachev to reduce defence spending and improve relations with the USA. As military expenditure dropped, Soviet ability to impose control over the Warsaw Pact countries diminished.

Overall, Gorbachev's reforms were central to the collapse of the communist system in eastern Europe. Glasnost, in particular, encouraged reformers and critics to question the Soviet system and openly promote democratic reforms. Gorbachev was not prepared to use force and believed the countries of eastern Europe were responsible for their own fates, as can be seen when the Berlin Wall came down in 1989 and East and West Germany were reunified.

7 Why did events in the Gulf matter, c.1970–2000?

Practice question, Paper 1 (page 58)
Explain why Saddam Hussein was able to rise to power by 1979. [6 marks]

Saddam Hussein was able to rise to power by 1979 because of his power in the ruling Baath Party in Iraq. He began by increasing his position in the party when he oversaw the intelligence service and quickly put family and friends into positions of influence. When there was a coup in 1968, called the July Revolution, he was made vice-president and vice-chairman of the Revolutionary Command Council. This allowed him to control many aspects of the Baath Party and wield a lot of power, second only to the president himself, so that by 1979 he was able to be declared president.

The introduction gives an overview of Gorbachev's views, but doesn't really address the question directly at this point.

These two paragraphs are more focused on answering the question. Solid examples are used when the student refers to the importance of *perestroika* and *glasnost* and how they led to calls for reform and democracy in eastern Europe.

The student balances their response here by examining how economic problems caused by war affected the Soviet ability to control eastern Europe. The links here between the finances of the USSR and its satellites is well made.

The student adds range and depth to their counter-argument by examining the arms race and the role of President Reagan. The explanation is clearly focused on addressing the question.

The student makes a clear judgement here by identifying one specific reform that led to the downfall of communism in eastern Europe. Additional evidence is used to explain why this factor had such a significant effect.

The first paragraph shows a clear knowledge and understanding of the significance of Saddam's position in the Baath Party and concisely explains how this helped him to rise to power.

Another factor was Saddam Hussein's use of repression. He controlled the army and secret police and used them to remove political opponents and execute those considered guilty of disloyalty. This created a feeling of terror in both the party and the population and left Saddam Hussein in a position where very few could remove him from power. He also filled the ranks of the armed forces with his own Sunni Muslims, which decreased the influence of the Shiite Muslims who might oppose him and his policies.

The candidate also examines how Saddam's position in the government gave him the ability to remove opponents on the way to the presidency. The explanations are well structured and supported by key examples.

Practice question, Paper 1 (page 59)
Describe the methods used by Saddam Hussein to control the Iraqi people. [4 marks]

One method used by Saddam Hussein to control the Iraqi people was to improve life for many Iraqis. The economy was improved through investment from oil sales, welfare services were created and there was massive expansion in electrification. Saddam Hussein also used terror and propaganda. A cult of personality grew up around him through the many statues, images and posters around Iraq of the great leader. He also used the secret police to arrest opponents and put on televised show trials to create a sense of fear and repression.

The response identifies a good range of methods used by Saddam and adds additional detail to add depth to the descriptions.

Practice question, Paper 1 (page 60)
'British influence in Iran was the main reason for the revolution in 1979.' How far do you agree with this statement? [10 marks]

British influence in Iran was a crucial reason for the revolution in 1979. Britain had paid the Shah's government for control of Iran's oil fields since the start of the twentieth century, which led to a growing sense of nationalism in Iran. When Mossadeq became leader and nationalised Iran's oil, it led to the British blockading Iran's ports and they then persuaded the USA to help them overthrow Mossadeq's government. The new government under the Shah was increasingly unpopular and led to the growth of opposition, especially from the religious leaders known as the mullahs. They criticised the Shah's government for working with the British to control Iran's resources, which gained the support of the ordinary people and helped lead to the overthrow of the Shah's government in 1979.

The student agrees with the statement and demonstrates a good knowledge and understanding of British influence in Iran as a cause of the revolution. Explanations are convincing.

However, there were other reasons for the revolution. Religion played a very important part in the revolution. The mullahs promoted a strict form of Islam in the mosques and criticised the corruption and unIslamic lifestyle promoted by the Shah's regime and its Western allies. They exploited the fact that the Shah was a mere pawn of the non-Muslim West and pointed the finger at the banks which were controlled by US and British companies and the cinemas which showed sexually explicit films which went against the religion of many Iranians. This increased support for an Islamic republic to be formed by abolishing the monarchy and the influence of the West in Iran.

Balance is provided and other factors are examined. The role of the mullahs is explained, and good evidence is provided to support the argument.

In conclusion, Britain did play a huge part in causing the Iranian revolution along with the intervention of the USA, which propped up an unpopular and corrupt government in Iran. This had seen only the supporters of the Shah benefit from the wealth of Iran, which was based on its oil reserves. Religion, on the other hand, united ordinary people who did not benefit from the Shah's government behind Ayatollah Khomeini. He, and other religious leaders, were able to explain the corruption as unIslamic and promote anti-Western feelings in the mosques and religious writings and speeches smuggled into Iran. Due to this, the factors are very linked and equally important as a cause of revolution in 1979.

The conclusion here suggests equal importance to the different arguments stated. The links between the factors are made explicit and the final judgement is clearly explained and supported.

Practice question, Paper 1 (page 62)
Why was Saddam Hussein unable to achieve a quick victory in the Iran–Iraq War? [6 marks]

One reason Saddam Hussein was unable to achieve a quick victory in the Iran–Iraq War was because he underestimated the resistance from Iran and its enthusiasm for resistance. Many young revolutionary Iranians were willing to become martyrs and die for the cause to save the Iranian revolution. Many joined the Basiji who were religious fighters equipped with modern weaponry. They were committed fighters and Iran had a much larger population than Iraq and therefore many more soldiers, which meant that a swift victory was impossible for Iraq.

Another reason was the fact that the war became a stalemate. By 1984, both sides had dug in and built defensive trenches across a 1000-mile border and found it almost impossible to advance. The stalemate was helped by the fact that foreign powers began to intervene in the war as France, for example, supplied arms to Iraq and Syria shut off supplies of oil to Iraq. This meant that neither side gained the advantage in the war, which was bogged down in the trenches until a ceasefire was agreed in 1988.

A well-structured explanation that uses key terminology to support. It directly addresses the question.

The explanation here is well supported and shows a wider knowledge of the Iran–Iraq War to support the argument.

Practice question, Paper 2 (page 64)
What is the message of the cartoonist? Explain your answer using details of the source and your knowledge. [8 marks]

The cartoonist is clearly critical of the actions of some of the United Nations' members and gives the message that they are just involving themselves in the Gulf War in Kuwait to protect their interests in Kuwaiti oil. In the source each of the leaders led by US President George Bush has an oil symbol on their tunic suggesting that their crusade to help Kuwait is about control over oil rather than to protect the Kuwaiti people from Iraq's soldiers. Kuwait was an oil-rich nation and Saddam Hussein had hoped he could pay off Iraq's debt by controlling the oil fields. The United Nations and especially the USA were horrified that Saddam Hussein might be able to control oil prices in the region and they quickly built up a large invasion force supported by many other countries. The cartoonist suggests that this invasion force was there only to regain control of the oil in Kuwait.

The student gives a focused start to their response. The main message of the cartoonist is correctly identified, and the view of the cartoonist is made clear.

Well-selected source details are used to support the student's explanation of the main message.

The student puts the message of the cartoon into context here by referring to key knowledge about the international response. This adds support to the explanation of the message.

The candidate finishes by reasserting the main message of the cartoonist.

8 Russia, 1905–41

Practice question, Paper 1 (page 68)
Why did the First World War weaken the tsarist autocracy? [6 marks]

The First World War weakened the tsarist autocracy because it made social and economic conditions in Russia much worse. There were food and fuel shortages as the railway network could not cope with the food and war materials being sent to the front line. This led to rapid inflation in the towns and cities and even bread rationing. This weakened the tsarist government because it was seen to be unable to cope with the total war effort needed to fight against the Germans. There were huge numbers of strikes and demonstrations in the cities, especially Petrograd, with many calling for the abdication of the Tsar. In the countryside, peasants began seizing land and even killing landlords. The effects of the war highlighted the weaknesses of the system.

The war also weakened the tsarist autocracy because of the actions of Tsar Nicholas II himself. In 1915, he decided to take personal command of the Russian army on the eastern front. Despite some victories, major defeats, poor conditions on the front line and the lack of weapons and munitions caused many soldiers to desert and return home to Russia. These failures were then personally blamed on the Tsar, which weakened his position in Russia.

The response is well focused on addressing the demands of the question and demonstrates a solid understanding of the socio-economic impact of the First World War on the tsarist autocracy.

There is adequate explanation here of the impact of Tsar Nicholas II's actions supported by a range of evidence.

Practice question, Paper 4 (page 69)

How important was the First World War as a cause of the revolution in March 1917?   [40 marks]

Essay section	Advice	Example content
Introduction	Begin by stating some reasons why the First World War might lead to the March Revolution.	*The social and economic effects of the First World War in the cities and the countryside* *The effect of military defeats*
	Then state other factors that led to the March Revolution to provide a balanced assessment.	*The personal role of the Tsar* *The actions of the Tsarina and Rasputin, which discredited the Russian government and monarchy* *The role of political opposition and the loss of support of the garrisons in the capital*
	You may also wish to look at long-term issues.	*The lack of political reform in Russia* *The continued calls to solve the peasant land issue*
	Try to assess which cause or causes were the most important so you can sustain your argument throughout your essay.	*The most important cause of the revolution in March 1917 was … because …*
First section	Address the cause given in the question – the First World War – even if you don't think it was the most important factor overall.	*The impact of the First World War was an important cause of the revolution in March because it meant that …*
	In each paragraph tackle a separate effect or impact.	*The social and economic problems such as the food and fuel shortages or the huge inflation in bread prices …*
	Finish the section by explaining how important you think the factor was and how it contributed to the March Revolution.	*This was an important effect that helped cause the March Revolution because/as it meant that/as it led to …*
Second section	In the second section you need to examine alternative factors to provide balance.	*However, the role of the Tsar/the actions of the Tsarina and Rasputin/political opposition … were also an important cause of the revolution in March 1917 because …*
	Follow the same process as in the first section by looking at one cause at a time, adding examples and explaining its importance in causing the March Revolution.	*The Tsarina and Rasputin were important in causing the March Revolution because they led to opposition in government, especially among the nobility …*
	Really strong responses will also start to evaluate and assess the relative importance of each cause with the factor of the First World War – if you can, try to sustain your argument from the introduction.	*The role of the Tsarina and Rasputin was not as important as the impact of the First World War because …*
Conclusion	Write a conclusion as the last paragraph. Here you can fully explain your judgement and the relative importance of the different causes.	*To conclude/overall, the most important cause/s of the revolution in March 1917 was/were … because …*
	Try to justify your argument by referring to some key evidence that helps support your judgement.	*This can be supported by the fact that …*

Practice question, Paper 1 (page 72)

'Bolshevik leadership and organisation was the main reason Lenin was able to seize power in November 1917.'

How far do you agree with this statement? Explain your answer. [10 marks]

Bolshevik leadership and organisation was an important reason why Lenin was able to seize power in November 1917. Lenin had united the Bolshevik Party when he returned to Russia in April 1917. He made his April Theses the official party programme which set the Bolsheviks out as the main party to oppose the Provisional Government and end the war. Bolshevik slogans became commonplace in Petrograd and Moscow such as 'Peace, bread, land' and 'All power to the Soviets'. These helped gain support from many industrial workers and even appealed to some poorer peasants, especially as the Provisional Government continued to fight the First World War, which was growing more and more unpopular with many Russians who faced hardship due to high bread prices and fuel shortages. Lenin and Trotsky were also key to the Bolshevik seizure of power when they stormed the Winter Palace in November 1917. Lenin chose the time and Trotsky used his well-organised and disciplined Red Guards to plan the coup, which was successful and gave the Bolsheviks control of the government when Kerensky and the Provisional Government fled.

However, the failures of the Provisional Government were also key to the Bolshevik seizure of power. The Provisional Government became more unpopular with the Soviets, which represented the workers and soldiers as it continued the war. More soldiers deserted the front line and the Summer Offensive launched by Kerensky was a massive failure with high casualties. This increased support and membership for the Bolsheviks who eventually controlled majorities in the Petrograd and Moscow Soviets by the autumn of 1917. This helped Lenin claim that he was seizing power in the name of the Soviets and that this was a popular revolution. The Provisional Government had also failed to solve the peasants' land issue and had decided to wait until elections for a Constituent Assembly to debate the issue. This was not radical enough for many poorer peasants who decided to seize land in the countryside. This increased the unpopularity of the Provisional Government with a key group in Russian society who made up about 80 per cent of the population. Without the support of many peasants, the Provisional Government was severely weakened and looked like it was unable to lead Russia after the March Revolution and solve its problems.

In conclusion, it was the failures of the Provisional Government, which were made worse by the impact of the First World War, which allowed Lenin and the Bolshevik leadership to take advantage of their position. They were able to increase their membership and support in the Soviets, which gave Lenin the confidence that the time was right for a rebellion.

Practice question, Paper 1 (page 73)

Why were the Bolsheviks victorious in the Russian Civil War? [6 marks]

The Bolsheviks won the Russian Civil War because of their superior geographical location. The Bolsheviks controlled the central parts of European Russia where most of the industry, major cities and railway links were. This allowed them to more easily supply the Red Army with the weapons and war supplies they needed to fight the Whites and quickly move troops from one region to another to fight off offensives by the White armies.

The Bolsheviks also won because of effective policies by Lenin. Lenin introduced War Communism and used the government to take control of all major industries so that they produced the supplies needed to win the Civil War. Lenin was able to mobilise the Russian workforce and unite them behind the aim of defeating the Whites at all costs to save the revolution.

The response demonstrates a strong knowledge and understanding of the role of Lenin as leader of the Bolsheviks.

The explanation here is well focused on addressing the question explicitly.

A second example of organisation and leadership is examined, which adds depth and range to the first section supporting the statement.

The counter-argument here gives balance to the response and shows a comprehensive knowledge of the role played by the Provisional Government.

The response adds breadth to the answer by looking at a long-term issue in Russia that had not been solved and helped contribute to the Bolshevik seizure of power.

The conclusion is short, but focused on addressing the question of 'How far ...?' by making a clear and concise judgement about the most important reason.

This is a well-structured paragraph that examines one reason the Bolsheviks were victorious. Key evidence supports the explanation.

A second reason is cited and demonstrates a wide knowledge and understanding of the topic. The explanation in the last sentence is well focused on addressing the question.

© Benjamin Harrison/Hodder & Stoughton

Lenin also used the Cheka to hunt out opponents, and requisition squads to take grain from the peasants to feed the soldiers and workers. This meant that although many Russians suffered in this period, the soldiers in the Red Army and the factory workers producing war supplies were always prioritised by the Bolsheviks so that they could keep fighting or contributing to the war effort, unlike the Whites who relied on foreign assistance.

Practice question, Paper 4 (page 78)

How significant were the purges in increasing Stalin's control of the Soviet Union?   [40 marks]

Essay section	Advice	Example content
Introduction	Begin by stating some reasons why the purges were significant in increasing Stalin's control.	*The purge of the Bolshevik Party* *The purge of the armed forces* *The purge of opposition in the general population*
	Then state other factors that allowed Stalin to increase his control in the Soviet Union.	*The role of the NKVD and terror* *The creation of the gulags* *The creation of Stalin's cult of personality* *Censorship*
	Try to assess which reason or reasons were the most significant so you can sustain your argument throughout your essay.	*The most significant reason why Stalin was able to increase his control of the Soviet Union was … because …*
First section	Address the cause given in the question – the purges– even if you don't think it was the most significant factor overall.	*The purges were a significant reason Stalin was able to increase his control of the Soviet Union because …*
	In each paragraph tackle a separate effect or impact.	*The purges targeted the old Bolshevik Party members first which meant that … For example …*
	Finish the section by explaining how significant you think the factor was and how it helped Stalin increase his control of the Soviet Union.	*This was significant in allowing Stalin to increase his control of the Soviet Union because/as it meant that/as it led to …*
Second section	In the second section you need to examine alternative factors to provide balance.	*However, censorship/Stalin's cult of personality/the role of the NKVD … was also a significant reason Stalin was able to increase his control of the Soviet Union because …*
	Follow the same process as in the first section by looking at one cause at a time, adding examples and explaining its significance in allowing Stalin to increase his control.	*Censorship was significant in increasing Stalin's control of the Soviet Union because it meant he could feed the Soviet population his version of history, especially the younger generation …*
	Really strong responses will also start to evaluate and assess the relative significance of each reason with the factor of the purges – if you can, try to sustain your argument from the introduction.	*Censorship was not as significant as the impact of the purges because …*
Conclusion	Write a conclusion as the last paragraph. Here you can fully explain your judgement and the relative significance of the different reasons.	*To conclude/overall, the most significant reason/s Stalin was able to increase his control of the Soviet Union was/were … because …*
	Try to justify your argument by referring to some key evidence that helps support your judgement.	*This can be supported by the fact that …*

Practice question, Paper 1 (page 80)
Why did Stalin introduce the policy of collectivisation?　[6 marks]

Stalin introduced collectivisation in the countryside so he could prevent future famine and feed the Russian cities. Russia had a long history of famine and Stalin needed to ensure that his industrialisation of the USSR would be successful. Collectivisation would ensure that the government had greater control over food production in the countryside by taking a percentage of the grain to send to the cities to feed the workers. This would then allow Stalin to increase production more rapidly and catch up with the West.

Stalin also wanted to take communism to the countryside. The peasants had always demanded their own private land, but this went against the ideals of communism which stressed communal ownership and no private property. Stalin viewed many peasants, especially the kulak class of rich peasants, as counter-revolutionary and therefore a threat to the Communist Party. Collectivisation forced the peasants to create collective farms called *kolkhoz* or state-owned farms called *sovkhoz*, so they no longer owned their own land. The kulaks were liquidised as a class and many peasants were encouraged to inform the authorities if they suspected a kulak of hoarding grain.

The first paragraph focuses on the question and provides a convincing explanation which is supported by general contextual knowledge – reference to the Five-Year Plans could enhance this section further.

The second paragraph is well developed and supported by more specific evidence. The explanation is more implicit in the last two sentences and could address the question more directly.

Practice question, Paper 1 (page 83)
'The Soviet people suffered more than they benefited from Stalin's modernisation of the Soviet Union.'
How far do you agree with this statement? Explain your answer.　[10 marks]

The Soviet people did suffer greatly during Stalin's modernisation of the Soviet Union. In the cities and towns where the Five-Year Plans were being implemented, workers faced harsh discipline and punishments for not meeting government-set targets for production. Many who failed to meet their targets, including managers, were accused of sabotage and could be fired, fined or even arrested and sent to a gulag. This created a sense of fear and intimidation for many working in the factories. In the countryside, peasants faced forced collectivisation and lost the private land given to them by Lenin in 1917. Many peasants slaughtered their livestock and refused to co-operate with the authorities, which led to brutal repression by the secret police and even a forced famine killing 13 million. In both the cities and the countryside, the workers and peasants were faced with constant propaganda and Communist Party messages to work hard for the Soviet Union. Their lives were closely monitored by the authorities and informers were used to root out suspected counter-revolutionaries who could be arrested and even executed by the NKVD.

However, some workers and peasants did benefit from Stalin's modernisation. In towns and cities women were employed in increasing numbers and gained opportunities for specialist training and education. Working mothers were able to use state-funded crèches. There were incentives to work hard and produce more, which included better housing and better services. Both peasants and workers had access to improved healthcare – there were even more doctors per head in the Soviet Union than the UK by 1940. This meant that many workers had a better standard of living and could lead healthier lives and women could compete for the same jobs and positions as men.

Overall though, the people suffered more than they benefited. Although many Soviet citizens had a higher standard of living by the late 1930s and famine had all but been eradicated, there was a huge human cost and the quality of life for many with repressive propaganda, censorship and the fear of intimidation and violence meant that Soviet citizens often suffered under communist rule during the process of modernisation. For Stalin, the outcomes in terms of production were more important than the lives of the people.

The response directly addresses the question and examines the suffering faced by the urban working class. Knowledge is good and explanations are explicit.

The response adds range to the answer by examining the countryside as well.

Further enhancement is given by looking at the role of propaganda and terror in both rural and urban areas.

Balance is provided by explaining the benefits many in the Soviet Union had access to. Strong evidence is used to support this argument.

The judgement is explicit and well supported by key evidence. This is a clinching argument.

Practice question, Paper 1 (page 87)
Why did the Treaty of Versailles lead to instability in the Weimar Republic? [6 marks]

The Treaty of Versailles was deeply unpopular with many Germans, especially the war guilt clause and the loss of much of Germany's armed forces, which led to great instability. The Treaty blamed Germany for starting the war and reduced its army to just 100,000. It was also allowed only six battleships, no tanks and no air force. This left Germany defenceless and caused outrage in the German army and among ex-soldiers in particular. Many ex-soldiers formed Freikorps brigades in 1919 and 1920 that fought the communists on the streets, which led to civil unrest. In 1920, Freikorps brigades, led by Wolfgang Kapp, even chased the government out of Berlin in an attempted coup.

The first paragraph uses well-selected and precise evidence to support a valid explanation of political instability in the Weimar Republic.

The Treaty also financially weakened Germany and this led to instability. The reparation payments were set at £6.6 billion in 1921. Germany could barely afford to pay the instalments and the printing of money was causing inflation. When the Government failed to pay in 1923, France and Belgium occupied the Ruhr region of Germany, which was the industrial heartland. Trade stopped and chaos followed. The Government printed more money to pay striking workers who were ordered not to co-operate with the French, and this led to a period of hyperinflation where commerce struggled to keep pace with the rising cost of goods and made trade impossible. The Nazis used this period as an incentive to attempt a putsch in Munich.

Detailed contextual knowledge is used here to add depth to the explanation on economic instability.

Practice question, Paper 1 (page 88)
'Germany was stable due to Stresemann's policies from 1923 to 1929.' How far do you agree with this statement? Explain your answer. [10 marks]

It could be argued that Stresemann's policies from 1923 to 1929 led to greater stability in Germany. Firstly, Stresemann managed to get the German economy up and running again. He burnt the worthless German marks and replaced them with the new Rentenmark. This temporary currency allowed trade and commerce to start up again, which stabilised the German economy and helped stop the hyperinflation. Also, Stresemann managed to negotiate French withdrawal from the Ruhr by ending the passive resistance. This improved relations with the French, who agreed to leave the Ruhr, and allowed production to restart, which was vital to German finances as the Ruhr was the industrial heartland of Germany.

The first part of this paragraph focuses on Stresemann's economic achievements and clearly explains how it helped stabilise Germany.

Stresemann also achieved significant stability in the arena of foreign affairs. The Locarno Treaties agreed Germany's western borders and essentially demonstrated that Germany would abide by the terms of the Treaty of Versailles. This improved Germany's relationship with the Allies and meant Germany was allowed into the League of Nations in 1926, which ended its time as an outcast in Europe. The Dawes and Young Plans of 1924 and 1929 lowered reparation payments and agreed loans with the USA worth over $800 million. This money was invested in infrastructure and public facilities, which helped boost production levels and fuel the Golden Age in German culture as the economy stabilised.

The second section examines one of Stresemann's international achievements and links it to economic stability in Germany.

This paragraph adds breadth to support the statement by examining more of Stresemann's international achievements. A clear explanation is provided.

However, it could also be argued that Stresemann failed to stabilise Germany. The US loans could have been called back, which would have left Germany in massive debt and would have threatened the prosperity of the mid-1920s. The stability provided by Stresemann was on thin ice at best. Furthermore, Stresemann's ending of passive resistance and signing of the Locarno Treaties was condemned by many nationalists and far-right politicians as giving in to the French and agreeing to the unpopular Treaty

Once again, international achievements in the form of foreign loans are linked to Germany's economic stability. A well-selected piece of evidence is used to support the explanation.

of Versailles settlement. This nationalist sentiment in Germany helped Hindenburg get elected as president in 1925, and showed that far-right politics was far from extinct.

Overall, Stresemann did stabilise Germany, but it was a temporary stability and one based on high risk. While the economy remained relatively strong, support for the Weimar Republic and moderate political parties remained high. When the Wall Street Crash plunged Germany into depression after 1929, the backlash was severe and extremist politics thrived, which suggests that stability was partially an illusion for many Germans.

Practice question, Paper 1 (page 92)
'The threat of communism was the most important reason for the increase in Nazi support.'
How far do you agree with this statement? Explain your answer. [10 marks]

The Nazis were a strongly anti-communist party on the far-right and anti-communism was always one of their most attractive polices for many middle-class Germans and German industrialists. These groups feared a situation like that in the Soviet Union where the Communist Party had nationalised businesses and abolished private property and individual wealth. Hitler, and his propaganda chief Goebbels, targeted the middle classes and the industrialists in the election campaigns of 1930 and 1932, at a time when the German Communist Party (KPD) was also attracting much of the working-class vote. In November 1932, the KPD won 100 seats in the Reichstag, for example. This electoral success for the Communists meant many moderate Germans began to support the Nazis because they promised to destroy communism. Some industrialists also began to help fund the Nazis, as the only party willing to take a hard-line stance against the Communists. This all helped the Nazis capture 37 per cent of the vote in July 1932, and become the largest party in the Reichstag.

However, there were other reasons for why Nazi support increased. Hitler's leadership was a key factor. He was a natural orator who drew huge audiences to his rallies and speeches. Many Germans were enthused by Hitler's apparent connection to the problems faced by ordinary Germans during the Depression of the early 1930s. The Nazis also made wide-ranging promises and changed unpopular policies when necessary so they could attract all classes in German society. For example, they promised better food prices for farmers and jobs for unemployed industrial workers. Hitler also used modern technology such as the radio to get the Nazi message across and flew around the country delivering speeches by plane in the 1932 presidential election, in which he received 37 per cent of the vote. Hitler's leadership and the organisation of the Nazi Party created a sense of discipline and order that attracted many German voters during the chaos and uncertainty of the Depression.

Finally, the most important reason for Nazi electoral success was the impact of the Great Depression. By 1932, nearly 6 million Germans were unemployed and the Government, under Chancellor Brüning, was able to achieve little to help the huge numbers of unemployed. Brüning cut benefits and salaries, which angered many, and required presidential decree using Article 48 to get policies made into law. To many Germans, Weimar democracy was failing, and the Nazis looked like a party of action that would bring strength back to Germany. The Depression also had the effect of increasing the Communist vote, which helped increase Nazi support significantly. The Depression was the key factor as in 1928 the Nazis polled just 2.6 per cent of the vote. The economic hardship of the Depression made them a viable alternative to the democratic parties in the early 1930s.

Balance is provided through a focused counter-argument. Well-selected examples are cited to support the explanations.

The conclusion makes a clear judgement and introduces new evidence to develop the argument.

The first paragraph tackles the factor in the question in great depth and detail. A strong knowledge and understanding of the importance of anti-communism is demonstrated and key examples are used well to develop the explanations.

Alternative factors are discussed in the next paragraph to give balance to the response. The explanations are concise and well focused on addressing the question.

The last paragraph examines a further factor and makes a judgement. The argument is convincing as the response links this factor to other factors discussed earlier in the answer.

Practice question, Paper 4 (page 94)

How significant was the Enabling Act in allowing Hitler to create a one-party state? Explain your answer.　　　　　　　　　　　　　[40 marks]

Essay section	Advice	Example content
Introduction	Begin by stating some reasons why the Enabling Act would help Hitler create a one-party state.	*The Enabling Act made Hitler a virtual dictator as he could make laws without the Reichstag.* *Hitler used the Act to ban political parties and trade unions.*
	Then state other factors that enabled Hitler to create a one-party state.	*The Reichstag Fire* *The Concordat with the Catholic Church* *The Night of the Long Knives* *The death of Hindenburg*
	Try to assess which cause or causes were the most important so you can sustain your argument throughout your answer.	*The most significant reason Hitler was able to create a one-party state was ...*
First section	Address the cause given in the question – the Enabling Act – even if you don't think it was the most important factor overall.	*First, the Enabling Act was a significant factor that allowed Hitler to create a one-party state because ...*
	In each paragraph tackle a separate effect or impact.	*The Act gave Hitler the power to pass new laws without consulting the Reichstag and Hitler used the Enabling Act to ban political parties and trade unions.*
	Finish the section by explaining how significant you think the factor was and how it enabled Hitler to create a one-party state.	*The Enabling Act was significant in allowing Hitler to create a one-party state because it meant that ...*
Second section	In the second section you need to examine the other factors.	*The Reichstag Fire* *The Concordat with the Catholic Church* *The Night of the Long Knives* *The death of Hindenburg*
	Follow the same process as in the first section by looking at one factor at a time, adding examples and explaining its significance in enabling Hitler to create a one-party state.	*However, the Reichstag Fire/the Concordat with the Catholic Church/the Night of the Long Knives/ the death of Hindenburg ... was also a significant reason that enabled Hitler to create a one-party state because ...*
	Really strong responses will also start to evaluate and assess the relative significance of each factor with the Enabling Act – if you can, try to sustain your argument from the introduction.	*... was more/less significant in enabling Hitler to create a one-party state because ...*
Conclusion	Write a conclusion as the last paragraph. Here you can fully explain your judgement and the relative significance of the different causes.	*Overall ... In conclusion ... To conclude ...*
	Try to justify your argument by referring to some key evidence that helps support your judgement.	*The reason ... was the most significant factor because ... This can be supported by the fact that ...*

Cambridge IGCSE and O Level History Study and Revision Guide

Practice question, Paper 1 (page 96)

'The SS was the most important aspect of the Nazi police state after 1933.'
How far do you agree with this statement? Explain your answer. [10 marks]

The SS was key to Hitler's creation of a police state after 1933, as it controlled the police and security forces and it also used violence and intimidation to control the German population. However, Goebbels' control of the media and the propaganda machine were also very important as they allowed the Nazi message to infiltrate every aspect of society on a daily basis.

The short but focused introduction sets out the factors that will be examined in the main body of the response and suggests a balanced answer.

The SS was very important in the creation of a Nazi police state because it controlled all the police and security forces after 1936. Himmler was given charge over the Gestapo in 1934, after the Night of the Long Knives, and he used it to spy and gather information on ordinary Germans. The Gestapo could arrest and detain people without charging them and would often rely on informers and tapping telephone lines to gather intelligence on possible opponents of the regime. Many who were arrested ended up in concentration camps. This spread fear in many Germans and forced many into silence in case someone overheard them say something negative about the Nazis or Hitler. The Nazis were able to create a police state based on surveillance of the population using the Gestapo.

This paragraph analyses various aspects of the SS state and demonstrates a wide knowledge and understanding of the topic.

The SS were also given control over the concentration camps. Camps like Dachau were used to hold thousands of enemies of the Nazi regime in brutal conditions. Food rations were very small, and the inmates were subject to regular beatings, torture and even executions. A few prisoners were released so that the general population heard about the horrors of the camps. This helped create a police state as the Nazis were able to remove their political enemies such as trade unionists and communists so they would not be able to speak out against the Nazis.

Extra range and depth are added in this paragraph and the explanation is well focused on addressing the question.

However, propaganda was also very important in creating the police state. Goebbels used the newspapers to print pro-Nazi messages and anti-Nazi newspapers were shut down using force. This meant the Nazis controlled the information in Germany and only exposed the German people to positive aspects of the regime, which meant they were unaware of Nazi failures that may have caused unrest or opposition. Goebbels also used posters and, most famously, the radio, to spread Nazi ideas. The People's Receiver was a low-cost radio that meant German families were exposed to Nazi propaganda on a daily basis. The Nazi message of loyalty to Hitler and the Nazis was a constant theme. This helped create a police state because it helped indoctrinate young people with Nazi ideas and ensured ordinary Germans were told who their enemies were in German society, such as the communists and socialists.

A range of examples are cited in the counter-argument and the explanation is well-developed.

Overall, the SS and the propaganda machine were equally important in the creation of a police state because the two different forms of control were highly reliant on each other. The propaganda spread the Nazi message, but relied on the brute force and violence of the SS to enforce it, which meant many Germans did not speak out against the Nazi dictatorship and some openly supported it.

A well-thought-out judgement is reached in the conclusion and the links between the different factors are developed convincingly.

Practice question, Paper 1 (page 100)

Explain why young people were important to the Nazi regime. [6 marks]

The Nazis valued young people because they were the future Aryan master race for Germany. Hitler wanted to create a Greater Germany and *Lebensraum* in the East and fill it with pure-blooded Aryans. Young people were vital to achieve this aim and they could be more easily indoctrinated with Nazi ideas and grow up as loyal Nazis. Girls in particular were targeted with Nazi racial theory in schools and the League of German Maidens,

The first paragraph focuses on the importance of young people in the Nazis' racial policies. A strong knowledge and understanding of this are demonstrated in the material.

where they were taught how to find a suitable Aryan husband and were educated not to mix their blood with Jews or other undesirables.

Young people were also important because Hitler needed future soldiers to fight his wars against the West and to conquer *Lebensraum* in the East, as well as claim back the territory lost in the Treaty of Versailles. Hitler introduced conscription in 1936, and needed a large military to realise his goals. Boys were given more PE in the school curriculum and taught basic military drill and discipline in the Hitler Youth because they would be the future soldiers Hitler needed to fight his wars.

The importance of young people in relation to the Nazis' military ambitions are explained here. Key evidence is included to develop the explanation.

Practice question, Paper 1 (page 102)
'The German workers benefited the most from Nazi rule.'
How far do you agree with this statement? Explain your answer. [10 marks]

German workers did benefit from Nazi rule to an extent, but in many ways, they were worse off compared to other groups such as farmers and big business interests.

German workers were promised jobs during the Nazi election campaign and the Nazis managed to cut unemployment from 6 million in 1932 to under 100,000 by 1937. This gave many workers an income and helped bring them out of poverty. Much of this was achieved by removing women from paid work in many sectors, conscription and the creation of the National Labour Service, which created jobs through public building projects such as the *autobahns*. Workers were also able to access cheaper holidays, cinema tickets and sporting events through the Nazi Strength Through Joy organisation. Working conditions were also improved in many factories by the Beauty of Labour movement. This meant many workers did benefit from Nazi rule under Dr Hjalmar Schacht, who spent huge amounts of public money creating employment.

This is a general albeit balanced start to the response.

This paragraph is well focused on addressing the question and the factor in the statement. A wide range of evidence is used to explain how the workers did benefit under Nazi rule.

However, workers did not completely benefit from Nazi rule because they lost their right to strike and their right to join a trade union. The Nazis quickly banned trade unions, which were mainly left wing in their views and therefore opposed the Nazis. They also banned the communist and socialist parties in 1933, which were the parties most workers supported. They were replaced by the German Workers' Front (DAF), which was a kind of Nazi trade union. This organisation tried to spread Nazi ideas and propaganda to the workers and controlled pay and conditions. It did not allow workers to bargain for their wages, which severely reduced their power as a group as well as their freedoms.

This paragraph offers a convincing counter-argument and explains in detail how workers did not benefit from Nazi rule, using well-selected examples.

Farmers probably benefited more than the workers because the Nazis viewed the peasant class as the purest example of the Aryan race. They introduced the Reich Food Estate, which gave guaranteed markets for food and protected their farms with the Reich Entailed Farm Law. The Nazi 'Blood and Soil' movement promoted the idea that the peasant family was the backbone of the new Nazi society and it meant they were given a good deal of protection under the Nazis.

An alternative group is examined providing further balance to the answer. Strong contextual knowledge is demonstrated here to support the explanation.

Big business really benefited the most under Nazi rule. The Nazis removed the problem of the communists, socialists and trade unions, which meant industrialists could pay lower wages and set longer working hours for workers. They also gained huge government contracts if they produced war materials such as chemicals, munitions or artificial oil. Owners of big business became very wealthy under the Nazis as long as they produced what the Nazis wanted and were able to use slave labour from the concentration camps and labour camps in the East, which increased their profits massively.

The final paragraph offers a convincing judgement by concluding that big business benefited the most under Nazi rule. This argument is developed by examining evidence in a wider context to include German occupation in the East.

Cambridge IGCSE and O Level History Study and Revision Guide

The USA, 1919–41

Practice question, Paper 4 (page 106)

How significant was mass production in allowing the US economy to prosper in the 1920s? Explain your answer. [40 marks]

Essay section	Advice	Example content
Introduction	Begin by stating some reasons why mass production allowed the US economy to prosper in the 1920s.	*The adoption of the assembly line, first used by Ford* *The motor industry and the knock-on effect with other industries*
	Then state other factors that allowed the US economy to prosper in the 1920s.	*Republican policies* *The USA's natural resources* *Confidence and speculation* *Mass advertising and mass consumption*
	Try to assess which factor or factors were the most significant so you can sustain your argument throughout your answer.	*The most significant factor that allowed the US economy to prosper in the 1920s was …*
First section	Address the factor given in the question – mass production – even if you don't think it was the most important factor overall.	*Firstly, mass production was a significant factor that allowed the US economy to prosper in the 1920s because …*
	In each paragraph tackle a separate effect or impact.	*The use of the assembly line; the motor industry and its knock-on effect with other secondary industries such as glass, rubber and oil*
	Finish the section by explaining how significant you think the factor was and how it allowed the US economy to prosper.	*Mass production was significant in allowing the US economy to prosper because it meant that …*
Second section	In the second section you need to examine the other factors.	*Republican policies* *The USA's natural resources* *Confidence and speculation* *Mass advertising and mass consumption*
	Follow the same process as in the first section by looking at one factor at a time, adding examples and explaining its significance in allowing the US economy to prosper in the 1920s.	*However, Republican policies/the USA's natural resources/confidence and speculation/mass advertising and mass consumption … was also a significant reason that allowed the US economy to prosper in the 1920s because …*
	Really strong responses will also start to evaluate and assess the relative significance of each factor with mass production. If you can, try to sustain your argument from the introduction.	*… was more/less significant in allowing the US economy to prosper because …*
Conclusion	Write a conclusion as the last paragraph. Here you can fully explain your judgement and the relative significance of the different factors.	*Overall … In conclusion … To conclude …*
	Try to justify your argument by referring to some key evidence that helps support your judgement.	*The reason … was the most significant factor because … This can be supported by the fact that …*

Practice question, Paper 1 (page 108)

'The economic boom led to great prosperity in the USA in the 1920s.'
How far do you agree with this statement? Explain your answer. [10 marks]

Many different groups did benefit from the economic boom in the 1920s. First, new industries like the motor industry prospered. Ford and other car manufacturers made huge profits during the economic boom as sales increased due to the lowering of prices, which was a result of mass production. Lowering prices increased the market for cars and meant sales increased massively in the 1920s – by 1928, one in five people in the USA owned a car. The motor industry provided hundreds of thousands of jobs for workers who generally had better wages and therefore more disposable income to spend on leisure activities. It also had a knock-on effect with other related industries such as the rubber, glass and oil industries; in fact, the motor industry used up 75 per cent of US glass production in the 1920s. It also provided contracts for road building, which in turn encouraged the building of suburbs, motels and restaurants. Many of these industries prospered thanks to the motor industry.

> The first paragraph focuses its argument on the huge economic impact of the motor industry. Links between other industries are well made and contextual knowledge is strong.

Professionals in the cities also prospered from the economic boom as they could use their disposable income to speculate on the stock market. Many were able to borrow money from the banks 'on the margin' and invest in hundreds of companies. Up until 1929, the value of many companies continued to rise and investors made profits from dividends or by selling their shares when the price reached a high point. This gave many Americans in the cities the opportunity to get rich quickly and have extra income to buy the new goods available thanks to mass production, such as refrigerators, radios and the motor car.

> Investors and speculators are examined here. The explanations of how they benefited from the opportunities in the stock market are convincingly explained and well developed.

However, many in the USA did not prosper due to the economic boom. Farmers in particular struggled throughout the 1920s and only a few large landowners were able to diversify their crops enough to benefit from the changing demands in the cities. Farmers had been overproducing since the First World War due to mechanisation and the loss of overseas markets in Europe. Government tariffs meant they could not sell their produce easily to other countries and so the market became flooded with surplus foodstuffs. This meant that prices remained very low throughout the 1920s and dropped by 50 per cent in 1921 alone. This led to many farmers going bankrupt and being forced off their land – a total of 6 million throughout the 1920s, most of them farm labourers.

> A counter-argument is given which provides balance to the response. The material on farmers demonstrates a good grasp of the key knowledge.

Older industries did not prosper due to the economic boom of the 1920s. Textile industries such as cotton and fuel-based industries such as coal declined, and their workers suffered lower wages, higher unemployment and poorer working conditions as newer industries and fuel types emerged to replace them. Cotton was gradually replaced by new man-made materials such as rayon and coal was losing out to new power sources like oil and electricity. This meant that many American workers were earning wages below the poverty line, especially women, who were heavily employed in the textile industry. They were unable to afford the new products or speculate on the stock market like those in new industries or the cities.

> Extra breadth is added to the response here by examining older industries in the USA. Well-selected examples are used to explain.

To conclude, on the whole rural Americans and those in older industries did not prosper in the boom years and this accounted for nearly 60 per cent of the US population. It was mainly big business, investors and those in the cities where the newer industries were that had access to all the luxuries being produced due to the economic boom. Many poorer Americans were left out and did not prosper or share in the wealth being generated in urban areas, resulting in a growing divide between the rich and poor.

> A convincing and balanced judgement is reached in the conclusion supported by a clear and concise explanation.

Practice question, Paper 1 (page 111)
How significant was immigration as a cause of growing intolerance in US society in the 1920s? Explain your answer.　　　　[40 marks]

Essay section	Advice	Example content
Introduction	Begin by stating some reasons why immigration caused intolerance in US society in the 1920s.	*Fear of unAmerican ideas such as communism and anarchism – the Red Scare* *Other religions such as Catholicism and Judaism* *Eastern and southern European immigrants might compete for jobs*
	Then state other factors that caused intolerance in US society in the 1920s.	*Racism, especially in the Southern states* *The role of the Ku Klux Klan* *Religious fundamentalism*
	Try to assess which factor or factors were the most significant so you can sustain your argument throughout your answer.	*The most significant factor that caused intolerance in US society in the 1920s was …*
First section	Address the factor given in the question – immigration – even if you don't think it was the most important factor overall.	*Firstly, immigration was a significant factor that caused intolerance in US society in the 1920s because …*
	In each paragraph tackle a separate effect or impact.	*Competition for jobs; fear of rising crime and criminal gangs; Red Scare*
	Finish the section by explaining how significant you think the factor was and how it caused intolerance in US society in the 1920s.	*Immigration was significant in causing intolerance in US society because it meant that …*
Second section	In the second section you need to examine the other factors.	*Racism, especially in the Southern states* *The role of the Ku Klux Klan* *Religious fundamentalism*
	Follow the same process as in the first section by looking at one factor at a time, adding examples and explaining its significance in causing intolerance in US society in the 1920s.	*However, racism, especially in the Southern states/the role of the Ku Klux Klan/religious fundamentalism … was also a significant cause of growing intolerance in US society in the 1920s because …*
	Really strong responses will also start to evaluate and assess the relative significance of each factor with immigration – if you can, try to sustain your argument from the introduction.	*… was more/less significant in causing intolerance in US society because …*
Conclusion	Write a conclusion as the last paragraph. Here you can fully explain your judgement and the relative significance of the different factors.	*Overall … In conclusion … To conclude …*
	Try to justify your argument by referring to some key evidence that helps support your judgement.	*The reason … was the most significant factor because … This can be supported by the fact that …*

Practice question, Paper 1 (page 112)
Why was the Volstead Act repealed in 1933?　　　　[6 marks]

The Volstead Act was repealed in 1933 because of the problem of organised crime. Criminal gangs such Al Capone's in Chicago made over $2 billion out of the sale of illegal alcohol in the USA during Prohibition. This led to violence on the streets such as the St Valentine's Day Massacre in 1929, and between 1926 and 1927 over 130 gangland murders had taken place with no arrests. This showed US society and the government that Prohibition was failing and leading to more problems than it was solving. In the cities in particular, criminal gangs bribed the authorities and made law enforcement

The first paragraph is clearly focused on addressing the question and gets straight into explaining the first factor on organised crime. Strong contextual knowledge is demonstrated here.

completely ineffective, which highlighted the amount of corruption in US society during Prohibition and contributed to the Volstead Act being repealed.

Another reason the Act was repealed was due to the need for increased government revenue during the Depression. The Depression had led to nearly a quarter of the workforce being unemployed by 1933 and farmers as a group were hit hardest as their food prices dropped rapidly. The government needed an extra source of income to pay for reforms and help farmers. If alcohol was legalised again then it could be taxed by the government to pay for reforms and farmers could start selling their grains to beer and whisky breweries again, which would increase demand and, with it, their income.

A valid second reason is cited and explained in some depth.

Practice question, Paper 1 (page 116)
'Farmers were the worst affected by the Depression in the 1930s in the USA.' How far do you agree with this statement? Explain your answer. [10 marks]

Farmers were hit especially hard by the Depression in the 1930s. This was partly due to the fact that they been suffering for most of the 1920s because a lack of demand had led to surplus food in the marketplace. This had caused prices to drop rapidly in the 1920s. The Depression led to even larger drops in income for farmers and many were unable to pay their mortgages and had their farms and homes seized by the banks. Black farmers and labourers were the worst off and many moved to the cities to look for work. This led to starvation for many as there was no welfare system to help, and many farmers and labourers relied on charitable handouts to survive. They also found themselves homeless and without shelter for their families, with many dying from malnutrition and disease. The dustbowl in the Southern and Midwest states made their plight even worse as the dust turned farmland into desert.

The first paragraph focuses on the factor stated in the question. The evidence is wide-ranging and well selected leading to detailed explanations.

However, those in the cities were also hit hard by the effects of the Depression. Unemployment among workers rose rapidly with nearly 12 million out of work by 1932. In some cities the situation was even worse – in Cleveland, for example, 50 per cent of workers were unemployed in 1932. Many workers were forced to sell their homes or had to move out of their accommodation because they could not afford the rent and relied on charity to feed, clothe and shelter them. Many towns had shanty towns on their outskirts known as Hoovervilles, where unemployed workers lived without proper facilities and many suffered from malnutrition and disease. Migrant and black workers who had the lowest paid jobs and often got fired first were worst hit by the Depression in the cities.

Balance is provided here by examining those in urban areas. Strong examples have been chosen to support the explanations.

Overall, it was not really farmers or those working in the cities that were exclusively worst hit by the effects of the Depression as both groups suffered the same consequences such as homelessness, hunger and, of course, no work. However, immigrants and black Americans were the worst affected by the Depression in both rural and urban areas. On the one hand they were the first to lose their farms or jobs as employers fired them first, and on the other hand they were the ones least likely to find work as employers often discriminated against them in the job market.

The conclusion shows balance and judgement. The response shows a clinching argument in relation to the wider social problems faced specifically by black Americans and immigrants.

Practice question, Paper 1 (page 117)
Why was Roosevelt able to beat Hoover in the 1932 presidential election? [6 marks]

One reason Roosevelt was able to beat Hoover in the 1932 presidential election was because Hoover had become deeply unpopular in the eyes of many Americans due to the way in which he was dealing with the effects of the Depression. Many Americans regarded Hoover as the 'do-nothing' president and although this was not entirely true, the fact that the

This is a well-developed first paragraph that examines Hoover's failings. The explanation offered explicitly addresses the question.

Republicans believed in self-help meant that most unemployed workers had to rely on charity to survive rather than government relief and welfare. This alienated many unemployed Americans because Hoover seemed to be doing nothing to help those worst affected by the Depression.

Another reason Roosevelt won the presidential election in 1932 was because of his campaign promises. Roosevelt ran a vigorous campaign across the USA, much of it from his train, and his personality and energy attracted many voters. Roosevelt promised action and wanted to spend public money to get people back to work. This campaign, and his promises, connected with many Americans who were sick of Hoover's lack of action and Roosevelt was able to win a landslide victory in 1932.

A good knowledge of Roosevelt's campaign and policies is demonstrated, although the explanation is less convincing than the one in the first paragraph.

Practice question, Paper 1 (page 118)
'The First New Deal benefited the farmers the most.'
How far do you agree with this statement? Explain your answer. [10 marks]

Farmers did benefit from the First New Deal. Roosevelt set up the Agricultural Adjustment Administration (AAA) in 1933 to try to improve food prices, and therefore income, for farmers who had been suffering low prices since the 1920s due to overproduction and government tariffs. The AAA set quotas to reduce production and this helped food prices to rise. Farmers' income doubled between 1932 and 1935 and those that were still struggling had access to government loans to help pay their mortgages. The AAA also helped share new farming practices to conserve the soil and help prevent the drought caused by the dustbowl.

The response begins by agreeing with the factor in the question. Good knowledge of the alphabet agencies linked to farming is demonstrated to develop the explanations.

Farmers in the Tennessee Valley area also benefited from the creation of the Tennessee Valley Authority (TVA). This New Deal agency benefited farmers across seven states. River flooding and drought were big problems in this area and the TVA funded the building of dams on the Tennessee River allowing farmers to more easily irrigate their farmland properly and prevent drought. This increased the profitability and production of the farms in the area and gave farmers access to electricity, thanks to the hydroelectric power stations.

The TVA is also specifically examined in relation to how it helped farmers. The explanation here is clear and explicitly addresses the question.

However, other groups also benefited from the First New Deal. Unemployed workers were helped by the Civilian Conservation Corps (CCC) and the Public Works Administration (PWA). The CCC employed young unemployed people for six months on conservation projects and helped around 2.5 million people. The PWA used public money to build new airports, highways, hospitals and schools, which also created millions of jobs. This helped provide a basic income for millions of Americans during the Depression and brought them out of absolute poverty.

Balance is provided by examining another group helped by the First New Deal – the unemployed. Knowledge of the reforms is once again strong with some well-selected and precise examples used to develop the response.

A final group that benefited from the First New Deal was the poor – those hit hardest by the Depression. There were 14 million unemployed in the USA by 1933, and many of these were in the cities living in Hoovervilles and begging for food. Charity was unable to clothe, feed and shelter all of them and the government under Hoover gave nothing to help them. The Federal Emergency Relief Administration (FERA) was set up to provide relief for those worst hit, such as families and children. Over $500 million was spent on soup kitchens, nursery schools, clothing and employment schemes, which stopped the suffering of many and helped prevent malnutrition and disease.

Breadth is added to the counter-argument by also analysing the impact of the First New Deal on the poorest in US society. Key evidence is cited in support.

Overall, farmers did benefit the most as they were helped considerably by a rise in income and government help throughout most of the First New Deal reforms, but only the landowners rather than the labourers. The modernisation of farming techniques encouraged by the AAA had the effect of putting more farm labourers out of work and the AAA did not focus its efforts on helping labourers, many of whom were black Americans. The unemployed were given considerable help, but much of the work was short-term. For example, the CCC only employed young men for six months. It did not include women and segregated black Americans. Furthermore, the PWA relied on government funding and when it dried up, unemployment rose again in 1937.

The conclusion shows a strong understanding of the relative benefits each group received from the First New Deal reforms. The judgement is well argued and convincing.

© Benjamin Harrison/Hodder & Stoughton

Practice question, Paper 1 (page 119)
What were the main reforms introduced as part of the Second New Deal?   [4 marks]

The Second New Deal introduced reforms that were aimed at helping ordinary Americans. The Wagner Act 1935 made companies recognise trade unions and made it illegal for employers to sack employees if they were a member. The Social Securities Act 1935 helped provide state pensions for the elderly and for widows. It also introduced a scheme for unemployment insurance whereby employers, employees and state and federal governments all contributed a small amount of money each week into a fund. If the worker lost their job they would then receive a small amount of money to help them survive until they found a new job.

The response is well focused on addressing the main reforms of the Second New Deal. It makes a number of detailed points with accurate supporting material while remaining concise enough for a four-mark question.

Practice question, Paper 1 (page 120)
Why did Roosevelt face opposition to the New Deal?   [6 marks]

Roosevelt faced opposition to the New Deal because Republicans and big business did not approve of the high levels of government intervention and public spending. Republicans believed in laissez-faire and thought that Roosevelt's support for the trade unions in the Wagner Act meant he was anti-business. Big business also disliked the increase in taxation to pay for the New Deal agencies and accused Roosevelt of being a socialist. Some set up a group called the Liberty League in 1934, to oppose government intervention and high spending.

The response focuses on conservative opposition first and uses some good examples of how and why Republicans and big business criticised Roosevelt.

Another reason Roosevelt faced opposition was because radical critics claimed the New Deal was not doing enough to help those affected by the Depression. Dr Townsend set up Townsend Clubs across the USA, which demanded a pension of $200 per month for those over 60, to stimulate the economy. The Catholic priest, Father Coughlin, used his own radio company to criticise Roosevelt for not doing enough to help the poor. Huey Long proposed sharing the wealth of the USA and taxing big business more to help those most in need. All these radical critics believed the New Deal did not do enough to help the poorest in society.

Radical critics are tackled next. A good range of examples are used in the explanation. Alternatively, the response could have examined Supreme Court opposition.

Practice question, Paper 1 (page 122)
'The New Deal was largely a failure in solving the effects of the Depression.'
How far do you agree with this statement? Explain your answer.   [10 marks]

The New Deal ultimately did fail to solve the effects of the Depression as only the onset of the Second World War finally brought it to an end. However, the New Deal did alleviate the worst effects of the Depression and provided much-needed employment to many Americans to help them out of extreme poverty.

The response starts with a well-defined and focused line of argument, which demonstrates a balanced approach to answering the question.

The New Deal could be said to have failed because unemployment never fell below 14 per cent and actually increased during the budget cuts of 1937. The New Deal led to a huge amount of public spending and an increase in regulations for businesses and the stock market, which meant it was more difficult for industry and investors to make a profit. This, in turn, meant that confidence was never fully restored to the stock market or to the consumer. Smaller tenant farmers and farm labourers never got the same amount of help that larger farms received, and many remained unemployed or in poverty. The AAA and TVA even ended up forcing many labourers and smaller farmers off their land and so increased the worst effects of the Depression. Those hardest hit by the effects of the Depression, such as migrant workers and black Americans, were helped the least. Some did find temporary work in the CCC for example, but overall, they were still discriminated against when looking for work, and the New Deal never passed any civil rights legislation to help improve the chances of black Americans.

The next paragraph uses a wide range of evidence to show support for the statement in the question. Multiple explanations are given and are developed with suitable examples.

Cambridge IGCSE and O Level History Study and Revision Guide

However, the New Deal did help alleviate the worst effects of the Depression for many Americans. Unemployment still fell by 30 per cent between 1930 and 1939, thanks to the job creation schemes of the CCC, PWA and WPA. Government spending even created jobs for out-of-work artists, actors and photographers. The poorest in society were given some relief through the FERA, which gave necessities to them such as food and clothing. Most importantly, much of the confidence in the banking system, which was lost after the Wall Street Crash, was restored after the Emergency Banking Act of 1933. All the banks in the USA were closed and only 5000 trusted ones were reopened after experts had checked them over. This caused many Americans to start putting their wages and savings back into the banks and prevented further bank failures. It also allowed banks to start lending money to businesses again, which helped create some jobs.

Balance is provided with a counter-argument on the successes of the New Deal. The help given to a range of different groups is examined and analysed.

Overall, the New Deal failed to solve the effects of the Depression, but it did alleviate many of its worst effects across many sections of US society. The New Deal attempted to help a large cross-section of the USA, including business, banks, the unemployed, those in poverty and it even introduced social security for pensioners and those who were sick with the Second New Deal. However, the most significant effect of the Depression, which was unemployment, was never solved and only the revitalising of the economy due to the demand for food, war supplies and war loans caused by the Second World War would bring unemployment down to normal levels again.

The conclusion returns to the original argument in the introduction and develops it further with a convincing explanation.

Index